Species, Phantasms, and Images

Species, Phantasms, and Images

Vision and Medieval Psychology in
The Canterbury Tales

CAROLYN P. COLLETTE

Ann Arbor

THE UNIVERSITY OF MICHIGAN PRESS

2004   2003   2002   2001   4   3   2   1

A CIP catalog record for this book is available from the British Library.

Library of Congress Cataloging-in-Publication Data

Collette, Carolyn P.
    Species, phantasms, and images : vision and medieval psychology in
The Canterbury tales / Carolyn P. Collette.
        p.   cm.
    Includes bibliographical references (p.   ) and index.
    ISBN 0-472-11161-2 (cloth : alk. paper)
    1. Chaucer, Geoffrey, d. 1400. Canterbury tales.   2. Chaucer, Geoffrey,
d. 1400 — Knowledge — Psychology.   3. Christian pilgrims and pilgrimages
in literature.   4. Tales, Medieval — History and criticism.   5. Visual
perception in literature.   6. Psychology in literature.   7. Vision in
literature.   I. Title.

PR1875.P79 C65   2000 2001
821'.1 — dc21   00-51175

To David
For the *pilgrim soul in you*
— Yeats

Preface

When the Wife of Bath says, "But yet I praye to al this compaignye / If that I speke after my fantasye, / As taketh not agrief of that I seye" (3.189–90), or when the Merchant describes Januarie's choosing a wife as a matter of "Heigh fantasye and curious bisynesse" (4.1577), a modern reader, supported by notes and by current usage, will likely assume that the term *fantasye* refers to some sort of daydream or imaginary world. In fact, in both of these cases the term refers to a specific feature of medieval psychology — the belief that through sensory experience in general and sight in particular, each human mind is a unique repository of various experientially generated images — the medieval term is *phantasms* — that it uses to comprehend immediate circumstances and form generalizations, or recalls as memory. In passages like these, when Chaucer or his characters talk of *fantasye* they refer to an important element in a complex late medieval psychology devoted to explaining how people see, imagine, and remember.

This book situates *The Canterbury Tales* within this late medieval context of thinking about the nature and function of the senses in human psychology, especially the chief sense, sight. The sensual basis of knowledge, the role and function of images in worship, the nature and promise of spiritual alchemy, the function of verbal signs to stimulate the individual imagination both in response to an author's invention and beyond an author's control — all topical issues in Chaucer's intellectual milieu — figure prominently in the tales he gathered together in his last, unfinished work.

But while allusion, verbal patterns, and explicit themes in *The Canterbury Tales* build on and grow out of a body of common knowledge familiar to medieval audiences, this system remains largely unknown to modern readers. Ironically our unfamiliarity with this material stems in part from the fact that we retain the words, the *signs,* that once evoked it, but use them to signify modern, not medieval, ideas. Modern English and Middle English share a basic vocabulary and a basic grammatical structure that makes Chaucer's poetry accessible and seemingly familiar in ways that *Beowulf,* for instance, is not. But in the six hundred years since Chaucer wrote, the ideas that our common vocabulary evokes have changed significantly. A case in point is what has happened to the word *fantasye.* For us it is inevitably colored with Coleridgean, romantic connotations of secondary imagination, or of chimeras, whereas in the late fourteenth century the term referred specifically to mental images derived originally from some kind of sensory experience. Recognizing the play of issues, wit, and ideas in moments of seeing and imagining in the *Canterbury Tales* depends on recovering at least the broad outlines of late medieval thinking about vision and imagination. In semiotic terms, we seek the medieval interpretants and referents of verbal signs that seem deceptively familiar.

The book that follows begins by describing the complex nexus of ideas about human cognition and psychology comprising late medieval theories of how sight, imagination, and *fantasye* function within the individual human mind. It moves on to discuss the role of sight and imagination as they affect action and desire in several fragments of *The Canterbury Tales.* The second chapter, on "The Knight's Tale," identifies a previously unrecognized theme centered in the limits of vision, articulated in different ways but to the same end by the three major male charaters as well as by the narrator; this chapter argues that the dark tone of the tale, which most recent criticism has imputed to anxiety about chivalric culture, derives as well from the tale's depiction of the constrained range of imagination and conceptualization each of the main characters exhibits. The third chapter deconstructs the "Marriage Group," breaking it into two pairs of tales that explore the power of will and *fantasye* in destabilizing human relations. In the first pair, "The Wife of Bath's Tale" and "The Clerk's Tale," Chaucer presents stories of uncontrolled male will linked directly to problems in perception. In the second pair, "The Merchant's Tale" and "The Franklin's Tale," he presents parallel cases of male and female obsession derived from mental images that direct action by simultaneously arising from and feeding desire. This third chapter argues that because medieval marriage is constructed as a union of two people into one, strains between partners in a marriage figure strains within individual human psyches. The fourth chapter reads the odd pairing of "The Physician's Tale" and "The Pardoner's Tale" as an inquiry into the dynamic effect of images of the beautiful on human desire, judgment, and greed; it does so by situating both tales within the general context of a late medieval psychology of vision as well as within a specific element of that context, Lollard anxiety about how the mind responds to images. The fifth chapter of the book reads Fragment VIII, "The Second Nun's Tale," and "The Canon's Yeoman's Tale," as a comparison of true alchemy to false alchemy. The action of both tales centers in vision and the preparation of the mind to see through physical to evidence of the metaphysical. The final chapter contextualizes the language of "The Parson's Tale" by reference to Lollard discourse and to Chaucer's own patterns of philosophic language; it argues that the tale is Chaucer's experiment in language and style to achieve what the Parson terms *undirstondynge,* direct, undistorted communication free of the mental images metaphor and *fable* encourage. The Retraction, read within the context of this tale, appears less concerned with repudiation of Chaucer's art than as one final attempt to call attention to the uncontrollable nature of human imagination, this time in response to literature.

In his last work Chaucer explored the effect and power of mental images on desire, conceptualization, and action. Read against the background of late medieval thinking about sight, Chaucer's art appears to negotiate a late medieval tension between affirmation of sight as the premier human sense and anxiety about the mental images vision might produce. But whereas the philosophic tradition closely tied to theology situates human psychology within a moral paradigm whose apogee is salvation, Chaucer's art problematizes the nature of human psychology and, in each fragment or tale where vision and psychology figure prominently, directs attention away from moral judgment and toward representing the complex bases of human relations and the uncertainty of human knowledge.

Acknowledgments

I am grateful for the help of many of my colleagues whose interest and criticism has sustained me through the long process of researching and writing this book. I want to thank Professor Bruce Arnold of the Classics Department at Mount Holyoke College for his help with Vincent of Beauvais's writing. I would also like to thank Professor Michael Davis of the Mount Holyoke Art Department for his interest in the subject, for his enthusiastic exploration of the concept of *multiplication of species* in his own work, and for his steady encouragement. To my colleagues Nancy Bradbury, Chick Chickering, Vincent Di Marco, Nancy Coiner, and David Benson, all of whom have read several drafts of chapters in this book, thanks for honest, helpful criticism and many excellent suggestions. I would like to thank Yvonne Nicholson, administrative assistant in the English Department at Mount Holyoke for careful proofreading of two entire drafts of this book. In particular I would like to thank Arlyn Diamond for always being ready to listen and to offer suggestions that many times helped me usefully rethink my topic and my approach. My special thanks go to Elaine Beilin for sharing her time and skill with me, for her faith in this project and her patience in listening to me work through my ideas. Finally, I would like to thank my husband David, whose unflagging and ready support made this book a reality.

I am grateful for permission to use material from the following articles in this book:

In chapter 3, Carolyn P. Collette, "Seeing and Believing in the Franklin's Tale," *Chaucer Review* 26, no. 4 (1992): 396–410. Copyright 1992 by the Pennsylvania State University. Reproduced by permission of the publisher.

In chapter 4, Carolyn P. Collette, "'Peyntyng with Greet Cost': Virginia as Image in the *Physician's Tale*," *Chaucer Yearbook II,* ed. Michael N. Salda and Jean E. Jost (Woodbridge: D. S. Brewer, 1995), 49–62. Reproduced by permission of the publisher.

Contents

1

The Psychology of Sight

Sight in Late Medieval Art and Culture

Vision, what people see and imagine that they see, figures prominently in the themes and structure of English poetry during the late fourteenth century. Gower's *Confessio Amantis* begins in earnest with Gower in a wood where, under the pain of unrequited love, he calls on Cupid and Venus to hear his prayer (1.115–35); immediately upon his conclusion he sees the king and queen of love. Seeing Criseyde in a temple, Troilus falls in love with her. Langland's *Vision of Piers Plowman* begins as a dream vision, with Will falling asleep and dreaming he sees a fair field full of folk. *Pearl* is a dream vision in which the narrator describes in graphic visual terms a complex allegorical explication of the theology of grace. What is equally true, but much less obvious, is that *The Canterbury Tales* are also full of moments when the plot turns on a significant moment of sight: the sight of gold in "The Pardoner's Tale," the sight of Virginia in "The Physician's Tale," the sight of Emelye in "The Knight's Tale," Dorigen's fixation on the sight of the rocky coast of Bretaigne, Januarie's daydreams of the perfect wife — all are moments of vision or of envisioning that move forward the plots of their respective tales. The centrality of sight to plot in these stories is so natural that we hardly notice it. But in fact the recurrent importance of moments of vision in *The Canterbury Tales* reflects Chaucer's knowledge of medieval psychology and of a complex, evolving, and ambivalent medieval attitude toward the processes involved in seeing, imagining, and understanding.

We think of sight as central to our lives because it is central to our physical existence. Seeing means being able to navigate in the world — to comprehend it, to move in it. Throughout the Middle Ages the sense of sight was similarly regarded as central, but for different reasons. Sight was commonly described as chief among all the human senses because it was the sense that apprehended light, God's primary medium in creating the physical world. Moreover, sight was not just more important than other senses, it was also regarded as generically different because of its close association, both literal and metaphoric, with the state of the soul. To possess sight meant being able to see clearly in the physical world, as well as being open to wisdom and understanding. Being blind meant not only being unable to see physically, but also being unaware of God's truths, being unable to read the index of God's power and love in creation. Trevisa's translation of Bartholomew Anglicus's *De Proprietatibus Rerum* attests to the broad popular medieval understanding of sight as "more sotile and more lifliche þan þe oþir wittis," for "he is more worthi þan oþir wittis."[1] The eyes both see and function as indices to the state of the soul: "Among alle þe wittes þe yen beþ next to þe soule, for in yȝen is token of þe soule. For in þe yȝen is iknowe and iseye al þe dome of mynde, desturbaunce and gladnes of þe soule, and also loue and wraþþe and oþir passiouns" (1:178). The sense of sight allows visual experience of the world at the same time that the eye itself provides an index to how inclinations and judgments based on sight have tempered and shaped the soul.

In Chaucer's immediate cultural context the primal importance of vision was axiomatic in philosophic discourse, appearing in a rich continuum of metaphors. As the following excerpt from an early-fifteenth-century Lollard sermon for Quinquagesima Sunday shows, physical sight was a metaphor for spiritual insight or understanding in the popular discourse of the time:

> But, for as myche as blyndenesse in soule letteþ man ofte þat he mai not knowe þe weie, ne see to goo þerynne to heuenli Jerusalem, þerfore as þe gospel telleþ suyngli oure Lord Jesus helide a man of his bodili blyndenesse þat criede bisili after his siȝt, and made him for to see, to teche vs to desire fulli in herte, and to crie bisili to God wiþ mouþe after goostli siȝt, whiche is þe grettist helpe þat mai beo to knowe þis weie and redili wiþoute errynge to go þerynne.[2]

Heather Phillips has shown that Wyclif was one of many late medieval theologians who adapted perspectivist ideas about vision to theology,

---

1. *On the Properties of Things: John Trevisa's Translation of Bartholomaeus Anglicus De Proprietatibus Rerum*, ed. M. C. Seymour et al., 3 vols. (Oxford: Clarendon Press, 1975), 1:111.

2. *Lollard Sermons*, ed. Gloria Cigman, Early English Text Society, o.s. 294 (Oxford, 1989), 111.

using the metaphor of a mirror.[3] In both *De Logica* and *De Benedicta Incarnacione* Wyclif argued for the presence of God in the Eucharist by analogy to an image in a mirror. Just as the mirror remains a mirror when an image is in it, so the elements remain bread and wine, he argued, even though God inheres in them. Similarly, God is present in the Eucharist when the bread is broken, just as an image is present in the shards of a broken mirror. What previously was in the whole subsequently appears fully in the pieces. From his earliest work to his latest, Phillips argues, Wyclif's writings reveal his familiarity with optical texts and "presuppose the existence of a sympathetic milieu and a receptive audience" (258). Phillips observes, "Wyclif, it seems, perceived the world around him, space itself, very visually. In this he was not alone. Indeed, in some way or other, his mind appears to have been very finely attuned to the *mentalité* of his age, to its unspoken habits of perception" (257).

Although he was working in a very different tradition from the realist assumptions implied in the passages above, Ockham's epistemology also centered in vision. William Courtenay makes a special point of the fact that Ockham's philosophy builds on the eye as the primary sense organ. For Ockham, "The rapidity with which the mind reaches out to know the object is particularly appropriate to (and in fact is based on and illustrated by) visual experience. 'Knowing' in Ockhamism is primarily 'seeing.'"[4]

At the same time, the primacy of sight among human senses was complicated by a correlative distrust. In part this distrust was generated by the commonly accepted notion that things in the perceptible world — *visibilia* — were inferior to those in the imperceptible world — *invisibilia*. Sight was also deemed untrustworthy because it could easily be deceived by magic or by desire. To see what is really there as opposed to what they wish were there, humans had to exercise the will to prevent remembered mental images from altering or shaping what the eye sees in any one moment. It was thought that the memory of sight, manifested in the formation and recall of mental images, could both alter the immediate

---

3. "John Wyclif and the Optics of the Eucharist," in *From Ockham to Wyclif,* ed. Anne Hudson and Michael Wilks (Oxford: Ecclesiastical History Society, Basil Blackwell, 1987), 245–58.

4. William Courtenay, "Nominalism and Late Medieval Religion," in *Pursuit of Holiness in Late Medieval and Renaissance Religion,* ed. Charles Trinkaus and Heiko A. Oberman (Leiden: J. S. Brill, 1974), 57.

perception of material reality as well as easily deceive the rational mind into "false" judgment. Trevisa, reflecting these attitudes, put it this way, "And it nediþ to take hede, for ʒif þe soule be ocupied about oþir þinges þan longiþ to þe siʒt, þe siʒt is þe lasse parfite, for he demiþ nouʒt of þe þing þat is isene" (*Properties of Things,* 1:109). Thus, the "simple" act of seeing could become a moral issue because it depended on an act of will. The belief that physical sight is linked to spiritual insight, that it can link the creation and the creator in the individual mind, coexisted with deep anxiety about the fallibility of the processes involved in seeing and remembering and their susceptibility to a variety of influences. This coexistence of affirmation and uncertainty created an epistemological conundrum, as well as a fertile source for writing about the follies of human wishes, will, and desire.[5]

---

5. Chaucer's acquaintance with this material is, of course, of paramount interest. Martin Irvine's article "Medieval Grammatical Theory and Chaucer's *House of Fame,*" *Speculum* 60 (1985): 850–76, demonstrated that the *House of Fame* contains a consistent and full treatment of late medieval physics of sound; Nicholas Davis's "The *Tretise of Myraclis Pleyinge:* On Milieu and Authorship," *Medieval English Theatre* 12 (1990): 124–51, discussing the Oxford Calculators and the Mertonians of the mid–fourteenth century, assumes Chaucer's active interest in late medieval science in this wry comment: "The Calculators much impressed their academic contemporaries, and their findings were later to form the basis for Galileo's researches into differential velocity, but knowledge of their achievements seems not to have travelled much outside the academic world during the 14th century. Possibly the bemused reception of their work by one 14th-century layman of unusually wide intellectual interests who is also known to have had a good deal of contact with academic Oxford should be counted as the exception which proves the rule: the physics of *The House of Fame* (see in particular lines 782–822) seems to owe as much to the Mertonians as to a more traditional Aristotelianism" (135–36). "The Nun's Priest's Tale" reveals Chaucer's acquaintance with the names and broad knowledge of the issues of fourteenth-century theology; "The Squire's Tale," lines 225–35, refers to "Alocen [Alhazen] and Vitulon" [Witelo] (on science in the tale see Vincent DiMarco, "The Dialogue of Science and Magic in Chaucer's *Squire's Tale,*" in *Dialogic Structures,* ed. Thomas Kuhn and Ursula Schaefer [Tübingen: Gunter Narr, 1996], 50–68); the *Treatise on the Astrolabe,* his position as clerk of the king's works, the dedication of the *Troilus* to the philosopher Ralph Strode — all reveal Chaucer's more than passing acquaintance with the science of his time. The standard work on Chaucer's connection with the world of the universities remains J. A. W. Bennett's *Chaucer at Oxford and at Cambridge* (Toronto: University of Toronto Press, 1974). Lois Roney's recent *Chaucer's Knight's Tale and Theories of Scholastic Psychology* (Tampa: University of South Florida Press, 1990) demonstrates the influence not only of faculty psychology but also of the rhetoric of Scholastic argument in Chaucer's thinking. On the subject of Chaucer's knowledge see, too, John Hill's *Chaucerian Belief: The Poetics of Reverence and Delight* (New Haven: Yale University Press, 1991); and Norman Klassen, *Chaucer on Love, Knowledge, and Sight* (Cambridge: D. S. Brewer, 1995). For general background on faculty psychology and its influence in literary texts, see Susan K. Hagen's *Allegorical Remembrance: A Study of the "Pilgrimage of the*

In *The Canterbury Tales* Chaucer drew on three separate but intersecting topics—faculty psychology, optics, and volition—for a complex, amorphous body of ideas about vision as a physical phenomenon, as a first step toward spiritual knowledge, and as a source of tension in human psychology. In all three areas continuous discussion in Scholastic circles throughout the late Middle Ages had defined and redefined terms, but the broad outlines within which discussion flourished remained surprisingly stable, entering the realm of medieval common knowledge. For the purposes of the literary critic seeking to understand the impact of this subject on literature, it is not necessary to retrace all the complexity of discussion so much as to delineate the paradigms of thinking that constituted late medieval understanding of the connection among the senses, the physical factors of vision, and the role of human will in seeing and remembering. Faculty psychology offers a good entry into the complex web of thinking that united psychology, optics, and will.

Faculty Psychology

Faculty psychology is an umbrella term designating a broad range of related theories that describe how the mind receives, processes, and stores information gained by all senses — the human faculties — especially sight. Following Aristotle and characterized by organization and systematization, medieval faculty psychology assigned each mental power its own proper cell or chamber in the brain according to its function.[6] Essen-

---

Life of Man" as a Medieval Treatise on Seeing and Remembering* (Athens: University of Georgia Press, 1990).

Of the works that treat the subject of vision, mind, and the function of both as part of the soul, we know that Chaucer certainly knew the discussion of these topics in Vincent of Beauvais's *Speculum Naturale*, in *Bibliotheca Mundi Vincenti Burgundi*, 4 vols. (Douay, 1624; rpt. 1964). Translations of this work cited in the text are provided by Professor Bruce Arnold of the Classics Department at Mount Holyoke College.

6. The two standard works on this topic are Murray Wright Bundy's *The Theory of Imagination in Classical and Medieval Thought*, University of Illinois Studies in Language and Literature, 12 (Urbana, 1927); and Ruth E. Harvey's *The Inward Wits: Psychological Theory in the Middle Ages and the Renaissance* (London: Warburg Institute, 1975). See also Katherine Tachau's *Vision and Certitude in the Age of Ockham: Optics, Epistemology and the Foundations of Semantics, 1250–1345* (Leiden: E. J. Brill, 1988); Henry Austryn Wolfson, "The Internal Senses in Latin, Arabic, and Hebrew Philosophic Texts," *Harvard Theological Review* 28 (1935): 69–133; Mary Carruthers, *The Book of Memory: A Study of Memory in Medieval Culture* (Cambridge: Cambridge University Press, 1990); and Janet Coleman, *Ancient and Medieval Memories: Studies in the Reconstruction of the Past* (Cambridge: Cambridge University Press, 1992).

tially three chambers execute functions of receiving, processing, and storing. While theories vary according to writer and over time, the following pattern from *De Proprietatibus Rerum* reflects common-knowledge understanding of the functions of the brain in the fourteenth century:

> The innere witte is departed aþre by þre regiouns of þe brayn, for in þe brayn beþ þre smalle celles. Þe formest hatte *ymaginatiua,* þerin þingis þat þe vttir witte apprehendiþ withoute beþ i-ordeyned and iput togedres withinne, *vt dicitur Iohannicio 1.* Þe middil chambre hatte *logica* þerin þe vertu estimatiue is maister. Þe þridde and þe laste is *memoratiua,* þe vertu of mynde. Þat vertu holdiþ and kepiþ in þe tresour of mynde þingis þat beþ apprehendid and iknowe by þe ymaginatif and *racio.* (Trevisa, *Properties of Things,* 1:98)[7]

The first chamber, imagination, is the place where sensations meet and in so doing constitute common sense, a kind of clearinghouse for sensory input, a place of mental assimilation of experience of the world. The second chamber, called variously *vis cogitativa, intellectus,*[8] or in some cases simply *reason,* receives the images produced by experience in the first chamber and operates on this data through reason to form an idea. This chamber in turn passes its processed images to the third chamber, the *vis memorativa,* in the back of the head. By the time experience has been so received, processed, assimilated, and stored it is no longer image but concept.

As this psychology sought to explain how ideas and memory function,

---

7. Trevisa describes the brain and its functions extensively in the third book of his work; here is a fuller discussion of the same point, appearing under the topic "De virtute animali":

> The vertu þat hatte *virtus animalis* haþ place in the *ouer*meste partie of a man, þat is in þe brayn, and haþ þre parties, *ordinatiua, sencitiua,* and *motiua.* Þat partie þat hatte *ordinatiua* eueleþ þe b[r]ayn by hisself allone. For in þe firste partie in þe formest chambre it ordeyneþ þe fantastik ymaginacioun; in þe middil chambre it ordeyneþ þe vertu estimatiue and [resoun. And þenne in þe laste chambre he makiþ parfite þe mynde and þe action of þe] mynde. For what þe vertu ymaginatif schapiþ and ymagineþ he sendiþ hit to þe doom *of* resoun. What resoun fongiþ of þe ymaginatiue, resoun demeþ hit as a iuge and sendiþ hit to þe vertu of mynde. þe vertu of mynde fongiþ what is [demed in] vndirstondinge and kepiþ it and saueþ it stedefastliche forto he bringe it forþ in acte and in dede. (*Properties of Things,* 1:107)

8. The terminology is not fixed and so varies from writer to writer; I have followed Bundy's lead and have tried to avoid describing complex terminological disputes and distinctions irrelevant to this discussion.

it drew upon and contributed to thinking about a closely related topic, images in the brain, termed *phantasms.* The neat compartmentalization of the tripartite brain appears over and over as conventionally accepted even while Arabic and later Western philosophers clearly recognized it as being too simplistic adequately to explain what really does happen in the mind. The human mind does not merely receive, process, and store information gained through the senses, it also works to classify, value, judge, combine, and recombine the images and sensations, creating fictions such as golden mountains or yellow horses. So, while this conventional compartmental description was accepted throughout the Middle Ages, within this schema the nature and function of the recombinative power of the mind, variously called the *phantasy* or *imaginatio,* continued to occupy medieval thinkers from Augustine to William Langland. Because so many theories existed simultaneously, it is helpful to know the broad outlines of some of the most influential work on this complex subject.

Early in the Middle Ages, Avicenna's highly influential writings linked the twin ideas of the creative potential of the imagination, storehouse of images or *phantasms,* and the role of will in controlling the creative process. Working with an inheritance of classical Aristotelian models, Avicenna assumed the basic tripartite division of the brain. For Avicenna the creative power, united to will, enters the process in the second chamber, enabling the mind both to abstract generalizations from particular experiences and to "compound and divide" sense experience received by common sense and stored by imagination.[9] Avicenna

---

9. Avicenna described the internal senses of the human mind this way:

One of the animal internal faculties of perception is the faculty of fantasy, i.e. *sensus communis,* located in the forepart of the front ventricle of the brain. It receives all the forms which are imprinted on the five senses and transmitted to it from them. Next is the faculty of representation located in the rear part of the front ventricle of the brain, which preserves what the *sensus communis* has received from the individual five senses even in the absence of the sensed objects.

It should be remembered that receptivity and preservation are functions of different faculties. For instance, water has the power of receiving an imprint, but lacks that of retaining it. Next is the faculty which is called "sensitive imagination" in relation to the animal soul, and "rational imagination" in relation to the human soul. This faculty is located in the middle ventricle of the brain near the vermiform process, and its function is to combine certain things with others in the faculty of representation, and to separate some things from others as it chooses. Then there is the estimative faculty located in the far end of the middle ventricle of the brain, which perceives the non-sensible

conceives of this process as variously calling on different aspects of the mind's powers, from the rational to the irrational. Avicenna understands *phantasia,* a property of the waking, conscious mind, to be an ability to call up the forms created by *formativa* and to regard them as real as sensory images. Thus by linking the active will and the waking consciousness, Avicenna's understanding of *phantasia* links the creative power of the mind to the exercise of the will. Because his writings were fundamental to medieval medicine, the linkage he articulated between the creative imagination and will became part of the basic assumptions of medieval psychology.

Two hundred years after Avicenna, Albertus Magnus (1206–1280) wrote what is now regarded as the most influential of medieval faculty psychologies. In his work the link between the creative potential of the mind's use of its storehouse of images and the will that drives that use becomes somewhat more complex. In *De Apprehensione* he describes mental apprehension of concepts as the product of five factors: common sense, imagination, opinion, phantasy, and memory. He classifies common sense, imagination, and memory as essentially retentive powers. Common sense retains the forms the sense receives in the presence of matter; imagination retains these forms in the absence of matter, and

---

intentions that exist in the individual sensible objects, like the faculty which judges that the wolf is to be avoided and the child is to be loved. Next there is the retentive and recollective faculty located in the rear ventricle of the brain, which retains what the estimative faculty perceives of non-sensible intentions existing in individual sensible objects. (*Avicenna's Psychology,* ed. F. Rahman [Oxford: Oxford University Press, 1952], chap. 31, "Concerning the Soul")

On the influence of the Avicennan model in late medieval English literature, see Alistair Minnis, "Langland's Ymaginatif and Late-Medieval Theories of Imagination," where he observes that by the late fourteenth century, "the *virtus imaginativa* was commonly believed to be of considerable value 'in practik or in speculatif.' However, on occasion the far-reaching imagination could over-reach itself. It is significant that the Gower passage quoted above [*Confessio Amantis,* 3067–74], forms part of an exemplum which warns against intellectual pride. There are many examples of the verb *imaginare* being used to designate the thinking of one's academic opponents, and here the implication of 'far-fetched' thinking is often present. . . . While the subtle and far-reaching qualities of imagination rendered it an immensely valuable kind of thinking, it had to be recognized for what it was: thinking which produced not certainties but possibilities" (in *Comparative Criticism: A Yearbook,* ed. E. S. Shaffer [Cambridge: Cambridge University Press, 1981], 71–103, 79; see, too, L. M. Eldredge, "Some Medical Evidence on Langland's Imaginatif," *The Yearbook of Langland Studies* 3 [1989]: 131–36; Ernest N. Kaulback, "The 'Vis Imaginativa Secundum Avicennam' and the Naturally Prophetic Powers of Ymaginatif in the B-Text of *Piers Plowman,*" *JEGP* 86 [1987]: 496–514; Britton J. Harwood, "Imaginative in *Piers Plowman,*" *Medium Aevum* 44 [1975]: 249–63).

memory retains them in the absence of matter over time. Imagination also serves reason by conjuring images and helping to form opinions (Bundy, *Theory of Imagination,* 188). Opinion and *phantasy* are the most complex factors in Albertus Magnus's theory of apprehension. Opinion finds out the intentions — *intentiones* — of what is perceived. Intentions are those inherent qualities of animals, people, and things that are real but beyond the power of the five external senses to determine. These "insensible forms" are received by the estimative faculty, which is uniquely equipped to judge them. The information the estimative faculty gains from these forms is then stored in the memorative faculty. Good, evil, fear, horror, pleasure are all apprehended by opinion operating on perception to determine intention. Just as imagination helps to form opinion, rendering an image for the mind to operate on, so opinion serves imagination, adding the dimension of emotion, the coloring, so to speak, to the form (Bundy, *Theory of Imagination,* 189).

But the most noteworthy addition in Albertus Magnus's description of the working of the mind is his theory of *phantasy,* the comparing, uniting, dividing faculty. *Phantasy* works on images stored in imagination and on the intentions determined by opinion. His theory puts *phantasy* at the center of human thought because it properly functions to serve reason and because it draws on both the anterior cell of imagination and the posterior cell of memory. In many ways *phantasy* in this psychology corresponds to our modern notion of imagination, the creative capacity of the mind that wills to draw upon stored material to combine, divide, and recombine it. In Magnus's philosophy imagination is always connected with actual experience, *phantasy* with the play of the mind based on the images experience generates. *Phantasy,* Albertus Magnus said, could serve reason in all the ways he outlined, but by its very nature, unchecked by will, it could also lead reason astray by feigning sensation or by misjudging. By its lively nature it could occupy the mind with chimeras, or with images drawn from the world of matter, interposing these between the individual and the steps of conceptualization and generalization that lead to reason and ultimate understanding, which he defined as true knowledge of God and of God in the created universe.

In spite of all the caveats and concerns about potential error, scholars of the thirteenth century affirmed the *phantasm* and its link to the material world as absolutely necessary to the mind's ability to think. Aquinas typifies this validation of the tie between the human senses and the material world. In discussing the human mind and soul he builds on

Aristotle's notion that *phantasms* enable one to abstract universal concepts from particular experiences, calling attention to Aristotle's dictum that there can be no idea without an image. In the *Summa Theologica* he questions "Whether the Intellect can actually understand through the intelligible species of which it is possessed, without turning to phantasms" (quoted in Bundy, *Theory of Imagination*, 219). In his opinion the soul understands nothing without a phantasm, a link to the corporeal world. In this theory the power of knowledge is "proportioned to the thing known" (Bundy, 219), and the thing known is retained in the mind through its *phantasm*, the image the mind retains in the thing's absence. The very fact that the human mind creates such *phantasms*, argues Aquinas, indicates that the Platonists are wrong: "if the proper object of our intellect were a separate form; or, if, as the Platonists say, the natures of sensible things subsisted apart from the individual; there would be no need for the intellect to turn to the phantasms whenever it understands" (*Summa Theologica*, quoted in Bundy, 220).

By the later Middle Ages, as these ideas about the nature and function of *phantasy* gained currency, there were attempts to smooth out strains and inconsistencies. Roger Bacon claimed for himself the role of synthesizer and reconciler of inconsistencies in the received tradition of faculty psychology and optics, attempting to combine Arabian, classical, and Western thinking. Bacon preserved the three-chamber or three-cell model, placing two faculties in the first cell. In the anterior resides the common sense, which "judges concerning each particular sensation." "For," as Bacon says, "the judgment is not completed in regard to what is seen before the form comes to the common sense."[10] The common sense forms a judgment about the differences of impressions on the senses, for example, that in milk whiteness is different from sweetness (422). But while the common sense judges, it does not retain the image. Another faculty in the back of the first cell does that — the imagination, what Bacon calls the "coffer and repository of the common sense" (422). The difference between the common sense and the imagination is like the difference between water and wax in their abilities to receive and retain impressions (422). The common sense and imagination together are the *phantasia* or *virtus phantastica* (422), whose purpose is to render a judgment about the external world. Cogitation, or *virtus cogitativa,* the

---

10. *The Opus Maius of Roger Bacon,* trans. Robert Belle Burke, 2 vols. (Philadelphia: University of Pennsylvania Press, 1928), 2:421.

property of the second chamber, makes judgments about the information received and processed by *phantasy*. This scheme redistributes the functions of the brain and in so doing moves *phantasy* "forward" in the process of sensory experience. Like the other theories about *phantasy*, Bacon's is centered in an effort to determine a site for the recombinative action of the human mind to function.

The influence of these discussions on the realm of "common knowledge" appears in the work of encyclopedists like Vincent of Beauvais, whose *Speculum Maius* deals with these topics in the volume titled *Speculum Naturale*. In discussing the close connection among vision, memory, and will, Vincent of Beauvais demonstrates that medieval faculty psychology in the thirteenth century develops around the idea of the image and depends on the knowledge of physical reality either experienced or gained vicariously through reading or listening, as the first step in all mental activity. Writing in an Augustinian tradition of epistemology, he asserts that all comprehension of new ideas depends on preexisting images in the mind:

> For I could not even understand one who is describing something, if I were listening for the first time to what he is saying, for he who describes to me some mountain stripped of forests and clothed with olive-trees is describing them to one who remembers the appearances of mountains, forests, and olive-trees, which, if I had forgotten, I would be completely ignorant of what he was saying, and for that reason I could not think of him describing that; so it happens that everyone who thinks of bodily things, whether he himself conceives something, or whether he hears or reads someone, whether describing the past or announcing the future, has resort to his own memory and finds there the manner and measure of all the forms which he observes while thinking. . . . For the sense receives an appearance from a body, which is sensed, and the memory from the sense, and finally the gaze of one who thinks from the memory. Furthermore, in this way the will joins the sense to the body, in this way is joined the memory to the sense, in this way it joins the gaze of one who thinks from memory.

> [Neque enim vel intelligere possem narrantem, si ea quae dicit, & si contexta tunc primum audirem, non tamen generaliter singula

meminissem, qui enim mihi narrat aliquem montem sylua exutum, & oleis indutum ei narrat, qui meminerim species & montium, & syluarum, & olearum, quae si oblitus essem, quid diceret omnino nescirem, & ideo narrationem illam cogitare non possem, ita sit vt omnis qui corporalia cogitat, siue ipse singat aliquid, siue audiat, aut legat, vel preterita narrantem, vel futura pronunciantem, ad memoriam suam recurrat, & ibi reperiat modum atque mensuram omnium formarum quas cogitans intuetur. . . .

Sensus enim accpit speciem à corpore, quod sentitur & à sensu memoria, à memoria vero acies cogitantis. Voluntas porro sic adiungit sensum corpori, sic memoria sensui, sic aciem cogitatis memoriae.] (chap. 22, 1667–68)

In Chaucer's time theology and philosophy would accept the essential features of this psychology of image, *phantasm,* and memory but would erode its comparative optimism about the close connection between knowledge and the material world, producing a rich literature of mystical experience and a heightened sense of doubt about the reliability of the senses in providing a basis for certain knowledge. Popular culture of the time is full of the dynamic tension between the necessarily sensual nature of experiential information and the belief that the mind must free itself of the material in order to function at its highest level. The Lollard argument against representation, both artistic and dramatic, reflects such a distrust. The early-fifteenth-century Lollard *Tretise of Miraclis Pleyinge* repeatedly opposes sensual pleasure to spiritual experience, worrying that miracle plays, "miraclis pleyinge," withdraw "not onely oon persone but alle the puple fro dedis of charite and of penaunce into dedis of lustis and likingis and of feding of houre wittis."[11] In an extended metaphor centered in the Old Testament contention between Isaac and Ishmael, the author of the treatise emphasizes the "distaunce of contrarite . . . bitwene fleyshly pley and the ernestful dedis of Crist" (107). Part of the reason for the deep dichotomy the text constructs between the fleshly and the *ernestful* is an identification of the fleshly with the semblance of reality, with accepting the material world as a source of empty signs in contrast to the "ernestful dedis" of spiritual reality. The *Tretise* concludes that one should "spende . . . nouther oure

---

11. *A Tretise of Miraclis Pleyinge,* ed. Clifford Davidson (Kalamazoo, Mich.: Medieval Institute Publications, 1993), 101.

wittis ne oure money aboute miraclis pleying" (114), for both are thrown away on such unprofitable activity as viewing representations.

Anxiety about the errors the mind commits when dealing with images stemmed from the bipolar paradigm that dominated philosophic discourse about sight: on the one hand philosophers asserted that images are absolutely necessary to the human brain; on the other hand, they warned that the images the brain requires can prevent the mind from moving beyond their form and texture. This philosophic/theological paradox in turn constructed human beings as creatures in whom a tension between their senses and the mental faculties the senses served produced a constant struggle. Humanity inhabited a world where the difference between affirmation and distrust of material information was slender indeed and where radical uncertainty was a natural human state.

Optics, Perspectiva, and Multiplication of Species

Faculty psychology deals with how the mind stores, recalls, and uses sensory stimuli from the world. But seeing is not merely a matter of looking, or at least it certainly wasn't during the Middle Ages. Optics contributed a complementary component to faculty psychology, holding that vision is a two-part process involving the powers of both seer and seen.[12] Vision and the images it depends on result from the phenomenon

---

12. For a discussion of the physics and theology of optics see David C. Lindberg, ed., *Roger Bacon's Philosophy of Nature: A Critical Edition, with English Translation, Introduction, and Notes, of* De multiplicatione specierum *and* De speculis comburentibus (Oxford: Oxford University Press, 1983). The association of God with light, and particularly with the light of grace, illumination of the mind, and understanding, is essential to understanding the metaphors of medieval philosophy and the assumptions behind theories of optics. In *Opus Maius* Bacon makes clear his sense of the preeminence of vision:

> Our experience of things here in the earth we owe to vision, because a blind man can have no experience worthy of the name concerning this world. Hearing causes us to believe because we believe our teachers, but we cannot try out what we learn except through vision. . . . But concerning vision alone is a separate science formed among philosophers, namely optics, and not concerning any other sense. Wherefore there must be a special utility in our knowledge through vision which is not found in the other senses. (2:419–20)

In discussing Grosseteste and the philosophy of light, Lindberg quotes the following passage from Bacon's *Opus Maius*, a passage that not only illustrates the broad metaphoric power of a discourse of light and optics, but implies the close connection between grace and will in its metaphor:

> Since the infusion of grace is supremely illustrated by the multiplication of light, it is useful in every way that by the multiplications of corporeal light should be revealed to

of *multiplication of species,* the natural property of matter to replicate its image through space. Vincent of Beauvais describes this principle when he describes vision as an interaction between viewer and viewed. Sight is

> produced from a visible thing, but not from it alone, unless someone is present and looking, on account of which vision is produced from a visible thing and a seeing person, in such a way indeed that the eye's sense derives from one who sees, and the concentrated attention of the one who is looking and observing (that conception of the sense which is called vision) is imprinted by the thing alone which has been seen, which once removed no form remains, which was in the sense as long as that which was being seen was present before it.

> [Gignitur ergo ex re visibili visio, sed non ex sola, nisi adsit & videns, quocirca ex visibili & vidente gignitur visio, ita sane vt ex vidente sit sensus oculorum, & aspicientis atque intuentis intentio, illa tamen informatio sensus, qua visio dicitur, a sola re visa imprimitur, qua detracta nulla remanet forma, que inerat sensui dum adesset illud, quod videbatur.] (*Speculum Naturale,* chap. 17, 1664)

Most modern readers assume control and power in the gaze located in the gazer. Certainly the influence of film and feminist theory has shaped our thinking in that direction. In contrast, the most influential late medieval thinking about optics assumed a degree of power in the object of vision itself. As a result, the subject one looked at was thought to be as important as the act of looking itself, and the act of looking always a dynamic interchange between viewer and viewed.

The thirteenth and fourteenth centuries produced a remarkable growth in theories of perspective, a topic that we now recognize as the begin-

---

us the properties of grace in the good and the rejection of it by the wicked. For the infusion of grace in perfectly good men is analogous to light incident directly and perpendicularly, since they do not reflect grace from themselves nor refract it from the direct path that extends along the way of perfection of life. But the infusion of grace in imperfect, but good, men is analogous to refracted light; for on account of their imperfections, grace does not maintain in them an altogether direct course. However, sinners who are in mortal sin reflect and repel God's grace from themselves, and therefore grace in their case is analogous to repelled or reflected light. (David C. Lindberg, *Theories of Vision from Al-kindi to Kepler* [Chicago: University of Chicago Press, 1976], 99)

ning of the modern science of optics, the study of how light and objects strike the human eye. But while the perspectivists' discussion was ultimately to lay the foundation for modern optics, scholars who have studied the field say that those philosophers who studied optics during this time were interested in cognition as much as perception.[13] A. Mark Smith suggests "that the ulterior concern of the perspectivists was epistemology and, therefore, that *perspectiva* should be understood as the science not of visual perception alone, but of visual *cognition.*"[14] Smith goes on to make this point: "Beneath a prepossessing tangle of virtues, intentions, and causes, the theoretical grounds of the perspectivist theory are almost intuitive in their simplicity. The fundamental purport of that theory is to explain how external objects affect us mentally through sight" (587).

In the fourteenth century the debate over how vision occurs, a debate between extramission theory, the idea that a beam of light radiates outward from the eye illuminating what it falls on, and intromission theory, the idea that all matter replicates its own image through intervening media until the image strikes the human eye, had tipped in favor of the latter, a concept that offered a wide scope for exploring the nature of light, color, and the angles of incidence and refraction that governed the transmission of images. The extramission theory of vision continued to exist in popular tradition — we see it, for example, as part of the conventions of love poetry as late as Shakespeare and Donne.[15]

---

13. See Zdzislaw Kuksewicz, "Criticisms of Aristotelian Psychology and the Augustinian-Aristotelian Synthesis," chap. 31, in *The Cambridge History of Later Medieval Philosophy from the Rediscovery of Aristotle to the Disintegration of Scholasticism, 1100–1600,* ed. Norman Kretzmann et al. (Cambridge: Cambridge University Press, 1982):

> In that period [fourteenth century], human cognition interested philosophers and theologians much more than the nature of the soul and its faculties. . . . [T]he main interest of these commentaries [on Aristotle's *De Anima*] was centered not on the nature of the possible and agent intellects, but on their function and the process of abstraction. Problems concerning the necessity of the active intellect, the production of intelligible species, the relation of the species to the act of intellection and the possibility of simultaneous intellection of several objects became the topics of chief interest. (628)

This focus developed in the wake of the Condemnations of Paris in 1277, which, according to Kuksewicz, found their "main target of criticism" in Aquinas's Aristotelianism and "the independence attributed to human cognition, unassisted by divine illumination" (623). Aquinas's ideas were thought to be particularly hostile to the Augustinian/Neoplatonic understanding of fundamental opposition between the human soul and matter.

14. "Getting the Big Picture in Perspectivist Optics," *Isis* 72 (1981): 569.

15. See Lindberg, *Theories of Vision,* 51f. for Avicenna's grounds of refutation.

The science of *perspectiva* during the late medieval period was devoted in large part to discussing and determining how intromission worked. The idea of intromission entered Western thought through the Arabic philosophers and doctors, chief among them Alhazen, whose name and influence continued throughout the Middle Ages: "Directly or indirectly, his *De aspectibus* inspired much of the activity in optics that occurred between the thirteenth and the seventeenth centuries, and among his followers we must number Roger Bacon, Witelo, John Pecham" (Lindberg, *Theories of Vision*, 86).[16] Alhazen's great contributions lay in his arguments against the extramission theories of Euclid and Galen, in support of a theory of intromission essentially Aristotelian in its foundation, but unique in its extensive grounding in classical mathematics, especially the work of Euclid, Ptolemy, and Al-Kindi. His work combined medical, physical, and mathematical traditions into a single comprehensive theory, laying the foundation for one of the principles of medieval psychology and optics, the theory of intromission (Lindberg, *Theories of Vision*, 49).

Intromission predicated the power of things to replicate images of themselves through the medium of air by a process termed *multiplication of species*, whereby images/*species* generated by matter strike the eye and, following the optic nerve, enter the mind as images.[17] Just how *species* worked in the mind to create ideas and abstractions was a central question in late medieval theology and philosophy. As an element in human psychology, the concept of *species* appeared in Christian philosophy as early as Augustine's *De Trinitate,* where he says every corporeal object gives rise to an incorporeal likeness, a species which exists in both the external and internal senses.[18]

In the late Middle Ages Roger Bacon's substantial treatment of the subject gathered and syncretized the many strands of thinking about the topic. Above all, Bacon was interested in how *species* exist physically. To the Augustinian understanding of the term as an element in human

---

16. On the importance of Alhazen's thinking in Western theories of vision, Lindberg says, "Alhazen's commitment to a theory of vision that combines the physical, the physiological, and the mathematical has defined the scope and the goals of optical theory from his day to the present" (*Theories of Vision*, 86).

17. For an informative and detailed discussion of *species* in late medieval philosophy, see DiMarco, "Dialogue of Science," 63; and Klassen, *Chaucer on Love*, 58–62.

18. All citations of *De Trinitate* are to book 9 and are taken from *A Select Library of Nicene and Post-Nicene Fathers of the Christian Church*, vol. 3, ed. Philip Schaff (Grand Rapids: Eerdmans, 1956), 147–50.

psychology, an understanding well known in the late Middle Ages, Bacon, following Grosseteste, added the sense that the term also denotes likeness emanating whether or not a percipient is there to receive it (*Bacon's Philosophy*, lv).[19] Once acknowledging the power of *species* to act with or without a receiver (percipient), philosophers opened the way to thinking about the term as signifying or at least implying the "force or power by which any object acts on its surroundings" (lv). Thus not only might humans receive and process sensory input they seek from the created world, but in Bacon's theory of nature the created world also has innate power to act on its surroundings, including humans, in a variety of subtle ways. Bacon developed a theory of *species* that accounted for various kinds of multiplication and of sensory reception. The proper sensibles, for instance, those qualities that can be perceived by the five basic human senses, color, sound, flavor, odor, touch, all produce *species* (lvii). Substance, too, produces *species,* but *species* apprehended only by the cogitative and estimative powers, not by external senses:

> the sensitive soul can easily perceive a substance through its species . . . although few people recognize this, since the common student of nature prefers that substantial form nòt alter sense . . . but it

---

19. Bacon allows for the operation of what others call the phantasy, the ability of the mind to combine, divide, and create new images out of what it has stored, through a more subtle and carefully worked-out combination of ideas based on the existence of accidental or sensible species and substantial and insensible *species.* The former, as we have seen, are received and judged in the anterior cell of the brain. The latter are judged by the second cell, but because the estimative faculty in this cell "does not retain a form although it receives it like the common sense," it requires memory to store its information. Thus the second cell, the seat of the cogitative faculty, is "the mistress of the sensitive [both physical and substantial] faculties":

> Man by means of this faculty sees wonderful things in dreams, and all the faculties both posterior and anterior of the sensitive soul serve and obey it, because they all exist on account of it. For the forms or species that are in the imagination multiply themselves into the cogitative faculty, although they exist in the imagination according to their nature primarily because of phantasia, which uses these forms; but the cogitative faculty holds these forms in a nobler way, and the forms of the estimative and memorative faculties exist in the cogitative faculty in accordance with the nature nobler than that existing in those faculties, and therefore the cogitative faculty uses all the other faculties as its instruments. In man there is in addition from without and from creation the rational soul, which is united with the cogitative faculty primarily and immediately, and uses this faculty chiefly as its own special instrument. Species are formed in the rational soul by this faculty. Wherefore when this faculty is impaired the judgment of reason is especially perverted, and when it is in a healthy condition the intellect functions in a sound and rational way. (*Opus Maius,* 2:426–27)

must be understood that this is true only of the exterior senses and the common sense, which retain the name "sense," for we do not call estimation and cogitation "senses," although they are parts of the sensitive soul. For the five specific senses and the common sense (and if we wish, we can easily add the imagination, as was evident above and will be touched on more fully below) perceive only accidents, although the species of substantial forms pass through them. (25)

This understanding of *species* accounts for how intentions can work on opinion in the psychological model offered by Albertus Magnus. The intentions the estimative faculty apprehends reach it as substantial *species;* we can see the process working, Bacon says, when a sheep meets a wolf and knows to fear it. Because of the existence of substantial *species,* all knowledge gained by sensible *species* is in essence secondary knowledge of accident and form, useful information from which to reason about action in the world, but not the highest form of knowing. Bacon cites Alhazen to make the point that wisdom exists on a different plane:

sight alone does not suffice for judging the truth of these things [the common sensibles]; nor is judgement concerning other [sensibles] attributed to sight, but to another power of the soul by the mediation of sight or touch or some other sense. (35)

Bacon accounts for the effect of a *species* on its receiver, saying that the reception of *species* alters a recipient:

The third conclusion is that every agent reaches to some part of the recipient that it can alter, in such a way that the alteration extends no further. . . . For the agent does not thrust or infuse something into the recipient, as was proved above, but alters it by contact with it. (*Bacon's Philosophy,* 63)

Species work to stimulate the potential in the recipient, rather than impart an action to it.

Archbishop Pecham's *Perspectiva Communis* (c. 1263), one of the most influential works on optics from this period of intense interest in the subject, makes a similar point about the power of all parts of creation to impact one another in the form of species.

Every natural body, visible or invisible, diffuses its power radiantly into other bodies. The proof of this is by a natural cause, for a natural body acts outside itself through the multiplication of its form. Therefore the more nobler it is the more strongly it acts.[20]

Because all creation emanates *species,* they can be received in different ways, and according to how they are received are given different names such as *species, idol, form, intention, phantasm and simulacrum, virtue, impression, passion.* But all forms of *species* result in the same effect in that all stimulate their receiver. This alteration inheres in the act of perception:

> Thus the wise and the foolish disagree about many things in their knowledge of species, but they agree in this, that the agent sends forth a species into the matter of the recipient, so that, through the species first produced, it can bring forth out of the potentiality of the matter [of the recipient] the complete effect that it intends. (*Bacon's Philosophy,* 7)

Ockham deliberately eliminated *species* from his theory of epistemology. His doing so testifies to the central and problematic nature of the idea in late medieval philosophy. Ockham stressed immediate existential knowledge of the mind in direct contact with material creation, denying a place for *species* in his philosophy. Humans, he maintained, possess intuitive cognition that allows them to gain existential knowledge by which to judge an object when it is present to the senses and by which to judge it not to be present—or not to exist verifiably—when it is not present to our senses. Moreover, Ockham asserted that this intuitive cognitive knowledge could never be mistaken about judgments of existence and nonexistence (a disputed point among theologians debating whether God could cause people to believe in the existence of a nonexistent object). While Ockham's thinking on this subject did not exert a wide influence, his engagement of the subject of epistemology directly through the issue of the existence or the nonexistence of *species* reveals how central *species* were to theories of cognition at the time.

---

20. David C. Lindberg, ed., *John Pecham and the Science of Optics: Perspectiva Communis* (Madison: University of Wisconsin Press, 1970), prop 1.27, p. 109.

The implications of this system of thought on the representation of reality in art are considerable. Human beings live in a world pulsing with vibrant energy. The human gaze does not merely fall upon inert creation; rather, all subjects are objects, all objects are subjects. To look is to participate in a web of connections, to open oneself to the power of things — human, created, inert, divine. Moreover, the system provides and accounts for a variety of levels of judgment based on sensible or substantial *species*. Individual moments of sight can function on any one of these levels. At the same time, this system of thinking implies a scale of perfection. It is clear that the highest level of vision occurs in the mind, based on substantial *species,* those that have little or nothing to do with accident. The highest level of vision is an act of pure intellection that is described metaphorically as insight. Such a scale of perfection seems inescapable because of the philosophical agreement that one of the dangers inherent in the model of vision relying on *species* is that *species* can fool the mind, create an apparent sufficiency in the workings of *phantasia* so as to short-circuit even the most basic processes of reason.

The system of thinking about vision as a combination of *species* and *phantasms* explains a lot of what happens in the action of *The Canterbury Tales* where characters see other people or parts of the material creation and find themselves overcome. Januarie is subject to *species* of May's beauty; his mind is literally impressed by her image. Dorigen is subject to *phantasms* of the rocks whose intentions she comprehends. But the most obvious instance of the operation of *species* in the human mind is the example of falling in love; Palamon and Arcite are overwhelmed by the sight of Emelye. Modern criticism focuses on the psychological state of the male lover, seeing him as agent. Medieval optics and theories about lovesickness explain the process of falling in love as having internalized the image of the beloved, in effect, being overwhelmed by the *species* of that person. Love is just as much a mental state, a result of the physics of sight, as an affective state; for the lover, agency and subjectivity are complicated by their interrelation with the external world. Nor is love the only emotion that, arising within an individual, can overwhelm: lust, greed, desire for an object or for a person can arise from the power of *species* to affect a gazer's sight, judgment, or will. Within such a system the question of how one controls the effects of sensory bombardment becomes paramount. Medieval philosophy constructed an answer in theories of the will at work both in the acts of seeing and remembering, the recollection of images and *phantasms.*

Sight, Will, and Self-Governance

A third topic crucial to late medieval thinking about the psychology of vision is the role of volition in seeing and remembering. Medieval theology and psychology both maintained that the mind could control what the eyes see and what the inner sight visualizes in the form of images and intentions recalled from memory. Theories of medieval faculty psychology, stressing the creative nature of *phantasy,* simultaneously stressed the need to control that creative power, to make it subservient to reason. Concern about the creative functions of the human mind comes out of the ancient tradition of Neoplatonic distrust of matter, a tradition attenuated under the influence of Aristotle in the schools of the thirteenth century, but alive and powerful in fourteenth-century Scholasticism's growing doubts about whether the material world and God are knowable through human sense.[21] To understand the relationship between will and sight it is necessary first to consider some of the basic late medieval ideas of how will affects both body and soul.

The idea that exercise of will lay at the heart of the theology of vision as well as the psychology of sight was extensively articulated in the early Middle Ages by Augustine in *De Trinitate.*[22] In vision, says Augustine, three things unite: the form of the body seen, the image impressed on the sense — the actual vision or the sense informed — and the will of the mind that applies the sense to the sensible body and retains the vision. The will, then, is central in Augustine's thinking in that it both initiates

---

21. Katherine Tachau's chapter on Oxford in the 1330s in *Vision and Certitude in the Age of Ockham* outlines the philosophical debate about the reliability of the senses, the ground of certainty, and, in the case of Crathorn, the sense that *species* "are not objectively existing, but instead are subjectively, i.e. really, existing entities in the mind or 'in some part of the brain.' Such a species is, moreover, immediately known — not formally, but 'by reflection and representatively, namely because the thing of which this is a word *(verbum)* is reflected and represented'" (261). Tachau's work delineates the recurrent, searching nature of this issue of what the mind is, and how dependent it is on the material world, whether and how the mind by itself is provisioned with conceptual knowledge, a debate framed in terms of abstractive and intuitive cognition (vision).

22. On the central, continuing tie in medieval thought between phantasy, sight, and the will, see Robert L. Montgomery, *The Reader's Eye: Studies in Didactic Literary Theory from Dante to Tasso* (Berkeley and Los Angeles: University of California Press, 1979), for a discussion of Augustine's use of phantasy and phantasm: "The image that remains in the memory Augustine calls a 'phantasy.' 'Phantasm' on the other hand, is a term he reserves for something different: it is recovery by an act of will, not of sense experience, but of an image constituted in the imagination from other remembered images. A phantasm is thus composite and in part invented, and the operation that produces it is akin to what was sometimes called 'phantasy' in later medieval concepts of the soul" (31).

vision and controls its retention: "even if the form of the body, which was corporeally perceived, be withdrawn, its likeness remains in the memory, to which the will may again direct its eye" (147). The unity of will and vision means that the will can impress the soul with what it causes the mind to see. The proofs of this in nature, says Augustine, are the chameleon, which changes color according to what color it sees, and, in the case of "other animals" who cannot easily change their bodies, offspring that frequently display in their bodies the effects of the "particular fancies" of their pregnant mothers (147).

Augustine developed a theory of perception that unites thinking, vision, and will apparently to prove that will, in controlling sight, controls our relation to this world. The end of the will in vision is a "connected series of right wills . . . a sort of road which consists . . . of certain steps whereby to ascend to blessedness." At the same time, he cautions that "the entanglement of depraved and distorted wills is a bond by which he will be bound who thus acts, so as to be cast into outer darkness" (*De Trinitate,* 150).

Will can fail in three ways: first, it can fail if the memory, the storehouse of our sense experience of the world, is not distinguished from external reality. Danger lies in thinking that the "corporeal and sensible nature" (*De Trinitate,* 152) of the forms in the mind exist "without, in the same mode in which it conceives them within either when they have already ceased to exist without, but are still retained in the memory, or when in any other way also, that which we remember is formed in the mind, not by faithful recollection, but after the variations of thought" (152). Second, if the will is not properly controlled, the generalizing faculty will not work (152). Third, the will can fail because it brings the collective memory to bear on individual experience, assimilating, matching, accepting, rejecting. This process can lead to true understanding or, if it is sidetracked by faulty will tied too closely to matter or to false forms, stay forever earthbound:

> For there are two kinds of vision. The one of [sensuous] perception *(sentientis),* the other of conception *(cogitantis).* But in order that the vision of conception may come to be, there is wrought for the purpose, in the memory, from the vision of [sensuous] perception something like it, to which the eye of the mind may turn itself in conceiving, as the glance *(acies)* of the eyes turns itself in [sensuously] perceiving to the bodily object. (152)

These ideas influenced later writers throughout the Middle Ages. Once more Vincent of Beauvais offers an example, for he structures his entire discussion of the connection between sight and imagination on the power of the will, as in these excerpts from chapter 18, "De imagine Trinitatis in memoria vel imaginatione":

> Furthermore, even when the appearance of the body has been re-moved, which was bodily sensed, its likeness remains in the memory, where the will may again turn its gaze so that it is thence inwardly formed, just as the sense is outwardly formed from a body that is present and able to be sensed, and thus would be that Trinity of memory and internal vision and that which joins both by means of the will.

> [Porro etiam detracta specie corporis, quae corporaliter sentiebatur, remanet in memoria eius similitudo, quo rursus voluntas aciem conuertat, vt inde formetur intrinsecus, sicut ex corpore subiecto sensibili sensus extrinsecus formabatur, atque ita sit illa Trinitas ex memoria, & interna visione, & que vtrúque copulat voluntate.] (*Speculum Naturale,* 1664)

So great is the power of the will that it can actually close off the mind and the senses from the world:

> But if the will, which moves this way and that way, and redirects the formation of the gaze, and joins together the things formed to the inward impression, should wholly gather itself together, and com-pletely turn away the mind's gaze from the senses of the body, and convert its image deeply to that which is perceived inwardly, so great a bodily likeness of the appearance is established clearly defined in memory that not even reason itself is allowed to distinguish whether the body is being seen outside or whether some such thing is being thought inwardly.

> [Si autem voluntas, quae hac atque illac fert, & refert aciem for-mandam, coniungitque formata ad interiorem phantasiam tota con-fluxerit, atque a sensibus corporis animi aciem omnino auerterit, atque ad eam, quae intus cernitur imaginem penitus conuerterit, tanta funditur similtudo speciei corporalis expressa in memoria, vt nec ipsa ratio discernere sinatur. Vtrum foris corpus ipsum videatur, an intus tale aliquid cogitetur.] (1665)

The will was crucial in the functioning of the sense of sight, long before images came into the brain. The precise relationship among the eyes, the soul, and the outer world was one philosophy and theology were at great pains to fix.[23] Trevisa puts it succinctly and typically when he says that eyes can be "enemyes and þeues and robbiþ mannes inwit. While we folewen þe desire of yӡen we beþ made sugettis to ful cruel enemies, as þe expositour seiþ *super illud Trenorum:* Mine iӡe haþ ispoiled and robbid my soule" (*Properties of Things,* 1:365). In the *Consolation of Philosophy* Boethius had argued that the perceiver was central in the process of vision, "for al that ever is iknowe, it is rather comprehendid and knowen, nat after his strengthe and his nature, but aftir the faculte (that is to seyn, the power and the nature) of hem that knowen."[24] In referring to "the power and nature of hem that knowen," Boethius had put responsibility for the processes involved in sight squarely on the individual and on individual will. This position contin-

---

23. This tie between soul and body constituted an abiding paradox in medieval Christian thought — an assurance of the validity of matter and of the divine sanction of the human mind's means of knowing matter, and a perpetual source of discomfort because the very act of apprehending the material world through the physical senses was subject to distortion and mistake. What fourteenth-century philosophy contributed was a different order of angst: it had long been said that the created world could blind Christians to the proper focus of love and attention, God. It had also been said that the human mind could play tricks on itself and, in so doing, drift away from its proper focus on God. Fourteenth-century thinkers raised this latter idea to a central debate, locating it in the question of how far and in what ways human faculties were at all capable of determining truth and leading to understanding of God. In "Scientific Thought in Fourteenth-Century Paris: Jean Buridan and Nicole Oresme," in *Machaut's World: Science and Art in the Fourteenth Century,* ed. Madeleine Pelner Cosman and Bruce Chandler, Annals of the New York Academy of Sciences, 314 (New York, 1978), 105–24, Edward Grant discusses Nicholas Oresme's philosophy of doubt (Oresme was a contemporary and friend of Machaut). While Grant points out that Oresme's work was "virtually ignored" (107) because his ideas were "either too technical or contained attacks against magic and astrology, thus severely limiting his appeal" (107), he maintains that Oresme's work (he was active 1335–79, d. 1382) represents a common strain of fourteenth-century philosophy, the unraveling of thirteenth-century Aristotelian pragmatism. According to Grant the thrust of Oresme's arguments was "to underscore the inability of human reason to arrive at certain knowledge about the physical world. . . . By suggesting sound alternatives to a variety of well-entrenched opinions, Oresme hoped to demonstrate that experience and natural reason were incapable of determining physical truth convincingly and unambiguously" (111). Grant points out that Buridan and Oresme "shared a general conviction that absolute truth was only to be found in faith and revelation and that knowledge of the physical world was at best provisional, probable, and approximate" (115).

24. Geoffrey Chaucer, *Boece,* book 5, prosa 4, 140, in *The Riverside Chaucer,* gen. ed. Larry D. Benson, 3d ed. (Boston: Houghton Mifflin, 1987). All citations of Chaucer's work are to this edition.

ued to be the dominant one throughout the Middle Ages. No matter how attractive, powerful, or compelling the images of creation were, the individual was responsible for controlling his or her response to them. The centrality of the individual appears over and over in the literature of this subject. Even the relatively scientific branch of the study of vision, optics, centered in the observer. David Lindberg, Pecham's twentieth-century translator and editor, says Pecham's principal objective in the *Perspectiva Communis* was to describe how objects appear to a single observer. Pecham's propositions depend on the individual's ability to exercise his will to reason individually about what he perceives (prop. 1.60, p. 137). On the one hand the observer finds him/herself in the midst of an attractive and compelling web of *species;* on the other hand, the percipient is not mere prey to vision, but participates in a cosmically ordained process linking understanding and the exercise of the will. In this process images and sensory experience are absolutely essential, yet potentially misleading.

The right orientation of the will was essential in negotiating the web of species in the world and controlling their correlative *phantasms* in the mind. Medieval psychology constructed the human psyche as a dynamic tension of oppositional but complementary capacities, built on the premise that ideally the will can control the senses. Trevisa reflects both the anxiety and the hope of this dynamic tension. Citing the authority of St. John Damascene, he says that God has made the human soul reasonable, intellectual, and tied to the body; that God has endowed it with grace and made it in his image. As the eye is in the body, so the intellect is in the soul. This soul, moreover, is free to act or not, for the soul has "fre avisement and wille and is changeable bi couenable will, for he may freliche worche oþir leue." But in the same passage he also cites Saint Bernard, who represents quite a different, and equally authoritative, tradition. Here is the passage where the two attitudes appear juxtaposed:

Iohannes Damascenus *capitulo 24ᵒ* comprehendiþ al þese diffini-ciouns vndir on general discripcioun and seiþ þat a soule is a sub-staunce, lyuynge, symple, and bodiles, in his oune kinde vnseye wiþ bodyliche yȝen, noþir schal deye, resonable, intellectual, wiþoute schap of lymes. And he vsiþ a body and ȝeueþ þerto herte of lif and of wexinge and of gendringe, and haþ none oþir intellect but in hitself he is ful clene. Also as þe yȝe is in þe body so is þe intellect, vndir-stondinge, in þe soule. And he haþ fre avisement and wille and is chaungeable bi couenable wille, for he may freliche worche oþir leue. Al þese þe spirit fongiþ of his grace þat made him; of him he haþ beinge and kinde. *Huc usque Iohannes Damascenus capitulo 5º supra.* Bernard descriueþ riȝt suche propirtees and seþ: O þou soule, ihiȝt and imade feir wiþ þe image and liknes of God, ispousid in spirit with fey, ibouȝt wiþ Cristis owne blood to take blisse, eir of sauacioun and of hele, partener of resoun, what hast þou to do wiþ þe fleische by þe whiche þou suffres moche, *et cetera?* By þese many and diuers diffiniciouns and descripciouns diuers propirtees of soule beþ iknowe, touchinge his beinge of kynde and of grace. (*Properties of Things,* 1:92–93)

Will's struggle to control the senses is a struggle to achieve real knowledge, for the soul has its own ways of knowing, at once closely tied to and distinct from the body's ways of knowing. Trevisa says that "þe soule haþ comparison [to þe body and to his ende and to his worchinge. In comparison to þe body] þe soule haþ fyue maner myȝtes and vertues" (*Properties of Things,* 1:95), which include feeling, wit, *ymaginacioune, resoun,* and *intellectus,* or understanding termed "inwit." The first three humans share in common with animals, but the latter two, *resoun* and *intellectus,* are uniquely properties of the human soul (1:95). Of these latter two *myȝtes and vertues,* Trevisa says that the soul *racionalis* is the "vertu of vndirstondinge þat hatte *intellectus,*" that it is "euerlastinge, incorruptibil," and that "þerfor his principal act and dede, þat is *intelligere* 'vndirstonde,' is noȝt dependaunt of the body," and

þerefore he lyueþ parfitliche and vndirstondiþ whan he is departid from þe body. And þe more he drenchiþ him into þe body, þe more slowliche and þe lasse parfiteliche he vndirstondiþ. And þe more he withdrawiþ him from þe boundis and likinge of fleissche, þe more esiliche and clereliche he vndirstondiþ. Here I clepe "drenchinge in" oþir by ymaginacioun of fantasie, oþir by likinge of fleisch, oþir loue of wordliche catel. (1:101)

Given a position between the beasts and the angels, the soul can turn by reason toward God and toward the highest kind of knowledge, understanding, or "by affecciouns toward creatures" turn "derk, corrupt, and apeired" (1:101). In this passage *affeccioun* denotes the emotional or volitional faculty of the soul. It can lead away from reason toward "drenchyng in" the body, a phrase that can variously mean surrendering to images of the *ymaginacioun* or *phantasy* or giving in to the pleasure of the flesh, love of worldly goods. As with the human faculties and their relationship to the mind, so medieval models of the soul, too, while stressing unity, also posit constituent elements that create a natural duality. Trevisa's compilation of sources reflects more than the contradictory thinking on this subject in the late Middle Ages; it also reflects the commonplace assumption that the strain between the reason and the *affecciouns* is located in the imagination and fantasy — it is not just deeds that turn the soul away from God, but thoughts, visions, imagination that can "drown" the soul in attachments to the created world. Finally, the passage reflects grave doubt that the soul can understand, know anything of real value about the creation and the creator, if it depends on the created world for information.

Understanding of God and of God's creation was the ultimate end of vision, both physical and spiritual. Although the discourse of understanding in the preceding passage favors an oppositional rhetoric pitting the soul against the senses, in fact the close connection between body and mind was assumed in the soul's journey to understanding. The soul was a pilgrim, a *viator* that used experience as a guide on its journey.[25] Nowhere was this interwoven nexus of physical sight, insight, and will so densely constructed as in late medieval English mysticism, which used a rhetoric of sight to express the Latin concept of *contemplatio* and of understanding to achieve what Wolfgang Riehle describes this way: the "seeing of the soul is the reception of knowledge which is shown to it by divine grace. Hence in Middle English texts *siʒt* is often linked with *understondyng* or *cnowyng*."[26]

At first it might seem that late medieval mysticism rejected the earthly in favor of visions of the divine. But mystical visions are yet one more instance of simultaneous affirmation of, and anxiety about, sensory knowledge. At its heart, a strong current of materialism inheres in the mystical writing of this period. It appears in Julian of Norwich's *Revelations*, for example, where she describes her visions as both bodily sight and ghostly sight, leading to understanding.

---

25. For an informative discussion of the topos of the soul/mind as *viator* see Russell A. Peck, "Chaucer and the Nominalist Question," *Speculum* 53 (1978): 745–60.

26. Wolfgang Riehle, *The Middle English Mystics*, trans. Bernard Standring (London: Routledge, 1981), 123–24.

And in that tyme that oure lorde schewyd this that I haue nowe saydene in the gastely syght, I saye the bodylye syght lastande of the plentyuouse bledynge of the hede, and als longe as y sawe that syght y sayde oftynn tymes: Benedicite Dominus. In this fyrste schewynge of oure lorde I saw sex thynges in myne vundyrstandynge.[27]

Julian's mystical discourse links bodily vision, understanding, and spiritual vision in this phrase, which recurs in both versions of the *Revelations:* "Alle this blyssede techyng of oure lorde was schewyd to me in thre partyes, that is by bodylye syght, and by worde formede in myne vndyrstandynge, and by gastelye syght" (1:224, 2:323, 666).

John Fleming identifies the widespread, popular dimension of the mystical tradition Julian participates in, citing the influence of Bonaventure's *Itinerarium Mentis in Deum,* in which "The mind rises to the understanding of the invisible divine nature by degrees; the first degree, of course, is the observation of 'those things that are made,' in St. Paul's famous words in Romans 1:20."[28] Fleming refers to this text as "typical of what might be called 'popular' or 'evangelical' mysticism of the fourteenth century" (213). The journey to eternal life and union with God "begin in a disciplined direction of the will, continue through the trained and graced exercise of the intellect to the spiritual union with God which is beyond the analysis of the rational faculties" (213).

Bonaventure says, "Corresponding, therefore, to the six steps in the ascent to God, there are six gradated powers of the soul, whereby we ascend from the lowest to the highest, from things outside us, to those that are within, and from the temporal to the eternal. These six powers are the senses, imagination, reason, understanding, intelligence, and the summit of the mind or the spark of synderesis.[29] The human mind begins any journey to God with the bodily senses, because they can perceive that the "supreme power, wisdom, and goodness of the Creator shines forth in created things" (*Journey of the Mind,* 8). The senses, in turn, especially the sight, depend on *species,* which embody the form, power, and activity of the created world in proportion to their

27. *A Book of Showings to the Anchoress Julian of Norwich,* 2 vols., ed. Edmund Colledge and James Walsh (Toronto: Pontifical Institute of Medieval Studies, 1978), 1:217.

28. John V. Fleming, *An Introduction to the Franciscan Literature of the Middle Ages* (Chicago: Franciscan Herald Press, 1977), 161.

29. Saint Bonaventure, *The Journey of the Mind to God,* trans. Philotheus Boehner, ed. Stephen F. Brown (Indianapolis: Hacket, 1993), 6–7.

source in God. From *species* one sees creation's "mode, species, and order, as well as substance, power, and activity. From all these considerations the observer can rise, as from a vestige, to the knowledge of the immense power, wisdom, and goodness of the Creator" (8). Judgment moves from the information of the senses via *species* to a "still more excellent and more immediate way to a surer beholding of eternal truth" (14). The operations of judgment work on what the reception of the senses has stored in memory, from which "comes forth intelligence as its offspring, because we understand only when the likeness which is in the memory emerges at the high point of our understanding and this is the mental word. From the memory and the intelligence is breathed forth love, as the bond of both. These three — the generating mind, the word, and love — exist in the soul as memory, intelligence, and will, which are consubstantial, coequal, and equally everlasting and mutually inclusive" (21). At the same time, Bonaventure cautions, this process of united intelligence and will can be lead astray if the will does not control the uses to which memory and intelligence are put:

Distracted by many cares, the human mind does not enter into itself through the memory; beclouded by sense images, it does not come back to itself through the intelligence; and drawn away by the concupiscences, it does not return to itself through the desire for interior sweetness and spiritual joy. Therefore, completely immersed in things of sense, the soul cannot re-enter into itself as the image of God. (23)[30]

---

30. The memory itself, storehouse of images and intentions, was a voluntary faculty that needed the will to retain, to summarize, or to erase its products. In *Seeing the Gawain Poet: Description and the Act of Perception* (Philadelphia: University of Pennsylvania Press, 1991), Sarah Stanbury recognizes this dualism and places it at the center of her discussion of the idea of seeing in the fourteenth-century English literature she discusses. On the one hand she cites the importance of the poetics of sight in English mysticism of the period.

A recognition and celebration of the role of the senses in leading to spiritual "vision" is at the heart of Franciscan spiritualism. . . . The role of direct experience in the hierarchy of knowledge is also important in the writings of Duns Scotus and William of Ockham. (128)

At the same time, she notes the dualism at the heart of late medieval epistemology.

In the mystical treatises and the poems describing the spiritual pilgrimage to God that proliferated in the later Middle Ages, sight becomes the primary metaphor and symbol for spiritual knowledge. Sight also becomes, paradoxically, both first task of the *viator*

The soul can return to itself, that is, to its proper and elemental state of union with God, through grace: "For into this heavenly Jerusalem no one enters unless it first comes down into his heart by grace, as St. John beheld in the Apocalypse. It comes down into our heart when, by the reformation of the image, the theological virtues, the delights of the spiritual senses, and uplifting transports, our spirit becomes hierarchical, that is purified, enlightened, and perfected" (23–25). In this tradition of mystical thinking the material world is not rejected so much as controlled through the will's longing for understanding.[31]

Within the context of these traditions of philosophic contradiction, aspiration, and uncertainty Chaucer creates his characters. In the interstices between affirmation and denigration he locates human beings struggling to know, to do, to love, to succeed. That they may fail is the source of his humor and the nature of the worldview he inherited. As the preceding pages have shown, discussions of human psychology in this period almost always comprise a dynamic balance between deprecation and celebration. As an artist Chaucer takes advantage of this inherent tension, exploiting it to produce his humorous characters, accepting its premises in creating his ideal characters as people who, like Griselda and Cecile, manage to live in the world without being of it.

Tracing the ideas current in late medieval culture about vision and the mind, about vision and mystical experience, and about vision and will, reveals broad-based agreement on several fundamental principles of medieval psychology: that physical sight is the chief human sense, that it is uniquely formulated to link humans to creation and to God. Rather than describing humans as observers of phenomena, the models of vision theory and of psychology assume that humans are part of a web of *species*, generated by matter, by accident and substance. This tradition

---

and his or her most deceptive faculty, the physical sense that must be stilled, whose "doors" must be closed before true spiritual vision can occur. (128)

Stanbury quotes the anonymous author of the *Cloud of Unknowing* as typical of fourteenth-century English mystics and, by implication, of popular piety: "þerfore leue þin outward wittes, & worche not wiþ hem, neiþer wiþ-inne ne wiþ-outen" (131).

31. Trevisa terms the soul's longing the *concupissibilis*. The "vertue" of the soul that "taketh hede to þing þat is good"; in the concupiscible "is wille and desire of goode þinge. . . . Al affecciouns and desire comeþ of the *concupiscibilis* and *irascibilis*. Affecciouns beþ foure: ioye, hope, drede, and sorwe. Þe first tweyne comeþ of þe concupiscibilis, for of þe þing [þat we] coueitiþ and desireþ we haue ioye and for ioye we hopiþ" (*Properties of Things*, 1:95–96).

stresses the fragile but essential links between human reason and material creation. It posits that will and a right orientation of will defined as a desire to understand ought to control seeing and remembering. In this culture vision and sight are fundamental both as experience and as metaphor for experience.

All this was part of the common, received knowledge of educated people in late-fourteenth-century England. While the chances that any one person would have known the specific passages and writers presented here in the way that I have organized them is slender indeed, that the people whom Chaucer wrote, worked, and lived with would have found many of these ideas familiar is a virtual certainty. Researching this topic one is struck by the redundancy of language, of metaphors, of arguments from one text to another. These are not arcane or specialized ideas — if Chaucer's audience did not know Bacon, they did know the theory of multiplication of *species;* if they did not know Augustine on the will, they surely knew that the will can impede the soul's journey to God by too great an attachment to the things of this world — they could have heard or read these ideas in a hundred places. Knowing this tradition, we can see that many of *The Canterbury Tales* that turn on moments of sight in fact also turn on knowledge of these traditions. It is not so much that ignorance of these ideas and traditions prevents a modern reader from understanding the tales, but rather that knowledge of these systems and theories enriches our readings of the tales, their jokes, their plots, their philosophy. Knowledge of these traditions creates a richer sense of the work, and of the author's creative mind. It also enriches our sense of the purpose and scope of Chaucer's art in his last work, revealing a fiction built on tension between affirmation and suspicion of the most basic processes of the human body and human mind.

2

The "Foule Prisoun of This Lyf": Limited Visions in "The Knight's Tale"

"The Knight's Tale" opens the *Canterbury Tales* in all manuscripts. By constructing the socially appropriate "accident" that the Knight tells the first tale, Chaucer sends multiple signals that this tale is a cornerstone, an important building block in the structure that will ultimately emerge as the completed *Canterbury Tales*. While the story is superficially a courtly one about love and arms, the knight-lovers are also philosophers, questioning whether any divinely ordained patterns govern events, whether human desire, choice, or action can shape events to human will. Readers who are familiar with late medieval astrology also recognize that the four planetary deities who dominate the tale — Venus, Mars, Diana, and Saturn — were thought to correspond to the four basic humors that comprise every human body. Their presence in the tale complements the philosophic theme, imbuing the action and the characters with a cosmic dimension that transcends the particulars of its pagan setting.[1]

Not surprisingly, so rich a tale has generated a vast amount of criticism, much of it attempting to explicate the theme of order within the tale, or, more recently, devoted to exploring its antichivalric ethos.[2] Part

---

1. On this topic see T. McAlindon, "Cosmology, Contrariety, and the 'Knight's Tale,'" *Medium Aevum* 55 (1986): 41–57. McAlindon notes, "The principal characters in the poem are so dominated by their emotions, and their emotions are so closely linked with the dynamics of universal nature, that the action seems propelled less by individuals than by psycho-physical forces which course through the human and non-human spheres of existence" (47–48).

2. Critics have pointed to the rich pattern of significance residing in the intersection of its diverse themes. Lee Patterson's discussion of the tale, its cultural milieu, and its twentieth-century critical reception in *Chaucer and the Subject of History* (Madison: University of Wisconsin Press, 1991), 165–230, categorizes the outpouring of criticism that has addressed the tale in the second half of this century. He begins by noting Muscatine's seminal influence on the terms of the discussion (Charles Muscatine, "Form, Texture, and Meaning in Chaucer's *Knight's Tale*," *PMLA* 65 [1950]: 911–29) in identifying the theme of the poem as "the struggle between noble designs and chaos" (165). Following Musca-

of the reason the tale has generated so much criticism lies in its thematic complexity: it bears multiple simultaneous interpretations, without seeming to validate one way of reading it over another. In its course, the story poses questions about how human beings know, love, and understand in a world of constant mutability. These basic questions lead to other, more complex issues such as whether free will exists and whether chivalric culture can help channel or control human passion. In addition to these well-recognized themes, the tale also develops a largely unrecognized theme centered in the visual experience of its characters and their attempts to deal with and use that experience. Late medieval theories about how human beings interact with the world through their sense of sight, and through the images the sense of sight stores in the mind, underlie the action of the tale at significant moments in its plot. The tale presents three distinct efforts to cope with, use, and transform visual experience. Palamon and Arcite, Theseus, and the Knight-narrator all contend with the effects of sight-created images as they strive to achieve their several desires and to make sense of their worlds. In each case the sense of sight, potentially the most useful of the senses, leads to three distinct yet narrow comprehensions of human and divine forces. The different responses these characters enact bear directly on the issues of self-governance, chivalry, and philosophy fundamental to the tale. The combination of these three responses contributes substantially to the dark, somber mood of the tale.

---

tine's lead, critics have investigated formalist concerns, asking whether the tale endorses or problematizes the possibilities of order and regulation in the world it images. See, for example, Kathleen A. Blake, "Order and the Noble Life in Chaucer's *Knight's Tale?*" *Modern Language Quarterly* 34 (1973): 3–19; Robert W. Hanning, "'The Struggle between Noble Designs and Chaos': The Literary Tradition of Chaucer's Knight's Tale," *Literary Review* 23 (1980): 519–41; Richard Neuse, "The Knight: The First Mover in Chaucer's Human Comedy," *University of Toronto Quarterly* 31 (1962): 299–315; Elizabeth Salter, *Chaucer: The Knight's Tale and the Clerk's Tale* (London: Edward Arnold, 1962); Joseph Westlund, "The *Knight's Tale* as an Impetus for Pilgrimage," *Philological Quarterly* 43 (1964): 526–37. But, says Patterson, the "formalist desire to stress the *Tale's* literariness and the liberalism that is its political analogue have been challenged by an opposing attitude — itself divided into two camps — committed instead to the historicity of cultural value" (166). One group, "ranked, under the banner of D. W. Robertson, [is] those who believe that all medieval writing was governed by a fully coherent and hierarchically organized world view" (166). This critical position naturally leads to reading disorder as a moral, spiritual failure, often attributable to human weakness — of a moral or spiritual nature. In the second or "opposing" camp are those who see the tale in general and Theseus in particular, as "a Chaucerian commentary on the decline of medieval chivalry into brutal exploitation" (167). Among such critics Patterson includes Terry Jones, David Aers, and Stephen Knight.

Palamon and Arcite: "Hurt Right Now thurghout Myn Ye"

The substantial action of the tale begins when the two cousins see
Emelye. As they respond to her image, Palamon and Arcite enter a
mental state where obsession impairs their ability to reason. To describe
their plight Chaucer draws on a discourse laden with complex philosophical, optical, and medical overtones — the discourse of lovesickness. As
early as 1914 John Livingston Lowes recognized that in describing the
love that arises from the vision of Emelye, that the knight/Chaucer was
describing the phenomenon and the symptoms of *amor hereos* — lovesickness.[3] Lowes suggested that the description of love's effect on Arcite
might "almost be a paraphrase of a chapter on *hereos* from one of
the medical treatises themselves" (525). Both Boccaccio and Chaucer
were familiar with this material, for, Lowes says, a reading of Boccaccio's
Teseide shows that "Chaucer found many of the *signa* already in the
Teseide, and proceeded to rearrange and combine them in the light of his
knowledge of the malady" (525).

Medieval theories of lovesickness familiar to Chaucer and Boccaccio
evolved from Constantine's eleventh-century translation of the Arabic
medical handbook of Abu Ja'far Ahmad ibn Ibrāhīm ibn abī Khālid al-
Jazzār, known in the West as the *Viaticum.* The popularity of the work is
attested to by the numerous commentaries, and by wills and university
records that cite the existence and circulation of manuscript copies. The
Viaticum explains the "disease" of lovesickness as a function of the sight.
An image enters the brain as imagination. Fantasy, unchecked by will
and separate from reason, transforms the image into an obsessive fixation. Eventually, in extreme cases, such obsession can lead to mania and
to melancholy, possibly even death. Lowes's research shows that Chaucer and his audience were familiar with the pathology of the disease.

Mary Frances Wack's more recent critical edition of Constantine's *Viaticum*[4] and several of its major commentaries emphasizes the same fundamental point: no matter how the details varied, lovesickness as *morbus*

---

3. John Livingston Lowes, "The Loveres Maladye of Hereos," *Modern Philology* 11
(1914): 491–546. A more recent analysis of the medieval psychological and medical thinking that the tale draws on and contributes to appears in Mary Frances Wack, ed., *Lovesickness in the Middle Ages: The* Viaticum *and Its Commentaries* (Philadelphia: University of
Pennsylvania Press, 1990).
   4. On the availability of this text and its commentaries in late-fourteenth-century
England, see Wack, *Lovesickness,* 47–48.

was described throughout the medieval period as a disease of the brain, initiated by vision. Wack outlines the various disputes and debates over the exact seat of love in the body and the mind, love's effect on the body, its function in the brain, and the morbidity it engenders. A connection among sight, image, and misjudgment appears in all descriptions. Avicenna, for example, located lovesickness in the misfunction of the estimative faculty in the middle ventricle of the brain, because estimation is "misled by an excessively pleasing sense perception, so strong that it eclipses other sense impressions that might contradict it" (Wack, 56). The gazer is acted upon by the image that overtakes him. Wack points out that at the heart of the theory of lovesickness in the later Middle Ages lay concepts of psychology, optics, and philosophy. The term *love* and lovesickness engendered from love represented a complex web of reference moving beyond affective emotion:

These authors' attention to *species* situates their work within a larger contemporary problematic, that of *species in medio,* a concept at the heart of interlocking controversies in optics, psychology, epistemology, and philosophy. The emergence of visual *species* in causal analyses of *amor hereos* in the late thirteenth and fourteenth centuries also placed lovesickness in a fertile nexus of debates on imagination and magic in natural philosophy and theology. (135)

Lovesickness makes its victim a prisoner of his own imagination and his own faculty of sight.

In the tale the idea of love as restrictive obsession contributes to the pervasive metaphor of life as a prison, for love leads to surrender of self and loss of self-control. Palamon and Arcite begin in a state of figurative imprisonment that will be compounded by the prison Theseus constructs, and by the psychological prison their eyes help build.[5] Caught in

---

5. Kolve identifies this overwhelming theme as a distinguishing feature of Chaucer's version of this story: "Chaucer's *Knight's Tale,* in contrast [to Boccaccio's], expands the prison image to make it totally inclusive, so that it furnishes the poem's final philosophic description of the world as well as its first substantial mise-en-scène. The scraps of philosophy we hear from within the prison of this world serve only to make it a little more bearable; they offer no release. In *The Knight's Tale,* the problem of freedom is never resolved—the poem remains locked in apparent determinism—and the problem of order reveals at its center nothing less than the problem of death itself. Neither Boethius nor Chaucer would have thought the *Consolation* a sufficient answer to that" (*Chaucer and the Imagery of Narrative: The First Five Canterbury Tales* [Stanford: Stanford University Press, 1984], 142). Judith Ferster, *Chaucer on Interpretation* (Cambridge: Cambridge

"this foule prisoun of this lyf" (1.3061), the two are incarcerated for the rest of their lives in a high tower from which they can survey the city and in particular a garden where Emelye gathers flowers "to make a subtil gerland for hire hede" (1.1054). In this prison they are free to use their faculties. They do so, look out the window, and each, to a different degree, finds himself bound mentally, as well as physically.

This process begins when Palamon, allowed by his jailer to ascend to a "chambre on heigh," sees Emelye. The two images of Palamon in the tower and Emelye in the garden are connected by the language that joins them. Palamon, imprisoned in the tower, "was risen and romed" (1.1065); Emelye, imprisoned in the garden, "Was in hire walk, and romed up and doun" (1.1069). The Middle English *romen* carried connotations similar to our modern word *pace* when used of caged animals. Palamon and Emelye, both caught by life, both *romynge,* pacing in their respective prison cells, he in the high tower, she in the garden, are united in their restless energy. But their situations might have been understood to differ in one significant regard: Palamon, situated in the tower, ought to be able to see further and more clearly than Emelye. In fact instead of looking out and away, he looks down and sees her.

Palamon's vision of Emelye, like Troilus's vision of Criseyde in the temple in book 1 of the *Troilus,* is overwhelming — a piercing experience in which the action of seeing and the image of the lady seen strike his heart:

> And so bifel, by aventure or cas,
> That thurgh a wyndow, thikke of many a barre
> Of iren greet and square as any sparre,
> He cast his eye upon Emelya,
> And therwithal he bleynte and cride, "A!"
> As though he stongen were unto the herte.
>
> (1.1074–79)

When exhorted by Arcite not to bewail his situation, but to "taak al in pacience," Palamon reveals that although he has had a vision and experienced its transformative power, he does not quite comprehend what he

University Press, 1985), discusses the absolute barrier that Arcite and Palamon erect between themselves, thereby imprisoning themselves in their alienation. Cut off from the world, cut off from understanding the nature/shape of things, they are also unable to understand each other.

has seen. Nevertheless, he emphasizes what the narrator has just told us, that the sight of Emelye has wounded him in the heart:[6]

Cosyn, for sothe, of this opinioun
Thow has a veyn ymaginacioun.
This prison caused me nat for to crye,
But I was hurt right now thurghout myn ye
Into myn herte, that wol my bane be.
The fairnesse of that lady that I see
Yond in the gardyn romen to and fro
Is cause of al my criyng and my wo.
I noot wher she be womman or goddesse,
But Venus is it soothly, as I gesse.

(1.1093–1102)

Thinking he has seen Venus, he prays to her. If he has not understood the essence of what he has seen, he has at least intimated from its *species* and *intentiones* some of its significance. Emelye represents a beautiful good in the tale. Palamon reveals that what he has fallen in love with is "the fairnesse of that lady" — she literally embodies an admirable universal quality that he desires. His love for her is not just for a person, but for the quality she represents.[7] Her presence in the garden, her melodious singing, mark her as a desirable image of the beautiful perpetually denied the two knights in the tower.

Arcite experiences a similar kind of response to Emelye, but it is different in degree. Hearing Palamon's speech, he looks out:

---

6. Wack explains that the Aristotelian physiology entering Europe during the thirteenth century strove for a time with the Arabic psychology of love, particularly over the question of where to locate the seat of the emotion. According to Aristotelian psychology the emotions resided in the heart; the Arabic medical and philosophical tradition regarded love as an obsession arising from sight and located as an obsession and a disease in the ventricles of the brain. By the time of Peter of Spain — and certainly by Chaucer's time — it was possible to distinguish between two types of love, one located in the heart and not morbid, the other located in the brain and truly morbid. Wack summarizes the distinction between the two theories of love: "'Cardiac love' may be a passionate emotion, but 'cerebral love' can become a disease" (*Lovesickness*, 96). Palamon is clearly stung in the heart.

7. Wack records that love was thought essentially to be a longing for something that completed the soul and was obtained through a woman. Love was not necessarily longing for an individual person or personality. This understanding accords with the cures suggested, for often they recommend intercourse with any woman as a relief from lovesickness. See Wack, *Lovesickness*, 66–73.

And with that word Arcite gan espye
Wher as this lady romed to and fro,
And with that sighte hir beautee hurte hym so,
That, if that Palamon was wounded sore,
Arcite is hurt as muche as he, or moore.
And with a sigh he seyde pitously,
"The fresshe beautee sleeth me sodeynly
Of hire that rometh in the yonder place;
And but I have hir mercy and hir grace,
That I may seen hire atte leeste weye,
I nam but deed; ther nis namoore to seye."

(1.1112–22)

Like Palamon, Arcite, too, responds to her beauty, tying the value and the very existence of his life to her. Concluding that his life depends on seeing her, he indicates that he, too, has perceived somewhat the depth of what she signifies, but is unable fully to understand who she is or what she portends for him. The narrator, foreshadowing what will come, suggests that Arcite is wounded more deeply than Palamon, for Arcite's response links love directly to death, not to Venus.

The jealous argument that ensues suggests that the vision of Emelye each has received and so deeply internalized becomes a *fantasye,* an image stored in the mind, but, because of the emotions attending it, an image that does not help either knight fully to understand what Emelye is, the nature of her beauty, or his own situation. Each knight comprehends some of her *intentiones.* But both seem infected with a disease of judgment. The sight of Emelye and desire for that sight become an obsession, severely impairing their brains' estimative as well as imaginative faculties, as her image almost totally occupies each knight's mind. Their "love" leads them into strife and contention so serious that it breaks the bonds of friendship, of chivalry, and of brotherhood. It also leads them into philosophic mazes. Each, desiring Emelye, questions the fortune that brings such a strong passion into his life but denies him freedom.

Arcite understands that his relationships to Emelye, to the prison house of life, and to free will are united. He is able to express his sense of helpless subjection to forces beyond his control. For Arcite, newly released from prison but still suffering, the central questions of life become questions about how to desire, recognize, and achieve real happiness, articulated in a speech that begins,

> Allas, why pleynen folk so in commune
> On purveiaunce of God, or of Fortune,
> That yeveth hem ful ofte in many a gyse
> Wel bettre than they kan hemself devyse?
>
>   (1.1251–54)

He goes on to enumerate the kinds of mistakes humans make in thinking they know where their happiness will lie:

> Som man desireth for to han richesse,
> That cause is of his mordre or greet siknesse;
> And som man wolde out of his prisoun fayn,
> That in his hous is of his meynee slayn.
> Infinite harmes been in this mateere.
> We witen nat what thing we preyen heere;
> We faren as he that dronke is as a mous.
> A dronke man woot wel he hath an hous,
> But he noot which the righte wey is thider,
> And to a dronke man the wey is slider.
> And certes, in this world so faren we;
> We seken faste after felicitee,
> But we goon wrong ful often, trewely.
>
>   (1.1255–67)

His conclusion is to abandon the subject and himself:

> Thus may we seyen alle, and namely I,
> That wende and hadde a greet opinioun
> That if I myghte escapen from prisoun,
> Thanne hadde I been in joye and parfit heele,
> Ther now I am exiled fro my wele.
> Syn that I may nat seen you, Emelye,
> I nam but deed; the nys no remedye.
>
>   (1.1268–74)

Palamon's questions are darker, centered in the nature of man's place in the hierarchy of the created universe and a fear of divine indifference toward human beings.

> O crueel goddes that governe
> This world with byndyng of youre word eterne,
> And writen in the table of atthamaunt
> Youre parlement and youre eterne graunt,
> What is mankynde moore unto you holde
> Than is the sheep that rouketh in the folde?
> For slayn is man right as another beest,
> And dwelleth eek in prison and arreest,
> And hath siknesse and greet adversitee,
> And ofte tymes giltelees, pardee.

(1.1303–12)

Where Arcite was able to acknowledge a shaping hand in the universe, saying, "Allas, why pleynen folk so in commune / On purveiaunce of God, or of Fortune," Palamon questions whether there is any benevolence in a universe which requires humans constantly to restrain their desires and which seems to torture the innocent:

> What governance is in this prescience,
> That giltelees tormenteth innocence?
> And yet encresseth this al my penaunce,
> That man is bounden to his observaunce,
> For Goddes sake, to letten of his wille,
> Ther as a beest may al his lust fulfille.

(1.1313–18)

Separate and distinct in their states and their reflections, both arrive at a common dead end. Their ability to formulate answers is limited in comparison to their ability to generate questions. Both speeches draw from *The Consolation of Philosophy* in which Philosophia provides answers to Boethius's questions; Arcite's is loosely based on prosa 2 of book 3, where Philosophia discourses on the nature of humans to desire the good, and the difficulties humans have in distinguishing between eternal good and transitory goods. Arcite's version is altogether more bleak than its source. Philosophia allows that riches, fame, and power are indeed worldly goods. Where she says that humans desire the good but, like a drunken man trying to find his house, have only a dim sense of how to find the good, Arcite asserts that humans really have no sense of the good, they have not forgotten, but are ignorant, they "noot which the righte wey is thider." Palamon's speech is based on book 1, metrum 5, Boethius's lamentation of despair to which Philosophia subsequently responds, correcting and instructing Boethius. No such correction appears in Palamon's nihilistic speech. Both Palamon and Arcite conclude their speeches with lamentation and despair; Arcite cries that "syn that I may nat seen you . . . I nam but deed," while Palamon resigns himself to being a victim of Saturn's and Juno's antipathy toward Thebes and of Venus's power: "And Venus sleeth me on that oother syde" (1.1327–33). In prison or out, each is obsessed by love generated through vision, ironically unable to "see" a way forward in philosophy; each poses questions but is unable to provide or recall answers. Their limited philosophy derives directly from their obsessive love centered in the image of Emelye.

As Arcite is exiled, the knight develops his condition separately from Palamon's. The tale explores the transformative power of the elemental passions generated by love as obsession. Without the actual sight of Emelye, Arcite feeds on the memory of her image, becoming lovesick to the point of melancholic mania, the image of Emelye having affected his "celle fantastik." He sorrows,

> For seen his lady shal he nevere mo.
> And shortly to concluden al his wo,
> So muche sorwe hadde nevere creature
> That is, or shal, whil that the world may dure.
> His slep, his mete, hys drynke, is hym biraft,
> That lene he wex and drye as is a shaft;
> His eyen holwe and grisly to biholde,
> His hewe falow and pale as asshen colde,
> And solitarie he was and evere allone,
> And waillynge al the nyght, makynge his mone.
>
>   (1.1357–66)

Finally, he succumbs,

> So feble eek were his spiritz, and so lowe,
> And chaunged so, that no man koude knowe

His speche nor his voys, though men it herde.
And in his geere for al the world he ferde
Nat oonly lik the loveris maladye
Of Hereos, but rather lyk manye,
Engendred of humour malencolik
Biforen, in his celle fantastik.

(1.1369–76)

Arcite is so *chaunged* that he is able to disguise himself as a servant and to reenter Theseus's domain unrecognized because of the effects of love. Lowes's extensive analysis of this passage demonstrates how closely lines 1372–79 follow medieval medical lore in their passing reference to the original site of his mania, engendered, "Biforen, in his celle fantastik." Wack points out that the classic symptoms of lovesickness often lead to loss of status, manliness, and "voice." In becoming a servant Arcite not only suffers mania, but he also finds himself "denatured" and "demasculinized." He voluntarily gives up his personal freedom to enter a new form of imprisonment, servitude.

Eventually, in part 2 of the tale, Palamon and Arcite come together by chance in the woods near Athens and agree to settle their dispute by force. The chaos of their emotions is played out in the extraordinarily rich descriptions of how they face each other, full of hostility. Although both are now free of Theseus's prison, each is yet enthralled to a vision and the deep emotion it has generated, bringing them to the brink of mutual destruction. Part of their essential humanity is stripped away as they face the real prospect of dying for love:

They foynen ech at oother wonder longe.
Thou myghtest wene that this Palamon
In his fightng were a wood leon,
And as a crueel tigre was Arcite;
As wilde bores gonne they to smyte,
That frothen whit as foom for ire wood.
Up to the ancle foghte they in hir blood.

(1.1654–60)

Theseus and the ladies of his court rescue them from this struggle. At first Theseus's intervention, transferring their struggle from the pathless forest to the highly wrought lists, seems to provide order and a sense of freedom. Each knight has a chance to shape events to his will. Yet the very champions the two enlist to help further their respective causes emphasize the passionate, physical nature of their struggle and suggest that although the site of struggle has changed, the essential nature of the struggle for Emelye, a struggle of elemental passion generated by the most basic imaginative function of the brain, remains the same. Each champion is described in terms of animals and mineral nature. Palamon's champion, Lygurge, "the grete kyng of Trace," looks about him "lik a grifphon," as he rides surrounded by "white alauntz . . . as greet as any steer" (1.2128–50). Emetrius, Arcite's champion, "Cam ridynge lyk the god of armes, Mars," "And as a leon he his lookyng caste" as he rides forth he bears "An egle tame, as any lilye whyt" (1.2155–89).

What happens in the lists is both surprising and, in retrospect, typical of the action of this story in which plans and rational expectations are continuously overturned. At the moment of victory, having achieved his dearest wish of winning the tournament and therefore, presumably, Emelye, Arcite is mortally wounded by Saturn's malevolent power in the form of an accidental fall. Arcite dies looking at Emelye — "Dusked his eyen two, and failled breeth, / But on his lady caste he his ye; / His laste word was, 'Mercy, Emelye!'" (1.2806–8), captive to her image to the end.

In spite of the subsequent "happy" resolution of reconciliation and the eventual marriage between Palamon and Emelye, the prospect of which concludes the tale, the story of Palamon and Arcite contains an element of Greek tragedy, because theirs is a story of inner blindness ironically caused by sight. Far from being in control of their choices and desires, they are at the mercy of their own faculties and their most elemental emotions. Their jealous competition, fueled by their obsession with Emelye, opens the way for a Saturnine power, closely associated with the root causes of discord and the worst symptoms of lovesickness, to enter directly into the world of the tale.[8] In Palamon and Arcite,

---

8. One of the most interesting changes Chaucer has made to his source is addition of the figure of Saturn to the group of planetary/tutelary deities. As Kathleen Blake notes in "Order and the Noble Life in Chaucer's Knight's Tale?" very little has been made of the fact. "In the *Teseida* we are told only that Venus has her way at the expense of Mars. Considering that Chaucer added Saturn and created for him a long speech generally acclaimed as good poetry, it is safe to assume that his role is important to Chaucer's purpose" (12). Saturn has some claim on being the tutelary genius of the tale, a point Lee Patterson makes this way: "the world over which Theseus presides has in fact allowed no room for the Jupiter whom he invokes but was driven instead by rivalries that only the malevolent Saturn could resolve" (*Subject of History,* 203).
Saturn fathered Venus when his son castrated him: "for his owne sone geldid him; and

the Knight's picture of chivalric heroes is finally of men who employ arms to help them cope with desires and feelings they cannot control. In turn, the code of arms is captive to a much stronger, unwritten natural code of uncontrollable passion, hostility, and aggression, part of a world where the highest values are entwined with the darkest forces.

The Knight-Narrator: The Limits of Memory

Palamon and Arcite enact one kind of response to visual experience, a mental state in which sensory information, minimally processed, possesses the mind. Theirs is the most narrow and limited response to vision in the tale. The Knight-narrator represents another kind of response. His mind, stored with images, moves beyond fixation to a degree of conceptualization as he describes the temples in the third section of the tale.

The Knight as narrator of this tale is a subject of perennial critical interest. Criticism about this tale in the last ten years seems dominated by the contention that, far from being a story about order within a chivalric code of love, arms, and polity, the tale actually reflects deep ambivalence about chivalric culture and that the Knight, his style, and his choice of tale symbolize this ambivalence.[9] As the narrator of the tale

---

his genytras weren iþrowe into þe see, and þerof come Venus" (Trevisa, *Properties of Things*, 1:479). According to Trevisa's description, Saturn is "an yuel-willid planete, colde and drye, a nyȝt planete, and heuy. . . . His cercle is most ferre fro þe erþe, and neþeles it is most noyfulle to þe erþe" (1:479). Saturn's influence is most obvious toward the end of the tale, when he decides the outcome of the joust will be the victory/death of Arcite. But his influence is also present in the medieval association among lovesickness, mania, and Saturn's melancholic influence, apparent in the tale's descriptions of Palamon's and Arcite's responses to the sight of Emelye. On the occurrence of Saturnine symbolism in the Middle Ages see Raymond Klibansky, Erwin Panofsky, and Fritz Saxl, *Saturn and Melancholy: Studies in the History of Natural Philosophy, Religion, and Art* (London: Thomas Nelson and Sons, 1964), especially p. 188: "The popularity of this professional astrology [in the later fourteenth century] enabled the idea of Saturn as a malevolent figure of menace to gain as decisive a victory over all other interpretations as had been the case with melancholy, thanks to the medical tracts and books on the four complexions."

9. In "The Struggle between Noble Designs and Chaos," Robert Hanning argues that Chaucer understood the "real paradox of chivalry—its imposition of moral idealism, on a deadly, and therefore potentially nihilistic, profession" (540). V. A. Kolve takes this idea one step further, locating the nihilism Hanning refers to in a more fundamental level of the tale: "The poem is finally less about questions of personal worth and moral values than about epistemological and teleological darkness" (*Imagery of Narrative*, 123). Judith Ferster's reading of the tale follows the same line of thinking. For her the tale turns on the

the Knight not only unfolds its plot but shapes its coherence, its themes, its emphases, its pace. Whatever issues of self-understanding, whatever criticism of chivalry the tale conveys are mediated through this narrator.[10] In describing the tale as one of epistemological and teleological darkness, one without purposive development, V. A. Kolve and Lee Patterson have argued that the narrator is either incapable of or unwilling to recognize the essential nihilism of his class and its values. But, reading the tale within a context of late medieval psychology, it is possible to argue the opposite, that Chaucer has fashioned the Knight as a narrator very much aware of his own narration and in control of at least some of the deep implications of his theme and discourse.

Part of the problem in accepting the Knight as a controlling narrator is the way Chaucer has created the Knight's voice. It is difficult to ascribe a consistent narratorial stance to him, for he is alternatively connected to and distant from his tale. On the one hand he is an active

---

existential isolation of characters who struggle toward right interpretation, toward building connections among and between themselves (*Chaucer on Interpretation,* 23). Lee Patterson has argued that in the tale nothing moves forward, that there is no "purposive" development (*Subject of History,* 208–9), that Chaucer's unresolved struggle with the idea and practice of chivalry lies at its heart: "At every level, then, the *Knight's Tale* demonstrates Chaucer's analysis of chivalry, not so much as a misplaced ideal or as a destructive sociopolitical practice (although both are implied) but as a failure of self-understanding" (227).

10. Hanning locates self-conscious criticism in Chaucer the author not the character of the Knight: "And behind Theseus lies yet a deeper level of unresolved tension: the ambivalence of the Knight about life's meaning, as revealed in his treatment of his characters. At this last, most profound level, Chaucer confronts the paradoxes inherent in chivalry, and thereby transforms Boccaccio's literary tour de force into a troubling anatomy of an archaic but, in his day, still influential ideal of the noble life." ("Struggle," 530–31).

Of the Knight's relationship to the author's position Hanning says, "It seems to me more useful to search out the source of this deep ambivalence about human happiness — about whether the golden bridle and the lists control human violence or merely license and intensify it. . . . And here, in my view, is where the fact that the tale is told by a professional warrior becomes extremely important" (534). Hanning writes of "this fatalistic sense of life" that stresses the "arbitrariness of events" and finally "succeeds in reducing all of his protagonists except Theseus to the level of playthings of large forces they cannot control" (537). Lee Patterson says, "We recognize here the voice of the professional soldier who knows the world to be a dangerous and unpredictable place and never lets down his guard" (*Subject of History,* 210). As a result of this wary and watchful mode, the Knight's narrative is constructed like a siege defense. Patterson notes that "one of the Knight's most common strategies of narrative containment is, literally, to build containers: it will help us to see how his version of narrative is in fact antinarrative by thinking of it as construction, as architectonics. Each narrative event is carefully sealed off from the others with a statement of finality: 'ther is namoore to telle' (974); 'what nedeth wordes mo?' (1029); 'This is th'effect' (1487); 'This is th'effect; there is namoore to seye' (2366); 'there is namoore to seyn' (2601)" (210–11).

presence in his own tale, interjecting, calling attention to his narrative style, offering editorial comments, modulating the level of discourse from the pithy proverbial to the semiheroic elegy. All the while, though, he seems to be at great pains to emphasize the fact that he is telling a story of lives and living very distant from his own life and world. In this alternation of distance and connection we can see that the Knight claims some issues as personal, treating others as interesting, but beyond his personal knowledge.

In treating the love theme, for example, the Knight-narrator attributes Palamon and Arcite's plight to the power of love that controls them, a power he associates with unproductive self-absorption, appropriation of physical and emotional energies better directed elsewhere. Love such as the love they experience is an emotion from which the narrator distances himself (1.1347, 1.1623–26). He knows that it occurs, but makes it clear that such love has not been part of his experience. Moreover, he seems to imply his disapproval of it in the way he weaves the love strand into the fabric of the plot. As it is presented in the tale, to be in love is to be in a state of alienation from the self. Love disrupts social patterns and the orderly hierarchies they support; it overwhelms the individual, destroying agency and initiative.

In contrast, the Knight comes alive as a narrator in the sections of the tale devoted to war. The fight in the woods and the description of the tournament are enlivened by a sense of the Knight's own familiarity with what he describes. This personal connection is most marked and sustained in the third part of the tale, where he drops all pretense of distance and bemusement about his own story and enters the narrative frame he has constructed. No longer guide to the action, he now testifies to the fact that the world of ancient Greece that he has conjured in his narrative shares a dark side with the world of a late-fourteenth-century Christian knight.

In this third section of the tale the Knight adopts a discourse that constructs the scenes painted in the temples as projections of his own psyche, formed by what he has lived through and seen. No longer the distant, struggling narrator of events, he becomes the teller of personal experience, of vision, and of such understanding as he has achieved from vision, memory, and recollection. In the third section of the story he repeatedly emphasizes that he has *seen,* that is, visually experienced, lived through, and conceptualized many of the forces and principles that operate within the tale as a whole. He does so within the well-recognized framework of an architectural memory system that he creates as a physical space in the story. The Knight conveys his *understanding* — his philosophy of life based on experience stored as images — through his descriptions of the three temples. By assigning to each of the three principals of the love triangle a tutelary deity, the Knight associates them with principles and forces he has already brought into the world of the tale and with the four planetary principles thought to govern the four humors — effectively creating the world of the tale as a projection of the human body. In this creation the descriptions of the temples become the thematic and philosophical center of the story. The irascible appetite represented by Mars is present in the battle theme and recurs throughout the tale; the concupiscible appetite represented by Venus symbolizes the forces that impel the two young knights to desire Emelye at the cost of their previous vows and their chivalric honor; in Diana the tale figures a principle of natural chaos, the flux and freedom of nature and nature's law of mutability. When these principles work at cross-purposes, the malevolent Saturn resolves the conflict. Chivalric ideals of love and arms are thus entwined with other, stronger forces into a pattern that reveals the power of purposeless change, a power associated with Diana and with Saturn, as the most basic force governing the tale.

In adapting his source Chaucer made several significant changes, radically altering what Boccaccio created as a poem to celebrate the joys of love and the sorrows of separation. Perhaps the most obvious of these changes is the order and structure of events in part 3 of the tale. Based on book 7 of the *Book of Theseus* and on the descriptions presented there, Chaucer's version in the third section of this tale transforms mere incidental detail to central narrative focus. Theseus may commission the lists and the temples the lists contain, but the Knight fashions them, shaping them as the loci of the passions and forces that range throughout the tale.

Boccaccio describes the temples in the course of the action of his tale; each of the knights and Emelye prays to his or her deity, and the prayers, personified, ascend to the gods, who are then described. In contrast, the Knight draws attention to the temples as located within the physical world of the tale and associates each petitioner with a temple. The temples represent the forces the gods exert and locate those forces in a specific place within the tale. The Knight draws on traditional associations and iconography in his descriptions, but he does so in a selective manner. Brooke Bergan points out that the temples "are a common medieval trope derived from an ancient memory technique. As described in the *Rhetorica Ad Herennium,* information can be stored in the mind by imposing striking visual images on an 'inter columnar space, a recess, an arch, or the like.'" "But," she continues, "the knight/narrator has undermined two of its most important elements — order and copiousness — by storing, or at least calling forth, only images of disorder."[11] Kolve notes this emphasis, too, comparing the representations of the images in the temples of Venus and Diana to medieval and late medieval illustrations of the connection between planetary gods and human life: "But more significant in terms of immediate poetic effect is Chaucer's nearly exclusive emphasis on all that is destructive or unhappy in either tradition" (*Imagery of Narrative,* 121). The knight achieves this effect by describing the painted interior of each temple as a series of semiotic representations of the qualities both of the deity to whom the temple is devoted and the effect of those qualities on those who serve that god and, more ominously, on the world in general. He has emphasized the dark side of all these forces in his version of a memory palace. Moreover, the Knight's rhetoric of "maistow see" and "I saw" invites the reader/listener to participate in his vision. The conventional rhetoric of vision as comprehension builds these passages. It invites the reader to use visual images stored in the mind to stimulate the imagination, to join with the Knight to comprehend the broader meaning of what is localized in the names Venus, Mars, and Diana. If we feel that the tale is nihilistic and dark it is so in large part because of our own ability to draw on similar images in our own minds in response to the Knight's stimulus.

What seems at first to be the governing spatial metaphor — the wall as screen on which these images are visible — actually dissolves into a series of mental images projected by a selective memory dominated by *fantasies* of destruction, of untamed emotion, and constant, undirected change. The Knight begins conventionally enough, describing the "noble kervyng and the portreitures / The shap, the contenaunce, and the figures / That weren in thise oratories thre" (1.1915–17). But his rhetoric alters significantly as he proceeds from the first to the second and third descriptions. Maintaining his distance from the experiences of love, the Knight describes the temple of Venus, stressing what one might see. Acting as our narrator/guide, he recounts and invites us to imagine through his narrative the space, the sights, and their implications. The passage's particular

---

11. "Surface and Secret in the *Knight's Tale,*" *Chaucer Review* 26 (1991): 1–16, 9.

details are marshaled by a recurrent verbal pattern reminding the reader that all this knowledge comes visually: "First in the temple of Venus maystow se" (1.1918); "Thus may ye seen that wysdom ne richesse" (1.1947); "The statue of Venus, glorious for to se" (1.1955); "And on hir heed, ful semely for to se" (1.1960); "And blynd he was, as it is often seene" (1.1965). All of this is standard rhetoric, drawing on a trope of vision as sight as well as comprehension, a rhetoric that, not surprisingly, given the Knight's implicit attitude toward the experience of love in the tale, claims little direct, experiential knowledge.

Something different happens after the description of Venus, as the Knight goes on to describe the attributes and the actions associated with Mars, the god of war, and Diana, the goddess of untamable nature. The Knight-narrator ceases to be the guide and becomes, rhetorically at least, the expositor of his own vision, and of his own understanding in a more urgent way. Patterson attributes these descriptions to repressed knowledge: "Insofar as the Knight truly does *see* these images, they witness to his repressed knowledge of military chivalry's darker, more malevolent valence. And many of the items in this catalogue of disasters could be applied, with only minor adjustments, to his own *Tale*" (*Subject of History*, 226). But the language of the descriptions argues that the knowledge the Knight brings forth here is not repressed, but conscious and overt. In the description of Mars's and Diana's temples, the Knight seems to enter his own story to testify to the horrors he has seen and remembered from life and built into the figurative temples of Mars and Diana. In these passages (1.1995–2087), the Knight attests to his own experience, his own vision and his *own* understanding of the darker forces that shape chivalric life. Part of the power of this poetry stems from the repetition throughout the passages of the personal witness, the personal experience that underlies the rich poetry, that piles image upon image in an overwhelming rush:

> Yet saugh I brent the shippes hoppesteres;
> The hunte strangled with the wilde beres;
> The sowe freten the child right in the cradel;
> The cook yscalded, for al his longe ladel.
> Noght was foryeten by the infortune of Marte.
> The cartere overryden with his carte —
> Under the wheel ful lowe he lay adoun.
> Ther were also, of Martes divisioun,

The barbour, and the bocher, and the smyth,
That forgeth sharpe swerdes in his styth.
And al above, depeynted in a tour,
Saugh I Conquest, sittynge in greet honour,
With the sharpe swerd over his heed
Hangynge by a soutil twynes threed.

(1.2017–30)

The space in the temple of Diana is full of descriptions of hapless mortals transformed, stripped of humanity, killed for unwitting or mistaken actions:

Depeynted been the walles up and doun
Of huntyng and of shamefast chastitee.
Ther saugh I how woful Calistopee,
When that Diane agreved was with here,
Was turned from a womman til a bere,
And after was she maad the loode-sterre.
Thus was it peynted; I kan sey yow no ferre.
Hir sone is eek a sterre, as men may see.
Ther saugh I Dane, yturned til a tree —
. . . .
Ther saugh I Attheon an hert ymaked,
For vengeaunce that he saugh Diane al naked;
I saugh how that his houndes have hym caught
And freeten hym, for that they knewe hym naught.

(1.2054–68)

And over all this mayhem, sits Diana, distant and cold:

This goddesse on an hert ful hye seet,
With smale houndes al aboute hir feet,
And undernethe hir feet she hadde a moone —
Wexynge it was and sholde wanye soone. . . .
. . . .
Hir eyen caste she ful lowe adoun
Ther Pluto hath his derke regioun.
A womman travaillynge was hire biforn;
But for hir child so longe was unborn,

Ful pitously Lucyna gan she calle
And seyde, "Help, for thou mayst best of alle!"

                                                    (1.2075–86)

The Knight concludes with this image of the woman laboring in child-
birth, an image of life on a cusp between survival and death. Nothing we
have seen in the picture of Diana painted here makes us feel that she will
intervene to help, although help lies in her power.

   In his descriptions the Knight does more than call forth random images; he moves from the particulars of his visual experience to generalization and conceptualization. In the first two descriptions of Venus and
Mars he generalizes incidents into categories by using the definite article,
suggesting the universality of what he is describing:

   The broken slepes, and the sikes colde,
   The sacred teeris, and the waymentynge,
   The firy strokes of the desirynge
   That loves servantz in this lyf enduren;
   The othes that hir covenantz assuren . . .

                                                    (1.1920–24)

   The toun destroyed . . .
   . . . brent the shippes hoppesteres;
   The hunte strangled . . .
   The sowe freten . . .
   The cook yscalded

                                                    (1.2016–20)

The rhetorical pattern of repetition is emphasized by the metrical pattern he uses, loading the beginning of each line with a vivid image
presented in regular metrical patterns. In addition, the use of the definite article suggests both the generalization implied in the specific instance and also the narrator's having internalized and conceptualized
that generalization for himself. The repeated emphasis on "I saw" along
with the generalization implied by the definite article emphasizes a degree of control and of understanding in the medieval sense of having
passed a received visual image through the chambers of the brain, having used the estimative powers of the mind on it, having determined the
intentions as well as the physical properties of the image, and finally

having moved from the experience of the individual instance to a generalization about what that individual experience may "mean."

With the shift of discourse from "you might see" to "I saw," the painted walls become a poetic projection of the visual experience of the Knight-narrator. Within the context of medieval thinking about vision, experience, and memory, they are the verbal representation of the *species* of vision that a reader/listener could justifiably infer to have entered the Knight's mind through lived experience and through reading or listening, as he says, to stories of how these forces are conventionally represented in his culture. These images are limned on the screen of the Knight's memory as much as on the walls of the temple. In a very real way the Knight becomes the temples — the visual memory system he uses becomes his memory, which in turn becomes the tale. Chaucer has constructed the rhetoric so that it seems that the Knight renders what he has seen and learned into art built out of memory. The quality of his experience, transformed and presented here in images of cyclic disorder, decay, strife, destruction, and transformation, informs the whole tale.

Theseus: Moving from the Physical to the Metaphysical

Theseus's Prime Mover speech presents a third distinct instance of the limited function of sight in the tale. Theseus attempts to use physical sight as a ground of philosophic understanding. His speech, structured by references to the experience of physical sight, asserts that physical sight can provide answers to life's deepest problems. But his attempt to reason from the "evidence" of physical sight to profound truth about stable order in the universe never really transcends the imagistic, for, as Bacon said, true reasoning takes place on a different level, a level that sensory experience merely supports: "sight alone does not suffice for judging the truth of these things [the common sensibles]; nor is judgement concerning other [sensibles] attributed to sight, but to another power of the soul by the mediation of sight or touch or some other sense" (*Bacon's Philosophy*, 35).

Theseus's Prime Mover speech is structured by a continuous appeal to the experience of physical sight and an assertion that physical sight can lead directly to metaphysical understanding. But his attempt to reason from the "evidence" of physical sight to profound truth about stable order in the universe never transends the physical. His attempt to conceptualize is limited to an acceptance of the idea of irreversible change as a principle of the world he inhabits, but it does not constitute the kind of profound understanding he promises, for awareness of change is awareness of accident, not substance. When he has finished his speech, it is clear that sight of the physical world has not led to any more profound insight than that all things wax and wane.

Limited though it may be, Theseus's acceptance of a principle of mutability at the heart of his universe is a new concept for him, and it is this sense of discovery that imbues the speech with its apparent message. Throughout the tale Theseus has striven to stop change and to establish stasis wherever possible. He seeks to "amend" the wrong done to the Theban women, in effect to restore something lost, to return their affairs to a former state.[12] He condemns Palamon and Arcite "to dwellen in prisoun / Perpetuelly" (1.1023–24). He designs the lists as a place where the two knights will "have his destynee / As hym is shape" (1.1842–43). He proposes Palamon and Emelye's wedding as "parfit joye, lastynge everemo" (1.3072). Theseus's famous desire for order is a desire to amend, fix, and maintain what is already established. For such a ruler the recognition of mutability as a governing principle in the universe is a major discovery. But because the essential Theseus is a character for whom stasis and perpetuity are inherently attractive, it is not surprising that his discovery of a principle of mutability in the world is rhetorically entwined with a language of stability. Hence the paradox and thematic tension at the heart of the passage.

Beginning with an exhortation to recall the "faire cheyne" of love that binds the universe and holds its chaos in "certeyn boundes," Theseus calls his audience to believe in this invisible right order by an appeal to their sensory experience, dispensing with authority:[13]

---

12. David Aers points out the cosmological and thematic significance of the scene with the widows, as Theseus turns from wedding and peace to war: "When we first meet Theseus in the *Knight's Tale* he is depicted, 'In al his wele and in his mooste pride.' There is an obvious ambiguity here which plays round the word 'pride'" (175). Aers goes on to observe the significance of Theseus as Mars's servant: "in a culture where Mars is valued, as he is by Theseus, there will not be much encouragement of creative human love, let alone a 'faire cheyne of love' binding all elements and events (cf. ll. 2987–93). We must emphasize that this is not to say such cultures lack 'order' or that Theseus is not the 'principle' of that order: only, that what matters is the nature of the order in question" (179). David Aers, *Chaucer, Langland, and the Creative Imagination* (London: Routledge and Kegan Paul, 1980).

13. In this passage Chaucer alters Boccaccio's original by excising part and giving it to Egeus (1.2843–49); he adds from Boethius's *Consolation of Philosophy* the ideas of the chain of love and the order such a chain guarantees even in a mutable universe. See

Ther nedeth noght noon auctoritee t'allegge,
For it is preeved by experience,
But that me list declaren my sentence.
Thanne may men by this ordere wel discerne
That thilke Moevere stable is and eterne.

(1.3000–3004)

His speech then moves on to paraphrase Teseo's from the Italian source, again directing his audience to understanding by vision, trusting the experience of sight and trusting to their ability to extrapolate from visual experience, that is, to reason rightly from the images they perceive and store:

This maystow understonde and seen at ye.
    Loo thé ook, that hath so long a norisshynge
From tyme that it first bigynneth to sprynge,
And hath so long a lif, as we may see,
Yet at the laste wasted is the tree.
    Considereth eek how that the harde stoon
Under oure feet, on which we trede and goon,
Yet wasteth it as it lyth by the weye.
The brode ryver somtyme wexeth dreye;
The grete tounes se we wane and wende.
Thanne may ye se that al this thyng hath ende.
    Of man and womman seen we wel also
That nedes, in oon of this termes two —
This is to seyn, in youthe or elles age —

Boethius's book 2, metrum 8; book 4, prosa 6; and book 3, prosa 10. While Chaucer follows Teseo's speech in form, he omits much of what Boccaccio has to say about the relative glory of dying young and the propriety of mourning (see Giovanni Boccaccio, *The Book of Theseus: Teseida delle Nozze d'Emilia,* trans. Bernadette Marie McCoy [New York: Medieval Text Association, 1974], book 12, stanza 8, 12–15). Chaucer does add the reference to 1.3025 to "grete tounes" to Teseo's list of waxing and waning forms in the world humans inhabit.

One of the most interesting changes Chaucer creates is the division of Teseo's speech between Theseus and Egeus. In part this separation reinforces the topos of inevitable decay, because Egeus's speech, in its single-minded theme of birth, death, and decay, both echoes and complements Theseus's more prolix version of the same theme, suggesting a degree of universality. Theseus's words not only have to be read along with his father's words, but Theseus, for all that he aligns himself with Jupiter as a conqueror, must also be read as acting within a universe, if not governed, then certainly deeply shaped by the power of Saturn.

He moot be deed, the kyng as shal a page;
Som in his bed, som in the depe see,
Som in the large feeld, as men may see;
Ther helpeth noght; al goth that ilke weye.
Thanne may I seyn that al this thyng moot deye.

(1.3016–34)[14]

This experience of sight is called forth to support the philosophic claim
that

men may be this ordre wel discerne
That thilke Moevere stable is and eterne.
Wel may men knowe, but it be a fool,
That every part dirryveth from his hool,
For nature hath nat taken his bigynnyng
Of no partie or cantel of a thyng,
But of a thyng that parfit is and stable,
Descendynge so til it be corrumpable.

(1.3003–10)

But something doesn't work here. The philosophy is too material, the
conclusion too wide a jump to the abstract. David Aers charges Theseus's words and reasoning with a cosmic, philosophical materialism:
"Rather than trying to maintain the existence of a real but hidden structure in the phenomenal world, one which may be grasped by philosophic
and religious reflection, he claims that the metaphysical order he ges-
tures towards can be proved by immediate and unstructured experience
(ll. 3000–4)" (*Chaucer, Langland,* 189). V. A. Kolve argues that while it
may strive for philosophical probity and deep understanding,

Theseus's speech of "philosophical resolution," so often celebrated in
the pages of Chaucer criticism, is preceded by a long silence (l. 2981–
86) and ends in a metaphor of despair. As an instance of human reason
attempting to understand on its own the nature and purpose of human
existence, it shows reason confounded, not triumphant. The movement out is pragmatic, not philosophic. (*Imagery of Narrative,* 148)

---

14. The emphasis on death and decay has led some critics to infer that Chaucer has
created Theseus's speech as a pagan statement. On this see Alistair Minnis, *Chaucer and
Pagan Antiquity* (Cambridge: D. S. Brewer, 1982), 125–31; and J. D. Burnley, *Chaucer's
Language and the Philosophers' Tradition* (Cambridge: D. S. Brewer, 1979), 79–81.

While a modern reader hears the verbal illogic in the passage, a medieval audience, as Kolve says, would also have been aware of the paradox of deep philosophy based largely on sensory evidence. In this passage philosophical conclusions are based on appeals to sight, structured in repeated forms of the verb *to seen,* a verb that had acquired multiple meanings in English well before Chaucer's time. This passage invokes the word in all its semiotic dimensions. Forms of the verb alternately signify actual sight in personal experience (1.3027), seeing as a result of having secondhand or indirect knowledge from history, written or oral (1.3025), and also comprehension (1.3026). The aim of this exhortation is clearly to "undirstonde" (1.3016). But the leap from sensory experience to metaphysics is too great. Theseus fails to provide the reasoned connection between visible experience and understanding. What Theseus can *prove* and what he seems to focus on, according to his own words, is the inevitable mutability of things. From this he infers that the best course of action is acceptance of the pattern of growth leading to senescence apparent in all natural life as the will of the gods:

> What maketh this but Juppiter, the kyng,
> That is prince and cause of alle thyng,
> Convertynge al unto his propre welle
> From which it is dirryved, sooth to telle?
> And heer-agayns no creature on lyve,
> Of no degree, availleth for to stryve.

(1.3035–40)

Accepting this, he concludes, with more of resignation than of insight:

> Thanne is it wysdom, as it thynketh me,
> To maken vertu of necessitee,
> And take it weel that we may nat eschue,
> And namely that to us alle is due.
> And whoso gruccheth ought, he dooth folye,
> And rebel is to hym that al may gye.
> And certeinly a man hath moost honour
> To dyen in his excellence and flour. . . .
> . . . .
> The contrarie of al this is wilfulnesse.
> Why grucchen we, why have we hevynesse,

That goode Arcite, of chivalrie flour,
Departed is with duetee and honour
Out of this foule prisoun of this lyf?
Why grucchen heere his cosyn and his wyf . . .

(1.3035–62)

At the end of this crucial passage marked by a poetic richness of imagery, metrical, and rhetorical smoothness, a passage whose verbal asso-
nance marks it as one of Chaucer's "set pieces," the message truly is "to
maken vertu of necessitee," to adjust to the world as it is. This is the
philosophy of reaction. Chaucer appears to have deliberately suppressed
the more positive elements in one of the speech's sources, Philosophia's
assurances to Boethius.[15] In the world as Philosophia explicates it to
Boethius, such accommodation is not necessary, because all necessity is
freedom. The element of duress that runs throughout Theseus's passage
is conspicuously absent from the *Consolation,* which argues a larger
perspective than appears in Theseus's *grucchynge* acceptance of a metaphysics of accommodation. But Theseus has to settle for a compromise
because he cannot transcend the evidence of earthly processes. What
those processes reveal is a closed, degenerating cycle of birth, growth,
and decay. He can assert that the evidence he adduces for his conclusion
sustains it, but he cannot prove it. For Theseus the link between what is
seen and what is proclaimed as understanding appears to be mis-
aligned — he reasons from visual experience to a conclusion about universal, cosmic patterns that his physical experience of sight does not justify.
He asserts stable, divine authority, but he proves and focuses our attention on mutability and decay in the world. Having announced his new
worldview, Theseus embarks on one last design when he arranges the
wedding of Palamon and Emelye. The marriage, the Knight tells us, is
marked by perpetual harmony, being the union of "sorwes two" in "O
parfit joye, lastynge everemo" (1.3072). Certainly no one who has read
or listened to the tale, especially to Theseus's speech, can expect that

---

15. Edward C. Schweitzer, in "Fate and Freedom in 'The Knight's Tale,'" *Studies in
the Age of Chaucer* 3 (1981): 13–45, uneasy with the simple identification of Theseus with a
principle of purposive order in this speech, points out that "the details have been so
extensively rearranged and the context so altered that the thrust of the speech runs directly
counter to that of the *Consolation,* for Theseus holds to the transience and corruption of
the world whereas Boethius turns from it to the simplicity and stability of God" (38).
Theseus, Schweitzer argues, describes fate, not Providence, emphasizes "inevitable ends"
rather than the potential inherent in new beginnings.

joy—or anything else—will last for long, much less "everemo," in its universe.

The Canterbury Tales begins with a noble tale, a story of love and arms, as well as an inquiry into the possibilities of knowledge—both on the cosmic, philosophical level, and the mundane, sublunar level. The topos of seeing, the theme of vision located in Theseus, the lovers, and the narrator, suggests the difficulty humans have in interpreting, acting, or philosophizing based on their own physical experience of the world. Cosmic patterns are inscrutable and ill defined in the world of the tale; the capacity of humans to control their own societies, their own lives, or even their faculties is called into question. The narrator reveals his own conception of the forces governing chivalric life as dark and bloody. In spite of the Knight's prayer at the end that God, "that al this wyde world hath wroght, / Sende hym his love that hath it deere aboght" (1.3099– 3100), the emphasis at the end of the tale is not on the joy of union after long striving, but on the price of love, the cost of achieving even tran- sient happiness. The world the Knight creates in this tale is one of limited horizons and even more limited options available to characters who clearly aspire to wider knowledge and deeper understanding than they can achieve. It is a closed, brutal world in which humanity's chief physical asset, sight, provides few answers, offers little help. Vision is a trap for Palamon and Arcite. It provides an insufficient foundation for Theseus's philosophical assertions. It generates a mental storehouse of images of destruction for the narrator to draw upon. The world of the tale is a world that repeatedly emphasizes the mutability of sublunar life while it pays lip service to an idea of fundamental harmony and stability at the center of the universe. The Boethian philosophic principle of mutability redeemed by God's eternal love is missing. Its absence would have been very clear to an audience, like Chaucer's circle of writers, familiar with the *Consolation.* Those, too, who knew Boccaccio's ver- sion would also have observed that in his version of the story of Palamon and Arcite Chaucer excises the moment of Arcite's wider vision, his understanding of the follies of human passion, will, and strife. In con- trast to Boccaccio, who sends Arcite into a realm of comprehension and understanding, Chaucer leaves the reader with the sense that Arcite is gone—no one knows where.

"The Knight's Tale" introduces a major topos that several of the tales will take up in turn—the limited capacity of human faculties, particularly the central faculty of vision, to interpret and construe the complex patterns and forces that inhere in the natural world and, by extension, in the world of human culture.[16] "The Knight's Tale" begins the *Canterbury Tales* by unbuckling a *male* very much like Pandora's box. A myriad of ills issue forth in its course: love that is more obsession than passion, war, violence, accident, and death. The characters who inhabit the tale cope as well as they can, but all find themselves thwarted in their dearest hopes. Emelye is denied the freedom she cherishes, Arcite dies for love, Theseus must finally recognize that mutability, not stability, is the principle of the world he inhabits. The instability and unreliability of human faculties contribute to the overwhelming sense of cosmic mutability the tale conveys. At the outset of *The Canterbury Tales* we enter a world of flux and change and, doing so, are reminded of the tentative and often insufficient efforts humans muster to deal with the cosmic flux that characterizes life as the Knight — and Chaucer — see it.

---

16. Chaucer's concern with these issues is, typically, latitudinarian. They form the basis of complex and serious philosophical inquiries, as in "The Knight's Tale." But the subject is not closed there, for in spite of the recurrence of philosophic issues in his art, Chaucer was a poet, not a philosopher. His art was capable of taking the theme so complexly and richly introduced and turning it on its head in the next two tales of the fragment, both of which include vision and understanding as major principles in the human psychology of their comic plots. If one had any doubts about the adaptability of this theme of the limits and pitfalls associated with human sight, one has only to consider that the other two tales that comprise the fragment turn, in different ways, on moments of sight. John the carpenter's concern with not looking too closely into "Goddes pryvetee" opens the way for his eventual, literal downfall. Nicholas's supposed discerning of the future in the stars is a species of sight and understanding. The denouement of "The Reeve's Tale" turns on the fact that no one can see in the dark. In the first fragment, then, Chaucer has introduced a theme that will recur throughout the tales, a theme basic to the topics of medieval philosophy, and in fact, basic to thinking about human psychology during the period.

3

Tales of Marriage, *Fantasye,* and *Wille*

"The Wife of Bath's Tale," "The Clerk's Tale," "The Merchant's Tale," and "The Franklin's Tale" are all stories of destabilized marriages brought into confusion because of what Chaucer's audience would have recognized as the destabilizing mental processes of one of the partners in the marriage. For most of this century Kittredge's construction of Fragments III, IV, and V of *The Canterbury Tales* as a "marriage group," stories about personal relations within marriage, has set the terms of critical thinking and debate.[1] Much has been written about the tales in these fragments, but until recently few have challenged the idea that the stories are fundamentally about human relations within the bond of marriage. Marriage is an important element of theme and plot in these stories, but the tales are more than simply stories of various kinds of marital experience. Because marriage was such a central and protean trope in the literature of medieval culture, its thematic presence in these tales invites a deeper understanding of their subjects as more than the difficulties of determining who will have *maistrye* within a union. Marriage served as a major metaphor in a wide variety of discourses in late

---

1. George Lyman Kittredge, "Chaucer's Discussion of Marriage," *Modern Philology* 9 (1911–12): 435–67. For dissenting critical opinions about the unity of the marriage group see Carleton Brown, "The Evolution of the Canterbury 'Marriage Group,'" *PMLA* 48 (1933): 1041–59; Donald R. Howard, "The Conclusion of the Marriage Group: Chaucer and the Human Condition," *Modern Philology* 57 (1959–60): 223–32, who argues "The Second Nun's Tale" as a pattern of ideal marriage; and Judson Boyce Allen and Theresa Anne Moritz, *A Distinction of Stories: The Medieval Unity of Chaucer's Fair Chain of Narratives for Canterbury* (Columbus: Ohio State University Press, 1981), 106–7, who divide the tales of this group into two separate groups dealing with moral issues and magic, respectively. See, too, Alfred David, *The Strumpet Muse: Art and Morals in Chaucer's Poetry* (Bloomington: Indiana University Press, 1976), 182–92, where he challenges the idea that "The Franklin's Tale" concludes the marriage group; and Warren Ginsberg, "The Lineaments of Desire: Wish-Fulfillment in Chaucer's Marriage Group," *Criticism* 25 (1983): 197–210. Under the pressure of feminist criticism, the old lines of thinking about this group of tales have given way to inquiries about the themes and dynamics of the separate tales that comprise the group.

medieval culture: it appears in the discourse of religion as the union of Christ and his Church, in alchemy as a means of expressing the chemical bond between the Red King (sulfur) and the White Queen (mercury), in politics as a way of expressing the union between the king and the country,[2] and in psychology, where it functioned as a symbol of the integration of elements within the individual psyche. Chaucer articulates the common perception of marriage as a metaphor for union of distinct elements of the self in the Parson's reference to the first human couple, Adam and Eve. In the Fall Eve's action in taking the fruit initiated, but did not realize, original sin. Adam's acceptance was necessary to complete the act. The two are described implicitly as two complementary parts of one person:

There may ye seen that deedly synne hath, first, suggestion of the feend, as sheweth heere by the naddre; and afterward, the delit of the flessh, as sheweth heere by Eve; and after that, the consentynge of resoun, as sheweth heere by Adam. For trust wel, though so were that the feend tempted Eve — that is to seyn, the flessh — and the flessh hadde delit in the beautee of the fruyt defended, yet certes, til that resoun — that is to seyn, Adam — consented to the etynge of the fruyt, yet stood he in th' estaat of innocence. (10.330f.)

Likewise, "The Parson's Tale" emphasizes the fact that in marriage two previously independent people are united into a new, single being. Adultery is a sin because it sunders in two what God has made whole.

Understoond eek that Avowtrie is set gladly in the ten commandementz bitwixe thefte and manslaughtre; for it is the gretteste thefte that may be, for it is thefte of body and of soule. / And it is lyk to homycide, for it kerveth atwo and breketh atwo hem that first were maked o flessh. (10.887)

The Parson's text evokes Mark 10:2–9, Jesus' discussion of divorce with the Pharisees, where he says, "For this reason a man shall leave his father and mother and be joined to his wife, and the two shall become one flesh. So they are no longer two but one flesh." These texts and

---

2. On Chaucer's use of this political trope, see David Wallace, *Chaucerian Polity: Absolutist Lineages and Associational Forms in England and Italy* (Stanford: Stanford University Press, 1997), 297.

others like them, designed to support the contention that the two parties to a marriage constitute one body and one mind, invite consideration of the tales of the "marriage group" as at once stories of marriages and also stories of tension and imbalance among component elements of the individual mind.

Woman, Will, and Marriage

The discourse of medieval marriage constructs the woman as unruly will, a lesser partner whom the sacramental texts of the Church regard as dangerous to the rational male, the dominant partner in the union. In the marriage service this assumption inheres in the way that marriage is described: the man takes a wife and the woman is married to the man, as the following blessing from the Sarum rite of marriage indicates. Appearing after the Host is broken and before the Communion, this prayer occurs at a crucially important point in the celebration of the Mass. Its language and terminology inevitably reflected and shaped attitudes toward the woman's subordinate and potentially destabilizing role in marriage. The prayer begins by recalling woman's role in original sin, introducing that lapse directly into each marriage:

> O God, by whom woman is joined to man, and the union, instituted in the beginning, is gifted with that bles+sing, which alone has not been taken away either through the punishment of original sin, or through the sentence of the deluge, look graciously, we beseech thee, on this thy handmaiden, who now to be joined in wedlock, seeketh to be guarded by thy protection.

If proceeds with a series of petitions to guide the woman joined to a husband, measuring her against Old Testament matriarchs:

> May the yoke of love and peace be upon her; may she be a faithful and chaste wife in Christ, and abide a follower of holy matrons. May she be amiable to her husband as Rachel, wise as Rebecca, long-lived and faithful as Sara.

It recalls the female weakness that led up to the Fall with this reference to Satan:

Let not the father of lies get any advantage over her through her doings; bound to thy faith and thy commandments may she remain united to one man; may she flee all unlawful unions; may she fortify her weakness with the strength of discipline.

And it moves on to define the ideal of the good woman:

May she be bashful and grave, reverential and modest, well-instructed in heavenly doctrine. May she be fruitful in child-bearing, innocent and of good report, attaining to a desired old age, seeing her children's children unto the third and fourth generation; and may she attain the rest of the blessed, and to the kingdom of heaven.[3]

The fact that there is no equivalent prayer for men underscores the pervasive nature of the assumption that women's behavior or misbehavior caused problems in medieval marriage. A brief glance through *The Goodman of Paris, The Book of the Knight of LaTour Landry,* or even Christine de Pizan's *Livre des Trois Vertus* provides ample evidence that it was the woman who was supposed to conform in dress, demeanor, attitude, and silence to her husband's wishes. Strains inevitably arose within this tenuous and unstable fiction of two people as one flesh and one mind, and from the cultural expectations that a good wife should conform to her husband's wishes, subordinating her will to his in all things.

Chaucer, typically, builds on and simultaneously complicates the received traditions of his culture. The *Canterbury Tales* that deal with couples in marriage explore patterns of female will in marriage, but they do more. They also explore how the union of sense, will, and imagination works within individuals in a marriage, and how the dynamics of that psychic union play out in human relations and actions.[4] Rather than tell

---

3. Cited in Robert P. Miller, *Chaucer: Sources and Backgrounds* (New York: Oxford University Press, 1977), 381.

4. David Aers makes a similar point within a context of acculturation rather than psychology: "In the *Canterbury Tales* Chaucer's fascination with the interactions between individual being, predominant social practices, and received ideas focussed on those living within the institution of marriage" ("Chaucer: Love, Sex, and Marriage," in *Chaucer, Langland,* 143). On the subject of marriage in this period and social expectations see, too, Henry A. Kelly, *Love and Marriage in the Age of Chaucer* (Ithaca, N.Y.: Cornell University Press, 1975). On the subject of dynamic relations in a marriage, especially in terms of *maistrye,* see Donald C. Green, "The Semantics of Power: *Maistrie* and *Soveraynetee* in

stories merely about the struggle between men and women within marriage, Chaucer broadens the frame of reference to explore how individuals, men as well as women, struggle with their senses, their imaginations, and their wills within their marriages, at times risking destroying the marriage or themselves.

Individual will is a basic force in these tales, for these stories of marriage are also stories of self-governance and individual obsession with imagination — Walter's "merveillous desir" (4.454) to "assaye" Griselda, Januarie's "Heigh fantasye and curious bisynesse" (4.1577) concerning his future wife, Dorigen's "derke fantasye" (5.844) of separation from her husband, all demonstrate the power of imagination. In these tales strength of *wille* determines the degree of control of imagination. As we have seen, in medieval psychology, *wille* was closely linked to sight, the ability to see and rightly recognize the essence — the *intentiones* — of what is visible. *Wille* has the potential to control or unleash *phantasms* — what Chaucer collectively refers to as both *fantasye* and *ymaginacioun* — that often shape, distort, or impede the harmony of marriage as a union of two people.

As it is used in late medieval psychology, the term *wille* denotes an affective response to what is cognitively present to consciousness, to what the mind knows from the senses. Loving, desiring, consenting, choosing, enjoying, like hating, repulsing, refusing, are all examples of the will in action. Cognition brings things of the world into the human mind, into the presence of the soul; appetite moves the mind/soul beyond the body toward some perceived good. In this psychological model *wille* can serve or oppose intellection. The will as appetite *(voluntas)* seeks what it judges good or desirable both in the material world and among universals. When the will desires a good in the physical world, two powers of sensory appetite, concupiscibility and irascibility, enable a person to incline toward or away from a sensory object. These two powers of sensory appetite relate to the will in the same way that imagination and fantasy relate to understanding — as part of a hierarchical structure in which all parts can work harmoniously, or break down in confusion. As men and women ought to work together in harmony in a marriage, will ought to work with reason, using, when available and appropriate, the informa-

---

The Canterbury Tales," Modern Philology 84 (1986): 18–23, where Green explores the medieval definition of *maistrie* as "individual power that can be won, usually to the detriment of someone else; if it conflicts with the natural order of things, the result is unfortunate" (21–22).

tion provided by the senses and stored as *phantasms* or images in the imagination. At times, however, as Augustine says, the will is faulty in that it overcomes and misleads reason into misjudging what is the good, or when it focuses on the appetites of the body.

In all of the marriage tales the will of one member of a marriage is weak or mistaken about the nature of the good; this mistake occasions discord within the marriage, just as it indicates disfunction in the individual psyche. The action of these tales of marriages almost always originates in the mind of one of the marriage partners, rather than in external causes.The plots that develop from the various individual psychologies share a metastructure of union, alienation, and reintegration of various degrees. In each tale the central protagonists endure distance and alienation that may or may not be resolved at the end of the tale into a reunion of husband and wife and a realignment of mental faculties.

"The Wife of Bath's Tale": Educating the Will

The action of "The Wife of Bath's Tale" centers in the appearance, disappearance, and shape-shifting of the old hag.[5] Read with a knowledge of the basic principles of faculty psychology outlined in the first chapter and at the beginning of this chapter, it may be interpreted as a story about the education of the will to desire the real good, not just the apparent good represented by female beauty. The knight whom Chaucer describes as a "lusty bacheler" is arguably a victim of his own sense of sight and his unrestrained will; the motivation for his initial crime, the rape, springs directly from his sight of the *mayde* and his immediate,

---

5. Among the vast critical resources available for a discussion of the tale, the following are particularly helpful: Lee Patterson, " 'For the Wyves Love of Bath': Feminine Rhetoric and Poetic Resolution in the *Roman de la Rose* and the *Canterbury Tales,*" *Speculum* 58 (1983): 656–95; Mary Carruthers, "The Wife of Bath and the Painting of Lions," *PMLA* 94 (1979): 209–22; the discussion of the Wife in Peter Brown and Andrew Butcher, *The Age of Saturn: Literature and History in the* Canterbury Tales (Oxford: Basil Blackwell, 1991); John A. Alford, "The Wife of Bath versus the Clerk of Oxford: What Their Rivalry Means," *Chaucer Review* 21 (1986): 108–32; Arlyn Diamond, "Chaucer's Women and Women's Chaucer," in *The Authority of Experience: Essays in Feminist Criticism,* ed. Arlyn Diamond and Lee R. Edwards (Amherst: University of Massachusetts Press, 1977), 60–83. I have also found the discussion of the Wife and her tale in Derek Pearsall, *The Canterbury Tales* (London: Allen and Unwin, 1985); and in Ferster, *Chaucer on Interpretation,* very helpful. Elaine Tuttle Hansen's *Chaucer and the Fictions of Gender* (Berkeley and Los Angeles: University of California Press, 1992), contains a chapter on the Wife of Bath, her Prologue and Tale, and their critical reception.

unthinking reaction to that sight. It also takes place while the knight is isolated and alone, a state that the text emphasizes through a modifying phrase, "allone as he was born," that carries three metrical stresses at the end of a line:

> And so bifel that this kyng Arthour
> Hadde in his hous a lusty bacheler,
> That on a day cam ridynge fro ryver;
> And happed that, allone as he was born,
> He saugh a mayde walkynge hym biforn,
> Of which mayde anon, maugree hir heed,
> By verray force, he rafte hire maydenhed
>
> (3.882–88)

It is fitting that the plot that develops from this incident should turn on the knight's perception, misperception, and ultimate understanding of the connection between appearance and sight. The corollary of his initial crime — seeing a maiden and raping her — is his marriage night in which he sees his ugly wife and will not touch her. In both cases he is mistaken in his perception: in the first case that he could commit such an aggressive act of will with impunity; in the second case that he is capable of wisely judging truth on the basis of what he sees.

On his quest to discover what women most want, the knight sees "ladyes foure and twenty, and yet mo" dancing in the wood (3.992). True to what we know of him so far, at first the knight is attracted to them, as he was in the initial rape scene, by the sight they represent, but they vanish, "he nyste where. / No creature saugh he that bar lyf, / Save on the grene he saugh sittynge a wyf — / A fouler wight ther may no man devyse" (3.996–99). The result of his attempt to engage the dancers proves not to be what his eyes would have led him to expect; however, the old woman does know the secret that the knight needs. She conveys it to him in return for his promise that he will grant "The nexte thyng that I requere thee" (3.1010). Together they return to court to find that his answer satisfies the queen, and all the women of the court: "In al the court ne was ther wyf, ne mayde, / Ne wydwe, that contraried that he sayde" (3.1043–44). At that point, the old hag claims his promise and asks him to marry her. Some of Chaucer's most sardonic lines follow here, describing the knight's dismay, the dismal wedding celebration, and the joyless bedding of the bride (3.1062–97). In response to the knight's explanation that he cannot stand to look at her much less to touch her, because, he accuses, "Thou art so loothly, and so oold also, / And therto comen of so lough a kynde" (3.1100–101), the old hag launches into a lecture instructing the knight to look beyond the surface of things for the true *gentillesse* that lies within, separate from pomp, riches, or position, for the spiritual good that glad poverty—freedom from destitution and freedom from attachment to the material things of this world—fosters. She teaches the truth that age, by common consent among the *gentils* of his culture, commands respect, even while it provides unlooked-for benefits in a wife: "Now ther ye seye that I am foul and old, / Than drede you noght to been a cokewold; / For filthe and eelde, also moot I thee, / Been grete wardeyns upon chastitee" (3.1213–16). But most of all the knight learns self-governance, not to follow his "worldly appetit" (3.1218). He learns to subordinate his will to someone else's wisdom. The queen had attempted to instruct him by requiring him to quest for the answer to the question "What is it that women most desire?" In setting him such a quest, the queen makes the knight subordinate his will for a time, as he seeks to understand the nature of female will. That subordination is also what the old hag achieves at the end of the pillow lecture and is, of course, what the Wife of Bath desires of her husbands. But mere subordination is not enough. In all three cases the women desire to educate male will, to change male desire, and to reintegrate men into the larger social community.

The old hag here is an example of what J. D. Burnley calls the "philosopher transformed," part of a literary convention in which women as "symbols of moral-religious idealism" carried double freight: "In a prevailing literary climate of anti-feminism the virtues of prudence, resolution, emotional stability were as unexpected in woman as in children, and for much the same reason. Both were regarded as relatively irrational creatures" (*Chaucer's Language,* 85). Chaucer gives this woman not only control of her husband, but also of the moral world she leads him into; she is a woman well acquainted with patience and control of the will. At the end of her effort the old hag offers the knight this choice,

"Chese now," quod she, "oon of thise thynges tweye:
To han me foul and old til that I deye,
And be to yow a trewe, humble wyf,
And nevere yow displese in al my lyf,

> Or elles ye wol han me yong and fair,
> And take youre aventure of the repair
> That shal be to youre hous by cause of me,
> Or in som oother place, may wel be.
> Now chese yourselven, wheither that yow liketh."
>
> (3.1219–27)

Offered the chance once more to assert his will, "Now chese yourselven, wheither that yow liketh," he demurs, and says,

> My lady and my love, and wyf so deere,
> I put me in your wise governance;
> Cheseth youreself which may be moost plesance
> And moost honour to yow and me also.
> I do no fors the wheither of the two,
> For as yow liketh, it suffiseth me.
>
> (3.1230–35)

At this point, the wife, now that his will has been subordinated sufficiently to merit reward, promises to be "bothe — / This is to seyn, ye, bothe fair and good" (3.1240–41).

Over its course the tale consistently draws upon a metaphor of intellectual insight dependent on recurrent attention to how physical sight is linked to *affeccioun* of the will. In the world of the tale true understanding is linked to a direction and control of the appetites that — ironically and happily — produces a transforming and transformative wisdom that literally changes the shape of the world — how things seem. For at the end of the tale the reader is left not with a magical transformation scene in which the old hag slowly changes, but with the strong implication that the change is in the knight. The old woman's speech stresses the knight's act of vision: in a series of stressed monosyllables she exhorts him to "looke how that it is":

> And but I be to-morn as fair to seene
> As any lady, emperice, or queene,
> That is bitwixe the est and eke the west,
> Dooth with my lyf and deth right as yow lest.
> Cast up the curtyn, looke how that it is.
>
> (3.1245–49)

The proof of change is placed in the knight's eyes: "And whan the knyght saugh verraily al this, / That she so fair was, and so yong therto . . ." (3.1250–51). Brown and Butcher in *The Age of Saturn* argue that the change in the old woman is linked to a transformation in the knight's way of thinking: "Finally, the tale does not suggest that such women as the transformed hag can exist only within the realms of fiction, but that the world of faery of which she is a part is, as much as anything, a psychological and emotional state which can actually be entered and enjoyed by those men able to admit the female principle into their marriages" (51). Whatever change has occurred has occurred as much in the knight's mind as in the wife's form. His newly tempered will allows him to see beyond the objects of its previously misdirected affection.[6]

At the end of the tale, in what seems to most readers a direct extension of the Wife's own story in the Prologue, the knight and his lovely wife are happily united. Presumably he will no longer find himself physically or mentally isolated, prey to the urgings of the will that led him to the initial rape, and therefore no longer subject to banishment and isolation, no longer doomed to wander by himself. With a reformed will, the knight is reintegrated into society.

"The Clerk's Tale": Unlimited Will

"The Clerk's Tale" apparently reverses the sovereignty topos introduced in "The Wife of Bath's Tale." This is not surprising because the Clerk is "quyting" the Wife's tale and her contention that no Clerk can speak well of a wife. He does so by reversing the thematic structure of the Wife's tale. No story of how women gain *maistrye* in marriage by educating male will, this tale tells of how a woman survives a marriage by complete control of her will. Griselda is so far from imposing her will on her husband that to many readers she has seemed without will at all. Walter's testing of her turns precisely on this issue — whether her will to deny her will can continue steadfast through all sorts of trials. Her initial promise to him is not only to do what he says, but also to surrender her will perfectly to his: "But as ye wole youreself, right so wol I. / And heere I swere that nevere willyngly, / In werk ne thought, I nyl yow

---

6. Arlyn Diamond has argued that the way the tale ends virtually rewards the knight for being a rapist ("Chaucer's Women," 71).

disobeye, / For to be deed, though me were looth to deye" (4.361–64). The words *wille* and *stille* occur frequently as rhymes throughout the tale (see 4.293–94, 524–25, 538–39, 580–81, 1077–78); like the words *assent, obeye, plese,* and *lust,* these words structure the narration. In virtually every case where these words appear, Griselda is the one who is still, who conforms her will, who assents, who obeys.[7]

Yet this is not only a tale of Griselda's strength of will and purpose; a secondary theme centered in Walter's will moves the action. While the tale reverses the thematic ground the Wife of Bath established, it shares

---

7. Charlotte Morse's review article, "Critical Approaches to the Clerk's Tale," in *Chaucer's Religious Tales,* ed. C. David Benson and Elizabeth Robertson (Cambridge: D. S. Brewer, 1990), 71–83, identifies the major strains of criticism as centered in discussions of how and in what way the tale functions as allegory, how and in what ways Griselda is to be received. Except as a figure for God or the devil within the allegorical context generally accepted for the tale — Griselda as a type of the human soul tested by God — Walter's character has received little attention. Critics who have discussed Walter include John McNamara, "Chaucer's Use of the Epistle of St. James in the *Clerk's Tale,*" *Chaucer Review* 7 (1972): 184–93, who says of Walter that since he "already has proof of his wife's fidelity, his continued tests exceed his rights as husband and lord. On a purely human level, he gives way to an internal temptation ('merveillous desir') to test the limits of his wife's patient service" (189). On the subject of *will* as important in the plot, see Denise N. Baker, "Chaucer and Moral Philosophy: The Virtuous Women of the *Canterbury Tales,*" *Medium Aevum* 60 (1991): 241–56, where she argues Griselda exhibits a species of medieval justice centered in the orientation of the will to grant unto each aspect of earthly hierarchy its proper due (244). John P. McCall's "The *Clerk's Tale* and the Theme of Obedience," *Modern Language Quarterly* 27 (1966): 260–69, suggests that "What his [the Clerk's] tale really does is develop a twofold theme: that by the free and total submission of the human will, the will itself becomes sovereign" (261). Aers notes that "Chaucer's text carefully brings out Walter's 'recalcitrant self-will' and its 'unambiguous censure' of his decision to afflict Griselda" ("Chaucer," 169). He goes on to say, "It is in Walter's 'lust' that a most important psychological dimension of the text resides, for the poet continually presents him as a man who is overwhelmed by a desire he cannot control. . . . Chaucer presents him as an authoritarian personality who fulfills his egotistic lust for dominion under the tyranny of his own sick will" (170–71). Aers recognizes the pattern in Saint Augustine, who "writes of himself: 'From a perverted act of will, desire had grown, and when desire is given satisfaction, habit is formed; and when habit passes unresisted, a compulsive urge sets in; by these knit links I was held'" (171). Aers goes on, however, to develop this idea in terms of the ruler possessed by a love of ruling, toward a political reading of the tale. On this theme see Lynn Staley [Johnson]'s "The Prince and His People: A Study of the Two Covenants in the *Clerk's Tale,*" *Chaucer Review* 10 (1975): 17–29; and Carol Falvo Heffernan's "Tyranny and *Commune Profit* in the *Clerk's Tale,*" *Chaucer Review* 17 (1983): 332–40. E. Pearlman's "The Psychological Basis of the *Clerk's Tale,*" *Chaucer Review* 11 (1977): 248–57, explores the ways in which modern critics can use psychology to analyze the tale; rejecting Freudian psychology as unhelpful in understanding Chaucer's characters, he develops a theory of Chaucerian psychology, which, is "descriptive and rhetorical . . . [a psychology] not an exploration of motive but a description of state of mind" (251).

some disturbing thematic features with the Wife's tale, for it, too, presents a male protagonist — Walter — whose will knows no bounds and, like the knight's will in "The Wife of Bath's Tale," becomes an impediment to the harmonious union of the marriage. In many ways the tale is an exploration of Walter's driving need to assure himself that what he has willed to happen — Griselda's total submission — has actually happened. In seeking to assure himself that the apparent and the real are one, he lets the disordered *phantasms* of his imagination virtually dismantle his marriage.

When we first meet him, Walter is in total control of himself, a master of the hunt, and a wise and perceptive reader of visual signs, able initially to see beyond Griselda's poverty:

Upon Grisilde, this povre creature,
Ful ofte sithe this markys sette his ye
As he on huntyng rood paraventure;
And whan it fil that he myghte hire espye,
He noght with wantown lookyng of folye
His eyen caste on hire, but in sad wyse
Upon hir chiere he wolde hym ofte avyse,

Commendynge in his herte hir wommanhede,
And eek hir vertu, passynge any wight
Of so yong age, as wel in chiere as dede.
For thogh the peple have no greet insight
In vertu, he considered ful right
Hir bountee, and disposed that he wolde
Wedde hir oonly, if evere he wedde sholde.

                                                        (4.232–45)

A distinct difference separates Walter, hunting and seeing Griselda as he rides, from the knight of the Wife's tale. In the one tale, the man acts directly, giving in to desire. In the other, the man is able to exercise *prudence,* a quality of being able to plan for future action, a quality that therefore implies exercise of will to control appetite. Chaucer initially constructs Walter's character to reflect both an ability to exercise prudent restraint and to see through apparent reality to essentials. Robin Kirkpatrick points out that while this passage of visual acuity occurs in both Petrarch's and Chaucer's versions of the story, Chaucer "seems to have recognized this contrast [Petrarch's Walter possesses a "mystic acuity of insight that contrasts with the crudity of the sensual eye"] and gone out of his way to preserve it. This is the more striking in that Chaucer's Marquis does not, overall, deserve to be credited with such a faculty as 'acer intuitus.'"[8]

But Walter does not long rest comfortably in the knowledge that he, unlike his *peple,* has had insight into virtue and understood it. Rather, once he becomes a husband, he becomes obsessed with testing his wife to determine if she really is what she seems to be, testing whether he can believe his sensory experience, particularly the experience of his eyes. The Clerk emphasizes that Walter's desire to know Griselda's nature is a wish of his heart, his affection and will, and that it intrudes into what has been a happy marriage:

Ther fil, as it bifalleth tymes mo,
Whan that this child had souked but a throwe,
This markys in his herte longeth so
To tempte his wyf, hir sadnesses for to knowe,
That he ne myghte out of his herte throwe
This merveillous desir his wyf t'assaye;
Nedelees, God woot, he thoghte hire for t'affraye.

(4.449–55)

Walter tests her will and his own ability rightly to discern it; he tests whether and in what ways her interior thoughts conform to her exterior — whether what he sees in her is apparently true or truly real. Ultimately he tests reality against his private fantasies, judging Griselda against his "ful faste ymaginyng." After the taking of the first child and Griselda's acceptance,

---

8. Robin Kirkpatrick, "The Griselda Story in Boccaccio, Petrarch, and Chaucer," in *Chaucer and the Italian Trecento,* ed. Piero Boitani and Anna Torti (Cambridge: Cambridge University Press, 1983), 239. Kathryn Lynch, "Despoiling Griselda: Chaucer's Walter and the Problem of Knowledge in *The Clerk's Tale," Studies in the Age of Chaucer* 10 (1988): 41–70, makes a similar point when she argues Walter as the focus of this tale, a "figure of human moral and epistemological confusion, which itself must be submitted to a higher truth. . . . Walter's frustrated attempts to provoke Griselda into moments of self-revelation . . . are framed by two instances of valid perception of her worth. Walter's problem is thus a failure to be true or constant to these perceptions, a failure that is opposed to Griselda's absolute fidelity" (44).

to this markys now retourne we.
For now gooth he ful faste ymaginyng
If by his wyves cheere he myghte se,
Or by hire word aperceyve, that she
Were chaunged; but he nevere hire koude fynde
But evere in oon ylike sad and kynde.

(4.597–602)

Nevertheless, once more Walter cannot rest quietly in the knowledge his sight provides. The Clerk makes it very clear that he is describing a case that modern psychology would call obsessive, which medieval psychology would attribute to an uncontrolled will within the specific context of power relations that medieval marriage provides:

This markys caughte yet another lest
To tempte his wyf yet ofter, if he may.
O nedelees was she tempted in assay!
But wedded men ne knowe no mesure,
Whan that they fynde a pacient creature.

(4.619–23)

But ther been folk of swich condicion
That whan they have a certein purpos take,
They kan nat stynte of hir entencion,
But, right as they were bounden to that stake,
They wol nat of that firste purpos slake.
Right so this markys fulliche hath purposed
To tempte his wyf as he was first disposed.

(4.701–7)

After taking the second child, he looks at Griselda to see "if by word or contenance / That she to hym was changed of corage, / But nevere koude he fynde variance. / She was ay oon in herte and in visage" (4.708–11). To his eye she continues to appear totally obedient. The Clerk underscores the hint of uncertainty that plagues Walter, who seems unable to trust his senses, when he describes the situation as one of apparent unity, using the term *semed:*

For which it semed thus: that of hem two
Ther nas but o wyl, for as Walter leste,
The same lust was hire plesance also.

(4.715–17)

Although theirs is a perfect marriage in terms of medieval expectation that in marriage two wills become one, Walter tests Griselda three times, obsessed with the question of whether Griselda can be what she seems. Amazingly, the answer is yes. The tale seems to end with Walter's recognition of this fact and with a feast, symbolic of Walter and Griselda's reunion and their joint reintegration into the community of human life as a married couple. But this reintegration is qualified. This is no simple happy ending, as in "The Wife of Bath's Tale." It is a triumph of Griselda's will that she can will to turn her own desires aside. But her own unlimited ability to negate her will makes her an absent presence in the story, far different from the dominant old hag/beautiful wife. Ironically her perfect will creates a subtext of alienation and isolation. At the end Walter admits his amazement at Griselda's steadfastness, proclaims himself satisfied, and presumably free of the disordered passions that allowed *fantasye* to overcome his reason. Now that he is psychically whole, he invites her to resume her place as his wife, to resume her role as mother, and to resume the unity of their marriage. But at the moment of reunification Griselda faints. In one sense this action epitomizes her actions throughout the tale. Griselda solves the problem of obsession, of will, desire, of affection by banishing them. Throughout the tale she does not allow herself to feel, a point underscored by the *wille/stille* rhyme associated with her. At the end, offered happiness, she removes herself from the possibility of deep feeling once more, by fainting. Her reintegration into the larger world of family, court, and polity, where she had once functioned so well, is highly qualified in Chaucer's version of the story. French versions of the story, like Philippe de Mézières' and Christine de Pizan's, stress not only Griselda's full reintegration into the world of the court, but also her ability to unite her family with Walter's world. But in Chaucer's version the end of the tale resists closure. Rather than feeling the relief of a reunion of the characters, the reader is left to ponder the inexplicable cause of Walter's testing, and to cope with a disquieting sense that assurances of a "happily ever after" ending aside, there is nothing to stop Walter from initiating another series of tests to measure Griselda against the fantasies of his mind.

Two Tales of Fantasye: "The Merchant's Tale" and "The Franklin's Tale"

Just as "The Wife of Bath's Tale" and "The Clerk's Tale" form a pair centered in the will, "The Merchant's Tale" and "The Franklin's Tale" form a unit. Different as they are in respect to tone and theme, they are yoked by their common interest in the power of *fantasye*. In both Januarie and Dorigen will runs riot with forms the imagination offers as objects of *affeccioun*. In "The Wife of Bath's Tale" and "The Clerk's Tale" will governed the action, blocking reason—the knight in the Wife's tale had to be educated in true values as opposed to his mistaken nature of the good, Walter was obsessed with a compulsion to test his wife. But in these two tales something more happens: not only does the will drive the action, but the fantastic dimension of the imagination also takes on a life of its own, literally becoming reality. These tales explore how that happens and what marital consequences ensue.

Winthrop Wetherbee cites Hugh of St. Victor's striking simile on the power of imagination when linked to desire. Because imagination is inherently material it clings naturally to the things of the world:

> Reason is light, but imagination, which can never transcend its material ties as *similitudo corporis,* is shadow. The two are joined by the soul's *affectio imaginaria,* and when this functions *secundum solam naturam,* reason is dominant, "circumscribing" by perfect understanding the nature whose image it perceives. But the bodily appeal of the image may subvert reason's power, and then, says Hugh in a brilliant image, imagination adheres to reason like a fleshly body, contaminating perception with desire and debasing their natural *coaptatio.*[9]

This is what happens to both Januarie and Dorigen—imagination, driven by desire, "adheres to reason like a fleshly body," totally dominating their perception of physical reality and their ability to make sound judgments. Januarie becomes a fool because of his wild, rushing desire to make his life conform to his imagination; that he should come to such an end is altogether consonant with the tone and attitude of the tale's

---

9. "The Theme of Imagination in Medieval Poetry and the Allegorical Figure 'Genius,'" *Medievalia et Humanistica,* n. s. 7 (1976): 48.

narrator, who seems to be telling the tale to highlight with acerbic irony the contrast between ideal notions of marriage and the realities of medieval marriage. Dorigen, in contrast, in a tale whose ending is problematic for modern readers, is apparently saved from ruin, identified as the catalyst for a multiplication of generosity. But in spite of all their differences in tone and ending, in both tales Chaucer explores how obsessive imagination distorts reality, effectively blinding his characters to objective truth and paralyzing their ability to act prudently.

In the case of "The Merchant's Tale" the male *fantasye* is very clearly a projected wish-fulfillment.[10] The beginning of "The Merchant's Tale" is another version of the Wife of Bath's Prologue — a rehearsal of authorities on marriage. In both cases the authorities have a life of their own; even though they are read and heard, not seen, the information they convey to the human brain is stored there in the form of *phantasms* and images that exist in the mind, assisting or distorting judgment.[11] It was a principle of medieval psychology that words written or heard could generate *species* and hence enter the mind as images. Tachau writes of this phenomenon,

> Like every other entity, the uttered (or written) word is capable of generating species that, in turn, multiply through the sense of hearing (or sight) into the inner senses. There the same operations of matching and sorting which allow the internal senses to perceive the relations among *intentiones,* allow the perception of the relation between the word (via the *species verbi*), the pre-existing concept *(species rei),* and the thing *(res)* the word was imposed to designate. (*Vision and Certitude,* 19)

---

10. In "Chaucer's Representations of Marriage and Sexual Relations," in *Critical Essays on Chaucer's* "Canterbury Tales," ed. Malcolm Andrew (Toronto: University of Toronto Press, 1991), 205–13, David Aers addresses this same point: "The poem opens with a lengthy and ironic reflection on normal male assumptions about the ends of marriage — that is, the 'paradys terrestre' the male hopes to experience in marriage, and the risks he runs of not having his expectations matched (ll. 1245–468). This passage is replete with long-lasting masculine stereotypes of women, fixing their role as the male's obedient economic, domestic, and, of course, sexual instrument. She is also, inevitably, the lost, nurturing and all-accepting mother. The old knight who wants a wife is affluent enough to afford a wide range of choice. Chaucer presents this activity in a brilliantly evocative image . . . [ll. 1577–85]. Here again are the possible psychic consequences of inhabiting a society where, in the Wife of Bath's words, 'al is for to selle.' In this imaging, women are, typically enough, denied all subjectivity — they only exist as objects in the acquisitive male field of vision, commodities to be purchased and consumed" (210–11).

11. See Mary Carruthers, "Memory and the Book," in *The Book of Memory,* 221–60.

The bitter tone and the dark humor of "The Merchant's Tale" spring in large part from the narrator/author's ironic summation of these verbal *species,* myths, spun out of misogyny and monastic isolation, tales men have told themselves about women. Lines 4.1267–1392 comprise a summary of the major arguments and exempla brought forth in medieval debates about marriage to support the idea of marriage as an institution created to better and to ease the life of the male:[12]

Mariage is a ful greet sacrement.
He which that hath no wyf, I holde hym shent;
He lyveth helplees and al desolat.

(4.1319–21)

The woman is "for mannes helpe ywroght," as we know from the creation story, for when God had created Adam, "And saugh him al allone, bely-naked," he created Eve:

God of his grete goodnesse seyde than,
"Lat us now make an helpe unto this man
Lyk to hymself"; and thanne he made him Eve.
Heere may ye se, and heerby may ye preve,
That wyf is mannes helpe and his confort,
His paradys terrestre, and his disport.

(4.1327–32)

---

12. Robert Edwards's "Narration and Doctrine in the Merchant's Tale," *Speculum* 66 (1991), 342–67, traces the changes and alterations Chaucer made in the sources for this "marriage encomium," noting that Chaucer's alterations of his sources turn conventional wisdom into a male-oriented and dominated fantasy of female subservience and compliance (354–56). Edwards points out that the encomium "defines the nature of marriage by defining the nature of a wife" (353). The sense that marriage as an institution depends on the wife's ability to conform to expectations is a point noted above in the beginning of the chapter in the discussion of the Sarum marriage rite.

Edwards notes (349) that the opening of "The Merchant's Tale" draws Januarie as a parallel to Walter. Edward F. J. Tucker, in "'Parfite Blisses Two': January's Dilemma and the Themes of Temptation and Doublemindedness in *The Merchant's Tale,*" *American Benedictine Review* 33 (1982): 172–81, also notes the parallels between the two tales' depictions of the males, particularly in the issue of will. Tucker picks up on McNamara's point that one could read "The Clerk's Tale" against the Epistle of James, to explore the same themes in "The Merchant's Tale," specifically the notion of double-mindedness in January's self-deception about why he wants to marry, and the presence of Justinus and Placebo as projections of January's divided self — will struggling against knowledge.

Building on these assumptions, it follows that the wife will be obedient and conforming, and that the wedded couple will live in unity of body and mind:

> So buxom and so vertuous is she,
> They moste nedes lyve in unitee.
> O flessh they been, and o fleesh, as I gesse,
> Hath but oon herte, in wele and in distresse.
>   A wyf! a, Seinte Marie, benedicite!
> How myghte a man han any adversitee
> That hath a wyf? Certes, I kan nat seye.
> The blisse which that is bitwixe hem tweye
> Ther may no tonge telle, or herte thynke.
> If he be povre, she helpeth hym to swynke;
> She kepeth his good, and wasteth never a deel;
> Al that hire housbonde lust, hire liketh weel;
> She seith nat ones "nay," whan he seith "ye."
> "Do this," seith he; "Al redy, sire," seith she.

> (4.1333–46)

Even six hundred years later one can hear the irony arising from Chaucer's poetic reformulation of these cultural bromides. The rhyme words he selects in this passage — sacrement/shent, desolat/estat, confort/disport, she/unitee, gesse/distresse, benedicite/adversitee, ye/she — are pairs in which one word opposes or modifies a previously "positive" noun, raising a question or creating an outright negative — *shent/sacrement.* These hints at the negative, the darker subtext of the issue, resonate through the text, which is assertive and confident, marked by frequent intertwining of authority and personal experience. The "I" of the narrator is not the questioning reader of authority, but the reader who has tested what he has read, assimilated it, and is proclaiming it as lived experience. In a very real way it does not matter who speaks these words in the tale, or conversely, it's appropriate that they float anchored only to the assertive, brash, knowing voice that proclaims them, because they formulate the cultural milieu in which the tale is played out. Ironic, sardonic, bitter, these lines give rise to verbal *species* that in turn generate the *fantasye* that Januarie subscribes to and to which he gives visual form, first in his private imaginings and later in his life with May. The folly and destruction that result directly from creating these verbal *fantasyes* literally become the plot of the story.

Januarie proposes to enter a marriage in which he is in total control. Apparently convinced that marriage is a sacrament instituted for the benefit of men, he builds on this premise, informing his courtiers that he must take a wife for the good of his soul as well as for the ease of his body. Moreover, he wants a young wife, one amenable to his wishes, "a yong thyng may men gye, / Right as men may warm wex with handes plye" (4.1429–30).[13] As in the case of the knight in "The Wife of Bath's Tale," the knight Januarie regards women as objects that he can model to his wishes. He has no doubt that he can mold May as wax, bend her to his will, make her be what he imagines as his ideal. It's interesting that Chaucer uses the conventional analogy of wax here, for it is used repeatedly in vision texts to explain how images appear, disappear, remain in the human mind. A medieval audience familiar with this tradition of analogy would have no trouble understanding May as a figment of Januarie's *ymaginacioun* shaped out of his *fantasye.* Justinus and Placebo, twin voices of reason and will, respond. Placebo urges him on in a course he has already announced he will follow. Justinus cautions him, in terms that not only contradict his general purpose, but specifically urge him to rethink some of the assumptions that have made that purpose so attractive, particularly his assumption that women in marriage are essentially extensions of the husband's will.[14] Man and wife may be one flesh, says Justinus, but which of the two will dominate the flesh is open to question.

Januarie replies with "Straw for thy Senek, and for thy proverbes!" (4.1567), rejecting any advice that counters his own proclaimed will and his own understanding of the institution he now intends to bring into his life. As if to symbolize and to seal his misunderstanding and his deafness

---

13. Mary Carruthers identifies this originally Aristotelian simile of an impression in wax to explain how the mind receives and stores experience, an analogy that appears frequently in discussions of psychology, as a "crucial feature" of Aquinas's thinking about cognition (*Book of Memory,* 55). Carruthers's work shows that the image was a widespread and useful analogy for mental activity in the late Middle Ages.

14. See Mary C. Schroeder [Carruthers], "Fantasy in the 'Merchant's Tale,'" *Criticism* 12 (1970): 167–79, on Justinus, whom she identifies as a principle of "reality" in the tale; when Januarie rejects Justinus's arguments, he in effect says that what he doesn't like or want is unreal. Once Justinus is gone, she points out, total fantasy reigns in the tale: "His imagination has expanded to include the ancient heroes and gods, themselves — the whole world is made to reflect January's idealized fantasy of it" (171).

to reason, the tale moves directly from his rejection of Justinus's caution to Januarie's unbridled imaginings of who his young wife might be. The image that dominates this section is the analogy of Januarie's mental reflections to a mirror set up in a marketplace.

> Heigh fantasye and curious bisynesse
> Fro day to day gan in the soule impresse
> Of Januarie aboute his mariage.
> Many fair shap and many a fair visage
> Ther passeth thurgh his herte nyght by nyght,
> As whoso tooke a mirour, polisshed bryght,
> And settle it in a commune market-place,
> Thanne sholde he se ful many a figure pace
> By his mirour; and in the same wyse
> Gan Januarie inwith his thoght devyse
> Of maydens whiche that dwelten hym bisyde.
>
> (4.1577–87)

Januarie's "heigh fantasye" is in fact an uncontrolled imagination, a riot of images in the brain, a feast of recombinative activity in which it is clear that Januarie is dealing with reality at several removes. His obsession is, of course, a variety of lovesickness; he is the *senex amans*. But the mirror is a complexly evocative image here. Mirrors figured prominently in optical treatises throughout the late Middle Ages. It was believed that through the use of mirrors properly aligned it was possible to see what was invisible to the unaided human eye. Chaucer alludes to this tradition in "The Squire's Tale," where one of the gifts to Cambyses is a magic mirror that allows him to see his enemies. But mirrors were also significant of unproductive narcissism. Writing of vision in *Piers Plowman*, Steven Kruger opens his discussion of mirrors, vision, and understanding with the observation that mirrors were the "instrument of self-reflection par excellence" in medieval culture.[15] The passage above, with its reference to impressions in the soul and to mirrors, combines two of the most potent analogies used to describe the operation of sensory experience on the mind and the recollection of that experience by the mind — the analogy of impression and of reflection.[16]

---

15. "Mirrors and the Trajectory of Vision in *Piers Plowman*," *Speculum* 66 (1991): 74.

16. John of Salisbury, *The Metalogicon of John of Salisbury: A Twelfth-Century Defense of the Verbal and Logical Arts of the Trivium*, trans. Daniel D. McGarry (Berkeley

J. D. Burnley interprets the mirror as a medieval analogy for hardness of heart, linking its reflective capacities with Januarie's odd combination of resisting advice and yielding to *fantasye* built on authority:

His mind is a mirror, and this suggests both his lack of consideration and his instability. . . . There is no doubt that the use of the mirror image in the description of Januarie, occurring as it does among accusations of *fol-haste,* is condemnatory. The *ymaginacioun* has an essential function in arriving at decisions on actions, but if it usurps the role of *prudence,* no good can result. What the fortunes of life deliver up to the individual should be subjected to the scrutiny of reason rather than the reflections of the sub-rational faculties. . . . The mirror, with its momentary images, can become the epitome of the hard heart which nothing can impress. (*Chaucer's Language,* 113–14)

The potential for distortion, for Januarie's imagination to fill his mind with chimeras that the mirror analogy underscores, is realized in the plot of the tale. The narrator tells us as much when he describes Januarie's final choice-making several lines later: "He atte laste apoynted hym on oon; / And leet alle othere from his herte goon, / And chees hire of his owene auctoritee." Unfortunately it is not an informed choice, "For love

and Los Angeles: University of California Press, 1955), says this of the retentive imagination, the quality of impressionability:

Aristotle asserts that sensation is a power of the soul, rather than a [mere] bodily state of passive receptivity. However, Aristotle admits that in order for this power to form an estimation of things, "it must be excited by a [bodily] state of being affected by action." As it perceives things, our soul stores up their images within itself, and in the process of retaining and often recalling them [to mind], builds up for itself a sort of treasury of the memory. And as it mentally revolves the images of [these] things, there arises imagination, which proceeds beyond the [mere] recollection of previous perceptions, to fashion, by its own [creative] activity, other representations similar to these. . . .

Imagination, accordingly, is the offspring of sensation. And it is nourished and fostered by memory. . . .

Aristotle asserts that opinion is "a state of the conscious soul wherein it is the recipient of action." This he says in view of the fact that when our imagination operates, the images of things are impressed on the soul. If one image is impressed instead of another, by a mistake whereby our act of judgment is deceived, the resultant opinion is called "fallacious" or "erroneous." For often our senses are duped. . . . Sensation deceives the untutored, and cannot pronounce sure judgment. A stick in the water seems bent, even to the most keen sighted. Since our mind perceives how we may be deceived by our senses, it strives to obtain knowledge which it can be sure is correct, and on which it can rely with confidence. It is this concern which gives birth to that virtue the Greeks term *fronesis,* and the Latin, "prudence." (217–21)

is blynd alday, and may nat see" (4.1595–98). Even after the choice, however, Januarie revels in his *fantasye:*

> And whan that he was in his bed ybroght,
> He purtreyed in his herte and in his thoght
> Hir fresshe beautee and hir age tendre,
> Hir myddel smal, hire armes longe and sklendre,
> Hir wise governaunce, hir gentillesse,
> Hir wommanly berynge, and hire sadnesse.
>
> (4.1599–1604)

He reenacts his choice as if he cannot let go of the process, but must visit and revisit his imagination:

> Hym thoughte his choys myghte nat ben amended.
> For whan that he hymself concluded hadde,
> Hym thoughte ech oother mannes wit so badde
> That inpossible it were to repplye
> Agayn his choys; this was his fantasye.
>
> (4.1606–10)

It is clear that Januarie's choice is formed entirely within the realm of his own mind. The blindness metaphor that governs so much of the theme and the plot of this tale comes into play in a very particular way here — Januarie is literally blinded by the creations of his own imagination. What's more, the tale tells us repeatedly, as in the passage above, that his blindness is compounded by deafness, total unwillingness to listen to others. He cuts himself off from others by retreating to the privacy of his bed. Januarie's will has run riot — he will marry, he will choose his own wife, he will stick with his choice, he will create her according to his own imaginings, he will not listen to advice contrary to his desire. His sense of sight, his imagination, and his will work together to isolate him. Because of this psychic disorder his marriage to May can never be a true union.

Given this state of affairs, existing from the beginning of the tale, there is a degree of ironic understatement in the narrator's description of Januarie's physical blindness:

Allas, this noble Januarie free,
Amydde his lust and his prosperitee,
Is woxen blynd, and that al sodeynly.

(4.2069–71)

Readers of the tale are quick to identify Januarie's physical blindness as a manifestation of his inner blindness, his state of self-deception.[17] As if to underscore the point, the narrator leads the audience to this understanding, in yet another authorial signpost directing the reader to the significance of the action:

O Januarie, what myghte it thee availle,
Thogh thou myghtest se as fer as shippes saille?
For as good is blynd deceyved be
As to be deceyved whan a man may se.

(4.2107–10)

The tale very clearly directs its audience to consider this sight/blindness theme as the foundation of Januarie's psychology. Januarie cannot break out of the confines of his imagination. To the contrary, he goes so far as to construct the walled garden as a tangible projection of his expectations of private pleasure in marriage. Januarie, a man who cannot or who chooses not to see the physical world clearly, apart from the distortions of his will, is determined to shape and mold that world—first in May, later in a garden—to conform to his mental picture of how things should be. His attempt is ironic because the shaping-molding motif creates the ideal environment for the very betrayal he has always most feared: the secret garden, with the blind husband at its center, is the ideal place for May and Damyan's tryst. It is ironic, too, that as a result of his attempts to mold and shape May to his will, she, who has been a fairly impassive character (4.1851–54), rebels. She, too, is capable of fantasy, or at least impression arising from visual experience, for after visiting the sick Damian, she is a different woman:

---

17. Neuse, among others, notes that Januarie's "sudden blindness (2057ff.) is perhaps no more than an outward, physical sign of his inward condition, his failure from the start to see May—or any woman—as other than an object for his 'bodily delit' (1249), a mirror for his priapic narcissism" ("Marriage," 125).

> But sooth is this, how that this fresshe May
> Hath take swich impression that day
> Of pitee of this sike Damyan
> That from hire herte she ne dryve kan
> The remembrance for to doon hym ese.
>
> (4.1977–81)

Ironically May is as impressionable as Januarie hopes—the only problem is that she is impressed with the image, thought, and desire for someone else. Her impression of Damyan inspires her to steal the key to the garden and to impress it in wax from which she creates a mold to make a new key to the secret garden, a key for her would-be lover, Damyan, to use.

The presence of Pluto and Proserpina in the garden presents another type of Januarie-May marriage.[18] Although Pluto here seems youthful, he is death and sterility who has raped springtime, attempting to graft onto himself her fertility and rejuvenation—much as Januarie has sought May to rejuvenate him. As Pluto and Proserpina debate, their citation of authorities raises once again the fundamental issue of the relationship of the sexes, the perennial medieval questions about how women, by their very nature, affect men. Pluto rehearses the treasons women visit on men every day, citing his agreement with Solomon, "wys, and richest of richesse, / Fulfild of sapience and of worldly glorie" (4.2242–43), and quoting Solomon's assertion that it is impossible to find a good woman: "Amonges a thousand men yet foond I oon, / But of wommen alle foond I noon" (4.2247–48), and so, for these reasons, he concludes, he will restore Januarie's sight. To this Proserpina responds, this time taking the role the narrator usually occupies in this story; she underscores the thematic significance of what is happening, and in so doing draws forth the "moral." She vows that she will provide all women "suffisant answere" to help them, "though they be in any gilt ytake."

> With face boold they shulle hemself excuse,
> And bere hem doun that wolden hem accuse.

---

18. On this section of the tale and its function see Marcia A. Dalbey, "The Devil in the Garden: Pluto and Proserpine in Chaucer's *Merchant's Tale*," *Neuphilologishe Mitteilungen* 75 (1974): 408–15; Charlotte F. Otten, "Proserpine: *Liberatrix Suae Gentis*," *Chaucer Review* 5 (1971): 277–87; Karl P. Wentersdorf, "Theme and Structure in *The Merchant's Tale*: The Function of the Pluto Episode," *PMLA* 80 (1965): 522–27.

For lak of answere noon of hem shal dyen.
Al hadde man seyn a thyng with bothe his yen,
Yit shul we wommen visage it hardily,
And wepe, and swere, and chyde subtilly,
So that ye men shul been as lewed as gees.

(4.2264–75)

She draws attention to the strength of male desire for women, so strong
it insures that even given clear visual evidence, the man will want to be
deceived by the woman. It is not so much that women will be able to fool
men as that men will become "lewed as gees," willing to deny the evidence of their own eyes. By their arrangement, Pluto and Proserpina
guarantee the status quo — that Januarie and men like him will continue
to live in and through the imagination. The tale strongly suggests that
men deceive themselves. Women are the focus of deception, perhaps the
efficient causes of deception, but men are predisposed to create their
own blindness.

And in fact the tale ends along lines predicted by Proserpina. Each
deity honors his/her vow. Januarie sees what is happening in the pear
tree and relies on his sight as proof: "God yeve yow bothe on shames
deth to dyen! / He swyved thee; I saugh it with myne yen, / And elles be
I hanged by the hals!" (4.2377–79). When May responds that if that is
so, then her medicine must be "fals," that surely he has seen mistakenly,
or only partially, he reiterates his certainty:

"I se," quod he, "as wel as evere I myghte,
Thonked be God! With bothe myne eyen two,
And by my trouthe, me thoughte he dide thee so."

(4.2384–86)

But even as he avows the truth of what he saw, he begins to recant,
begins to doubt the evidence of his senses, "me thoughte he did thee
so." When May responds, "Ye maze, maze, goode sire," he, "lewed as
gees," slides even further back into the world of *fantasye* and imagination, the world of his own creation:

"Now, dame," quod he, "lat al passe out of mynde.
Com doun, my lief, and if I have myssayd,
God helpe me so, as I am yvele apayd.

> But, by my fader soule, I wende han seyn
> How that this Damyan hadde by thee leyn,
> And that thy smok hadde leyn upon his brest."

(4.2390–95)

May draws on standard medieval optical theory — distorted vision on awakening — to explain Januarie's mistake:

> "Ye, sire," quod she, "ye may wene as yow lest.
> But, sire, a man that waketh out of his sleep,
> He may nat sodeynly wel taken keep
> Upon a thyng, ne seen it parfitly,
> Til that he be adawed verraily.
> Right so a man that longe hath blynd ybe,
> Ne may nat sodeynly so wel yse,
> First whan his sighte is newe come ageyn,
> As he that hath a day or two yseyn."

(4.2396–2604)

May's final warning to Januarie, "Til that your sighte ysatled be a while / Ther may ful many a sighte yow bigile" (4.2605–6), concludes with the observation, "He that mysconceyveth, he mysdemeth" (4.2410). This warning is the ironic, paradoxical heart of the tale, pointing directly to the relationship among will, imagination, and judgment. Januarie has cultivated his imagination to present images to his mind; with these images of nubile young women, and with the fantasies arising from medieval ideals of what a marriage should be, he has created a conception of marriage, its physical joys and his own future pleasures. Having so "mysconceyved," he is doomed forever to "mysdeme" even the factual information his senses present. He and May are reunited, but the action of the tale has so developed that the split mentality/psyche of the opening — Justinus and Placebo — is refigured in the conclusion, where, thanks to the deities that control the garden, Januarie will never be able to be certain of what he sees, or of his wife. His marriage will mirror his psychological state, which in turn creates the terms on which he lives with his wife: because he does not care to use his senses to determine the reality around him, she will have the power to make him doubt his own senses.

Peter Brown has shown that May's explanation to Januarie in the garden is based on medieval accounts of how and under what circumstances vision can be impeded and mistaken. Alhazen and Witelo both wrote on weak vision as the cause of visual error, Witelo describing various cases of discrepancy between actual and imagined sights: "For when some object appears to visual perception as another and as if it were the real one, then the mode of apprehension makes a visual error, because the form pre-existing in the mind is applied unsuitably to another form, to which it does not correspond."[19] Brown notes that Vincent of Beauvais's *Speculum Maius* identifies three "causes of defective vision like those which, according to May, afflict Januarie. These are staring too long at an object of extreme whiteness or brightness, waking suddenly from sleep and opening the eyes after a prolonged period in which they have been closed or in darkness, a circumstance close to January's as he stares amazed into the pear tree" (238).

Brown also establishes that Chaucer's well-developed theme of inner blindness is his addition to the story:

Sources for the earlier phases of The *Merchant's Tale,* the *Miroir de mariage* of Eustache Deschamps and the *Elegiae Maximiani,* contain passages with some reference to blindness, but Chaucer has not used them to any considerable extent. It was he who enriched the idea of inner blindness and he who introduced optical material into the closing passages of the tale. ("Optical Theme," 243)

Within the context of the other tales about marriage in Fragments III and IV, this tale shows that Chaucer's knowledge of *perspectiva,* optics, and the general literature of what Brown calls "visual phenomena" was fully integrated in his interest in how vision and its residual effects in imagination played out in human relations. Chaucer understood the senses within the larger dynamic of the self in the world. Building on what appears to have been an extensive acquaintance with the science of

---

19. Cited in Peter Brown, "An Optical Theme in *The Merchant's Tale,*" *Studies in the Age of Chaucer,* Proceedings 1 (1984), 236.

Brown cites "The Squire's Tale" as corroborative evidence that Chaucer likely was aware of scientific theories of optics (234). On the wide availability of texts on this subject he says, "At Oxford by 1350 it was possible to study optical texts by Alhazen and Witelo as substitutes for works by Euclid. Evidence of the widespread interest in optics during the fourteenth century may be found in a range of texts, from the highbrow scholastic treatise to the more popular and accessible encyclopedia, sermon exemplum, and vernacular poem" (235).

optics and faculty psychology, he created both characters and plots whose humor and meaning are fully apparent to those familiar with the philosophic context in which they were conceived and received.

"The Merchant's Tale" suggests that if not exclusively a male failing, the type of misconception arising from indulged imagination and the consequent misjudgment it creates is typically male. The reader is left to wonder if the appearance of Pluto and Proserpina, rulers of the underworld, are meant to suggest the hellish nature of this pattern of misconception. Or do they merely articulate the existing state of nature? The tale leaves us wondering if male will leads men like Januarie and, we may presume, the Merchant-narrator, to such unhappiness, or whether the will is directed externally as the mind comes into contact with the texts of *auctoritee.* Are men so blind about women because they are predisposed either by nature or by the action of their wills to self-deception? Harry Bailly raises just such questions by misunderstanding Januarie's blindness. In the Epilogue he exclaims about the "sleightes and subtilitees" in women who are "as bisy as bees . . . us sely men for to deceyve, / And from the soothe evere wol they weyve" (4.2421–24). In stating this "lesson" Harry Bailly calls attention to the subtle ways in which the tale actually points a very different lesson: it is not women who deceive, but men who create the circumstances in which deception can flourish. Januarie has deceived himself; it follows that his wife can deceive him as well.

Seeing and Believing in "The Franklin's Tale"

"The Merchant's Tale" is a brilliant representation laying bare the dynamic of a certain kind of medieval male libido. "The Franklin's Tale" is its companion piece in that it examines a female response to vision, the images and fantasies that sight produces, and the ways will, driven by *affeccioun,* creates a similar sensual instability and isolation, leading to a breakdown within a marriage. But while "The Merchant's Tale" seems to offer a generic criticism of a typically gender-bound phenomenon, "The Franklin's Tale" seems much less universal, much more specific. And, unlike "The Merchant's Tale," this story figures both a problem and a potential solution.

Chaucer added and developed an optical theme in "The Merchant's Tale," making explicit and central what his sources only hinted at. A reading of the sources and analogues for "The Franklin's Tale" reveals that there, too, Chaucer added a pattern of literal imagery of seeing and seeming to his sources for this tale.[20] This pattern in turn gives rise to a theme of perception and illusion that develops out of the marriage introduced at the beginning. The marriage contract Dorigen and Arveragus establish comes at the start of the tale, a sign that, within the tale at least, it is not so much conclusion as prologue. Their marriage pact once more recalls the issue of relationships within a marriage; but it does more than that. It also offers a model of integration that can apply both to a marriage and to an individual psyche. If medieval marriage is the creation of one flesh, one couple out of two people, then the aim must be a union more complete, more real than that which concludes "The Merchant's Tale," where only self-deception driven by lust joins husband to wife. In Dorigen and Arveragus's initial agreement each promises the other forbearance, a respect for free will, a disinclination to force obedience. Each in turn expects that temperance and self-governance will shape their married lives. The Franklin stresses the stasis their pact has established between lordship and servage. Each has, in effect, become the other's stay and support in this equilibrium:

Heere may men seen an humble, wys accord;
Thus hath she take hir servant and hir lord —
Servant in love, and lord in mariage.
Thanne was he bothe in lordshipe and servage.
Servage? Nay, but in lordshipe above,
Sith he hath bothe his lady and his love.

(5.791–96)

The action of the tale commences after the marriage pact; Arveragus leaves Brittany for England "To seke in armes worshipe and honour — / For al his lust he sette in swich labour" (5.811–12). In leaving thus, he

---

20. On the dimension of magic and illusion that Chaucer added to his sources see, W. Bryant Bachman Jr., "'To Maken Illusioun': The Philosophy of Magic and the Magic of Philosophy in the *Franklin's Tale,*" *Chaucer Review* 12 (1977): 55–67; A. M. Kearney, "Truth and Illusion in *The Franklin's Tale,*" *Essays in Criticism* 19 (1969): 245–53; Anthony E. Luengo, "Magic and Illusion in *The Franklin's Tale,*" *JEGP* 77 (1978): 1–16; Susan Mitchell, "Deception and Self-Deception in 'The Franklin's Tale,'" *Proceedings of the Patristic, Medieval, and Renaissance Conference* (Villanova: Augustinian Historical Institute, 1976), 67–72. On optical illusions, jugglers, and conjuring tricks see A. G. Molland, "Roger Bacon as Magician," *Traditio* 30 (1974): 456.

withdraws his support from his wife. By itself the statement "For al his lust he sette in swich labour" is neutral, perhaps even positive in a chivalric context; set against the careful verbal balancing, the rhetoric of moderation and equilibrium used to describe the marriage, however, the excess of the phrase strikes an odd, ominous note. Dorigen, left thus, enters on a life of sorrow so great that, the tale tells us,

> She moorneth, waketh, wayleth, fasteth, pleyneth;
> Desir of his presence hire so destreyneth
> That al this wyde world she sette at noght.
>
> (5.819–21)

Dorigen's grief is so great that it not only isolates her in self-obsession, but also signals that her connection to the rest of the world is tenuous. Her friends try, apparently with some success, to influence her thinking, to lure her back to their community, to alter her perception of how the world is:

> By proces, as ye knowen everichoon,
> Men may so longe graven in a stoon
> Til som figure therinne emprented be.
> So longe han they conforted hire till she
> Receyved hath, by hope and by resoun,
> The emprentyng of hire consolacioun,
> Thurgh which hir grete sorwe gan aswage.
>
> (5.829–35)

Once more, the tale moves to establish a state of equilibrium. As it happens, Arveragus is well and plans to return. Dorigen is urged by her friends to enjoy herself and to strive "Awey to dryve hire derke fantasye" (844). Responsive to their pleas, she rises to amuse herself, but on seeing the ocean and the rocky coasts that bound Brittany, gives in once more to sorrow, a direct result of what she sees. Once more sight — literally what she sees and how she reacts to what she sees — isolates her from her friends:

> Now stood hire castel faste by the see,
> And often with hir freendes walketh shee
> Hire to disporte upon the bank an heigh,

Where as she many a ship and barge seigh
Seillynge hir cours, where as hem liste go.
But thanne was that a parcel of hire wo,
For to hirself ful ofte, "Allas!" seith she,
"Is ther no ship, of so manye as I se,
Wol bryngen hom my lord?"

                                                    (5.847–55)

The interlace of the words "shee" and "see" and the homonyms of "see" and "sea" provide an intricate pattern of self-referentiality, also calling attention to the thematic center of the famous passage that follows, Dorigen's complaint about the rocks where she questions God's wisdom and providence. What is less remarked is that the structure of her complaint focuses on her own perceptions of how the rocks seem to her:

But, Lord, thise grisly feendly rokkes blake,
That semen rather a foul confusion
Of werk than any fair creacion
Of swich a parfit wys God and a stable,

                                                    (5.868–71)

In her thought/prayer, she exhorts God, saying, "Se ye nat, Lord, how," using sight as a metaphor for comprehension, attempting, in effect, to project her worldview, literally her sublunar perception of the nature of things, into the realm of eternal stability.

As the tale progresses, her thoughts and her affection for her husband are relayed to us through a discourse composed of references to her feelings of isolation generated in response to her sight. The May celebrations, arranged by her friends, once more trying to draw her into their community, sadden her (5.920). She holds herself aloof from their revel and makes "alwey hir compleint and hir moone, / For she ne saugh hym on the daunce go / That was hir housbonde and hir love also" (5.920–22). She is obsessed, lovesick; her will, focused on her absent husband, impedes her judgment; it certainly does not serve her reason, as we see shortly.

When Aurelius approaches her with word of his love, she offers a dual response indicative of her mental state. Initially she rejects his suit entirely (5.980f.), but she immediately qualifies her response in a passage whose language warrants careful attention, for it establishes the dual theme that governs the rest of the action of the tale: the question of how far and in what ways one's individual sight corresponds to actual reality:

Yet wolde I graunte yow to been youre love,
Syn I yow se so pitously complayne.
Looke what day that endelong Britayne
Ye remoeve alle the rokkes, stoon by stoon,
That they ne lette ship ne boot to goon —
I seye, whan ye han maad the coost so clene
Of rookes that ther nys no stoon ysene,
Thanne wol I love yow best of any man;
Have heer my trouthe, in al that evere I kan.

(5.990–98)

The plot moves to its next stage: Dorigen's speech has raised the issue of appearance and "reality." Arveragus returns home, he and Dorigen resume their happy life, and Aurelius, in despair, takes to his bed for two years. At last his compassionate brother remembers a fellow student at Orleans and his book "of magyk natureel" (5.1125), which deals with "operaciouns / Touchynge the eighte and twenty mansiouns / That longen to the moone" (5.1129–31), that is, astrology. But the Franklin immediately links astrology to illusion: "swich folye," he says, "is nat worth a flye — / For hooly chirches feith in our bileve / Ne suffreth noon illusioun us to greve" (5.1131–34). And clearly the book deals with controlling appearances, probably, as "The Squire's Tale" suggests, through mirrors, for Aurelius's brother says,

My brother shal be warisshed hastily;
For I am siker that ther be sciences
By whiche men make diverse apparences,
Swiche as this subtile tregetoures pleye.

(5.1138–41)

He observes further, "with an apparence a clerk may make, / To mannes sighte, that alle the rokkes blake / Of Britaigne weren yvoyded everichon" (5.1157–59).

Indeed, in Orelans they find just such a clerk whose skill in magic "natureel" enables him to convince people that they actually see things that are not there (5.1190f.). Not surprisingly, such a skilled magician demands a stiff price for his services, but the bargain being made, he proceeds, as the Franklin tells us, pulling out all the stops:

> This subtil clerk swich routhe had of this man
> That nyght and day he spedde hym that he kan
> To wayten a tyme of his conclusioun;
> This is to seye, to maken illusioun,
> By swich an apparence of jogelrye —
> I ne kan no termes of astrologye —
> That she and every wight sholde wene and seye
> That of Britaigne that rokkes were aweye,
> Or ellis they were sonken under grounde.
>
> (5.1261–69)

His skill prevailed to the extent that "for a wyke or tweye, / It semed that alle the rokkes were aweye" (5.1295–96). Chaucer here appears quite deliberately to move back and forth in this tale between saying, as here, that "it semed that all the rokkes were aweye" and asserting, as in 1301, that "voyded were thise rokkes everychon." He seems deliberately to be raising an issue that lay at the heart of a number of late medieval and early Renaissance debates about the nature of magic, namely the question of whether magic exists in the doing or in the perception. The tale in this section builds on ambiguity about whether indeed the rocks are there and not visible, or whether they are actually gone. Given this ambiguity, Aurelius's "wel I woot the rokkes been aweye" (5.1338) seems oddly absolute.

We know the result of the magician's skill — Dorigen's lamentation and despair, Arveragus's desire to preserve his and Dorigen's honor, and his concern to create an appearance that belies reality.

> I yow forbede, up peyne of deeth,
> That nevere, whil thee lasteth lyf ne breeth,
> To no wight telle thou of this aventure —
> As I may best, I wol my wo endure —
> Ne make no contenance of hevynesse,
> That folk of yow may demen harm or gesse.
>
> (5.1481–86)

Dorigen's plight arises in the context of a complicated pattern of references located in theories of magic, faculty psychology, and optics. Seen within the context of the other tales of the marriage group, it is clear that this tale involves elements of faculty psychology that they, too, draw on, to greater or lesser degrees. But while this tale deals with *fantasye,* as does the Merchant's, in this case *fantasye* arises less from figurative images of authority in the brain, and less through the lustful combination of images in the mind, than from physical reality. The *phantasms* that obsess Dorigen, *phantasms* she indulges and courts as symbols of, and aids in, her grief over the absent Arveragus, arise from actual sight of the physical world. Medieval faculty psychology would explain what happens to Dorigen as an instance of *species* entering her mind, which then overreacted to the *intentiones* of the images — those intangible but real qualities that evoke instinctual response in animals and subrational responses like fear, a sense of danger, in humans. Late medieval theories of optics, less concerned with reception and processing of information, emphasized another dimension of *species,* a notion of the power of the material world to affect the mind. As Archbishop Pecham maintained, every natural body can replicate itself through *species,* but some *species,* either by virtue of beauty or sheer power, are correspondingly stronger than others.[21]

In drawing attention to the power of things in this world to impress themselves on the human mind through sight, the theory would, for example, account for how the rocks come to dominate Dorigen's thinking. This aspect of optics contributes a second dimension to a reconstruction of late medieval theories of sight: seeing depends both on the mental capacities of the observer and on the multiplicative power of the things of this world.

"The Merchant's Tale" and "The Franklin's Tale" make explicit a theme implicit in the other two tales of the marriage group: the power of *phantasms* to affect behavior. Bacon observed that experience must be properly assimilated in order to serve various levels of intelligence, maintaining that "the species that are in the imagination" are essentially different from "the species of the estimative," which are of a "nature nobler" than the species of the imagination and the cogitative faculties, as the estimative faculty is nobler than the imaginative and cogitative

---

21. Cited in Pecham, *Perspectiva Communis,* 36.

faculties.[22] Medieval faculty psychology posited hierarchical degrees of cognition within the human mind[23] achieved by various exercises of the will in order to assimilate and control information received by the senses. Dorigen's *derke fantasye* is an example of sense experience producing *species,* which in turn generate *phantasms,* growing in power and number unchecked by will. Augustine described this dilemma in *De Trinitate,* commenting that the will can fail to regulate the images that crowd the mind, rendering the mind unable to deal with visual experience; in Dorigen's case the image of the rocks has fully occupied her mind. Rather than accept the rocks as part of creation and "looking" past them, she deals with them only at the physical level, unable to move the *phantasms* of the rocks from the imagination to the estimative faculty, unable to begin to deal rationally with them.

The magic subplot of the tale supports a psychological reading of the tale in medieval terms, for the nature of magic was disputed at the end of the fourteenth century: did it manifest power over matter, or over human perception of change in matter? Late medieval court culture demonstrated real concern about the nature of magic. Philippe de Mézières argues against magic in his letter to Richard II; Christine de Pizan's father fell out of favor with Charles V's heirs who suspected his medicine and his astrology as being based on magic. One way to attack magic was to deny its power and link its effect not so much to changes in matter but to the deceptibility of human perception. During the late fourteenth century alchemy, astrology, and natural magic were often written of as linked phenomena. In this tale Chaucer seems to draw on this tradition because he indicates that he and presumably his audience understand magic as a category of astrology. Magic appears in writings on astrology because magic often involved astrological necromancy, the performing of magic by invoking spirits — intelligences (often fallen angels) that dwelled in the constellations.[24] Nicholas Oresme (Bishop of Lisieux, d. 1382) and Henry of Hesse (1325–97) attacked astrology and such notions of invisible powers and defended the possibility that magic might be explained by reference to naturally occurring phenomena. In late-

---

22. From *Opus Maius,* V.I, distinction 1, chaps. 2–4, in Edward Grant, *Source Book in Medieval Science* (Cambridge: Harvard University Press, 1974), 410.

23. For a brief illustration of the distinctions drawn between the powers of the human soul and the animal, see Kretzmann et al., *Later Medieval Philosophy,* 607.

24. Lynn Thorndike, *A History of Magic and Experimental Science,* 8 vols. (New York: Macmillan, 1923–58), 3:605.

fourteenth-century debates about the relationship among magic, nature, and sight, Oresme and Hesse argued for the existence of natural magic, explained by natural phenomena, against those who believed in the power of spirits, intelligences, and demons. Thus magic was held to be both real — it effects a detectable change in matter — and not real — it is caused by natural rather than supernatural means. One recurrent explanation for the effect of magic, a natural explanation, is, according to Oresme, the nature of sight and the physical sense in general. He demonstrates the deceptibility "and the almost infinite possibilities for error which they (the senses) present. . . . [N]othing is perceived directly or solely by the senses, but interior virtue must cooperate and human judgement, which is often at fault, be exercised in perception."[25] He therefore concludes, "Such deceptibility of the senses and errors of human judgement serve to explain a large percentage of so-called marvels which are mistakenly attributed to God, demons, magic, or the stars" (425). The ambiguous language of the tale on whether the rocks are truly gone, or merely seem to be gone, exists within this context. This is *magic natureel* of the highest order.

In the light of knowledge about late medieval thinking on the operation of the faculty of vision in and on the world, one reads the tale somewhat differently. Modern criticism has located the heart of the tale in the relationship between Dorigen and Arveragus, as lovers. In fact this material suggests that we need to think of their relationship as husband and wife in medieval terms. Such a way of thinking, for example, can fix the initial event of the tale, the marriage of mutual support, as a first step in a sequence of logically related events. The marriage pact is not so much conclusion to the marriage group as prologue and setting for the action of the tale. On the most obvious level, the Augustinian tradition provides a way to link the marriage contract with the sight theme, a theme itself in turn directly tied to Arveragus's absence, to Dorigen's fixation on the rocks, even to her contemplation of suicide. The rocks become an obsession with Dorigen because her will, weakened by her separation from her husband, cannot order the *phantasms* of the rocks into their proper place. Her peculiar circumstances give rise to her own perspective on the world — one her friends find hard to comprehend and are at pains to reverse. Medieval theories

25. Thorndike, *History of Magic*, 3:451; see also Grant, *Source Book*, 488–94, for excerpts from Oresme's "An Attack upon Astrology."

of sight are individually oriented, exploring how individuals can know the world around them or be obsessed, mistaken, possessed by fantasy. The ability to see is not so much an absolute physical phenomenon as a function of personality and circumstance. Thus it is no accident that throughout the first half of the tale Dorigen's friends keep trying to counteract the effects of her lonely and distorted view of things by drawing her back into their community.

Dorigen's difficulties in dealing with what she sees or what she doesn't see, but wishes she could see — Arveragus — thus are tied to her relations to others. Just how ideal the marriage contract is, is a question.[26] Nevertheless, Chaucer interweaves through it such terms as *patience, governaunce, temperaunce,* suggesting at the least that their arrangement will provide a balance, an equilibrium for their two personalities, as well as for society's expectations — servage and lordship. Without Arveragus, Dorigen loses her support. She cannot deal with the rocks. Specifically, she cannot deal with her own reception of them into her mind in the form of *phantasms.* Neither can she deal with what they bring to her, in the *species* they generate. She cannot handle the *intentiones,* that is, the immaterial but very real qualities of fear and terror that sight can also translate to the brain.

But it is not only the rocks that obsess Dorigen. After Aurelius claims what she has promised, Dorigen, with Arveragus "out of town," spends a "day or tweye" rehearsing examples of classical women who chose death before dishonor. The rhetorical structure of that passage, which seems to conclude after forty-four lines (5.1355–98), and again after twenty-five more (5.1423), and yet continues for another thirty-three (5.1456) is another type of *derke fantasye* based either on reading or more likely on the *phantasms* produced in the brain by hearing. Without Arveragus, Dorigen seems to lose self-control, and her dark musings threaten the unity of her marriage through the image of suicide. When Arveragus returns, he brings her a plan, offers her a direction, and helps to restore her psychological balance.

Dorigen's obsession with the rocks, too, creates the magic subplot, out of which grows her obsession with the *phantasms* of the classical "good women." This plot, in turn, with its verbal ambiguity — the rocks have disappeared, the rocks seem to have disappeared — taps a rich vein

---

26. For a counterargument to the more generally accepted view that their marriage would have been understood as an ideal, see Robert P. Miller, "The Epicurean Homily on Marriage by Chaucer's Franklin," *Mediaevalia* 6 (1980): 151–86.

of late medieval thought about the location of reality, the centrality of individual observation of reality. The discussion of magic above indicates that some thinkers, at least, were trying to account for the marvelous as the yet unexplained natural. In the tale the casual remembrance of a magician (5.1117f.) and his book "upon his desk ylaft" (5.1128), the repeated stress on illusion, the somewhat commercial nature of the bargain, all work to demystify the magic element. They suggest great skill, but little sense of the supernatural. Rather, the center of the magic subplot seems to be the deception of sight.

Contextualized by faculty psychology, each of the marriage tales appears to correlate the harmonious union of imagination and will within the self to the marriage bond. In each of these tales sight and insight are tied to the orientation and the direction of the will, to what the individuals in the tales decide are objects of desire. The various marriages depicted are strained, tested, strengthened in relation to the psychic states of one of the partners. These texts play out the consequences and the ramifications of the medieval axiom that the two parties to a marriage constitute one body and one mind. Far from being the union of two people into one, marriage in these tales seems to offer the occasion for individual partners in the marriage to become less than they were singly. In several instances — the Clerk's tale, the Merchant's, and the Franklin's — we witness the profoundly isolating power of *imaginacioun,* the recombinative power of the mind, as it separates an individual from reality and isolates him/her within the products of the mind, rending the marriage pact and destroying any hope that two people can be as one flesh and one mind.

As much as these marital unions figure strains within a marriage, they figure strains in the individual mind, revealing the intense interplay among will, individual imagination, and expectation created on the basis of secondary sensory experience gained through reading or hearing stories based on authorities. If it is a group, Chaucer's marriage group is as much a series of tales about human psychology centered in mental images, as it is about marriage.

4

Objects of Desire: Sight, Judgment, and the Unity of Fragment VI

The fragment of the *Canterbury Tales* that contains both the Physician's and the Pardoner's tales seems to be an odd pairing, for the short fragment contains what are regarded as one of the best of the tales—the Pardoner's—and one of the worst—the Physician's. Yet there is apparently no doubt that the tales comprise a genuine fragment, and that they were understood to be one from the earliest manuscripts. Helen Storm Corsa notes that the two tales "are welded together by a link that is Chaucerian, and in the late-Chaucerian style."[1] Little critical attention has been paid to the unity of the fragment because the stories seem so

1. Helen Storm Corsa, ed., *A Variorum Edition of the Works of Geoffrey Chaucer*, vol. 2, *The Canterbury Tales, Part 17, The Physician's Tale* (Norman: University of Oklahoma Press, 1987), 53. For a full discussion of the critical history of "The Physician's Tale" up to the middle 1980s see pp. 28–41. The exact nature of what unifies these two tales, linked together in all but ten mss. (Corsa, 53), has never been fully agreed upon.

Articles particularly helpful to this reading include R. Howard Bloch, "Chaucer's Maiden's Head: 'The Physician's Tale' and the Politics of Virginity," *Representations* 28 (1989): 113–34; William H. Brown Jr., "Chaucer, Livy, and Bersuire: The Roman Materials in *The Physician's Tale*," in *On Language: Rhetorica, Phonologica, Syntactica; a Festschrift for Robert P. Stockwell from His Friends and Colleagues*, ed. Caroline Duncan-Rose and Theo Vennemann (London: Routledge, 1988), 39–51; Brian L. Lee, "The Position and Purpose of the Physician's Tale," *Chaucer Review* 22 (1987): 141–60; D. W. Robertson, "The Physician's Comic Tale," *Chaucer Review* 23 (1988): 129–39; Diane Speed, "Language and Perspective in the *Physician's Tale*," in *Words and Wordsmiths: A Volume for H. L. Rogers*, ed. Geraldine Barnes et al. (Sydney: University of Sydney Press, 1989), 119–36; Richard L. Hoffman, *Ovid and the Canterbury Tales* (Philadelphia: University of Pennsylvania Press, 1966), 179–82; Marta Powell Harley, "Last Things First in Chaucer's Physician's Tale: Final Judgment and the Worm of Conscience," *JEGP* 91 (1992): 1–16; Lee C. Ramsey, "'The Sentence of It Sooth Is': Chaucer's *Physician's Tale*," *Chaucer Review* 6 (1972): 185–97; Jay Ruud, "Natural Law and Chaucer's *Physician's Tale*," *Journal of the Rocky Mountain Medieval and Renaissance Association* 9 (1988): 29–45; Jerome Mandel, "Governance in the *Physician's Tale*," *Chaucer Review* 10 (1976): 316–25; Daniel Kempton, "*The Physician's Tale*: The Doctor of Physic's Diplomatic 'Cure,'" *Chaucer Review* 19 (1984): 24–38.

different. But in fact they share at least two common elements. First, the plot in both tales turns on a moment of vision — Apius's vision of Virginia and the rioters' vision of the gold under the oak tree. In both tales vision directs judgment as Apius and the three rioters respond to the sight of something that stirs their wills to immediate desire. Second, both tales contain substantial and well-integrated references to topical issues of the day; the Pardoner's tale to preachers and preaching,[2] the Physician's to the debate about the role and function of painted images in religious devotion. It may be that on both counts, trope and topicality, this apparently simple fragment is actually one of the more thematically complex units of the *Tales*.

Attempting to recover the complex web of reference these tales wove for a late-fourteenth-century audience means situating the tales within an appropriate semantic field. Michael Riffaterre describes the importance of recognizing how broadly medieval audiences contextualized medieval literature, specifically calling attention to remembered phrases, conventions, topoi, and characters as forming intertexts alive in people's minds:

> The intertext may be as written as the text, but being elsewhere, outside the text, the relationship between the two is memorial, as if

---

2. Alan Fletcher, "The Topical Hypocrisy of Chaucer's Pardoner," *Chaucer Review* 25 (1990): 110–26, and Alistair Minnis, "Chaucer's Pardoner and the 'Office of Preacher,'" in *Intellectuals and Writers in Fourteenth Century Europe*, ed. Piero Boitani and Anna Torti (Cambridge: D. S. Brewer, 1986), 88–119, have pointed out that the tale appears to reflect a wide range of concerns in late-fourteenth-century society about the nature and role of preachers and preaching, and about the place of figures like the Pardoner in the religious community. Minnis concludes that Chaucer's tale was certainly understood within a context of active debate about a subject that periodically surfaced in Christian thinking, rekindled in part by the Fourth Lateran Council's 1215 exhortation to clergy to preach, and by the growth of the preaching friars (88–89). Minnis concludes Chaucer's position is "quite clear": "He has, as it were, translated the orthodox view into literary terms. The bad life of a preacher does not necessarily destroy his preaching; the immorality of the Pardoner does not destroy the force and quality of his *exemplum*" (115).
Alan Fletcher in "Preaching and the Pardoner," *Studies in the Age of Chaucer* 11 (1989): 15–35, argues that the tale is an example of a kind of preaching Chaucer's audience would have recognized and "disdained," that the Prologue and tale together "could have been perceived to be polemical, even if only obliquely, about contemporary preaching" (16). In "The Topical Hypocrisy of Chaucer's Pardoner," Fletcher contends that "Modern readings of Chaucer's text have been interested in making psychological, rather than moral, sense of the Pardoner's religious hypocrisy. Perhaps their emphasis in this respect betrays a modern preoccupation and one very likely to predominate when describing a personality is an easier matter than reconstructing a long since defunct system for conveying moral meaning" (117).

the intertext had lost its written materiality and survived only in memory, to be read solely through the mind's eye. The reason why the intertext is relevant is that it is selected by the text. There is around us, in our minds, a vast terra incognita of other texts and also, and perhaps above all, a terra incognita of mythologemes, ideologemes, descriptive systems, and sememic structures that the sociolect feeds into texts, and which is the stuff, the precast, the prefabricated stuff of literature. . . . The relevant area is literally selected, carved out from the rest by that analogy, homology, or plain identity if the text actually quotes from or alludes to the intertext.[3]

Riffaterre writes generally about how medieval audiences contextualized fiction and the conventions, signs, topoi of fiction as they appeared in specific works, but his words hold particular relevance for understanding how a late medieval English audience might have contextualized Fragment VI and the individual tales that comprise it.

Alan Fletcher implies the existence of just such an intertext of referents,[4] contending that the Pardoner's hypocrisy "is likely to have been colored by the important issues it would have raised in any medieval reader's mind, particularly if he or she were living close to Chaucer's circle in London in the 1390s. At that date hypocrisy like the Pardoner's was a highly topical matter" ("Topical Hypocrisy," 110). Fletcher notes that the Prologue and tale refer to the Eucharistic debates of the time about substance and accident; to the question of whether a bad man can preach effectively; and to the ongoing controversy about the abuse of preaching, or preaching for personal gain (113).[5] Citing Chaucer's acquaintance with Gower, his possible acquaintance with "philosophical Strode," who debated Wyclif in the 1360s, his relationship with Archbishop Thomas Arundel, "the hammer of the heretics, and who acted as attorney for him in certain property transactions" (116),

---

3. "The Mind's Eye: Memory and Textuality," in *The New Medievalism,* ed. Marina S. Brownlee, Kevin Brownlee, and Stephen G. Nichols (Baltimore: Johns Hopkins University Press, 1991), 33.

4. On the typical offices, functions, and roles of a pardoner *(quaestor)* in fourteenth-century England, see Alfred L. Kellogg and Louis A. Haselmayer, "Chaucer's Satire of the Pardoner," *PMLA* 66 (1951): 251–77, which shows how closely the function of the pardoner was integrated into the financial and bureaucratic fabric of late-fourteenth-century Roman Catholicism, how suspect and liable to temptation pardoners seem to have been, and how closely Chaucer's Pardoner conforms to type.

5. On this topic see Rodney Delasanta, "Sacrament and Sacrifice in the *Pardoner's Tale,"* *Annuale Mediaevale* 14 (1973): 43–52.

Fletcher maintains that Chaucer "can hardly have been oblivious to the religious and political climate around him" (116). Similarly, any "reasonably informed" contemporary of Chaucer's would have been aware

> of the topicality surrounding the issue of such religious hypocrisy as the Pardoner's. He would not have failed to see how its distinctive emphasis, or even some of the very words and phrases used to express it, would have been colored by its treatment in the orthodox versus Lollard debate. (116)

The kind of topicality Fletcher recognizes in the figure of the Pardoner and in the issues raised by his Prologue appear in "The Physician's Tale" as well, for it is laden with words and phrases that recur in the contemporary religious discourse of the debate about images. The tale presents the figure of Virginia in such a way that she is both a human being, a natural image of the Creator, and a consciously crafted work of "true" art, nature's masterpiece. In her description a late medieval audience would have heard references to a variety of topical issues centered in discussion of true and false images of God, the respect properly given to images in religious art, and to individual human beings as living images of God.

Images and the Senses

In the late fourteenth century, debates about the acceptance or rejection of images as aids to worship occurred at both Oxford and Cambridge.[6] Further, Anne Hudson points out,

> In the last quarter of the fourteenth century a number of tracts were written both in defense of images and against them, the latter position coming rapidly to be identified with Lollardy. . . . Some of the more picturesque observations reported in the episcopal registers, observations which to judge by the way in which they break the conventional bareness of the accounts must have caught the ear of the notary, concern the honour of *stokkes and stones and ded mennes bones.* (*Premature Reformation,* 303–4)

---

6. Anne Hudson, *The Premature Reformation: Wycliffite Texts and Lollard History* (Oxford: Clarendon Press, 1988), 94.

The early-fifteenth-century *Dives and Pauper* reflects the issues on both sides of the debate. It defends the orthodox position that images are useful in three ways:

And þerfore God defendyȝt noght vttyrly [the] makyngge of ymagis but he defenyȝt vttyrly to makyn ymaagis to wurshepyn hem as godys and to settyn here feyȝt, her trost, here hope, here loue and here beleue in hem. . . . Þey seruyn of thre thynggys. For þey been ordeynyd to steryn manys mende to thynkyn of Cristys incarnacioun and of his passioun and of holye seyntys lyuys. Also þey been ordeynyd to steryn mannys affeccioun and his herte to deuocioun, for often man is more steryd by syghte þan by heryng or redyngge. Also þey been ordeynyd to been a tokene and a book to þe lewyd peple, þat þey moun redyn in ymagerye and peynture þat clerkys redyn in boke, as þe lawe seyȝt.[7]

Opposition to images was not necessarily a sign of heterodoxy. W. R. Jones documents a spectrum of opposition to the mistaken use of images, in the middle range of which he locates opposition that was critical, but not heretical.[8] The issue turned on the nature of the veneration offered to the image. Opposers feared that *latria,* the highest kind of veneration, belonging to the cross alone, might be offered to mere images, that people would forget that the images represented abstractions — an idea, a good, a saint's life and deeds — and would regard the physical image itself, the mere painting or carving, as deserving of veneration, or would regard it as a repository of magical power. In the early Middle Ages Augustine had explained images as a species of sign, using the example of royal insignia, which, as Jones says, "referred to a higher reality and thereby demanded respect" (45).[9] This process of transferring

---

7. *Dives and Pauper,* ed. Priscilla Heath Barnum, part 1, Early English Text Society, 275 (Oxford: Oxford University Press, 1976), 82.

8. W. R. Jones, "Lollards and Images: The Defense of Religious Art in Later Medieval England," *Journal of the History of Ideas* 34 (1973): 28–29.

9. For a discussion of contemporary English debates on this issue see Margaret Aston, *Lollards and Reformers: Images and Literacy in Late Medieval Religion* (London: Hambledon Press, 1984), 178–79, where she describes both *Dives and Pauper* and Walter Hilton's treatise "On the Worship of Images" (c. 1385–95). What is remarkable about these debates in light of the action of "The Physician's Tale" is the association Aston points out between opposing images and wishing to destroy them. On *Dives and Pauper* she says, "It was all too contentious an issue, and the very openness of the book's discussion as to how images could be worshipped without idolatry could have laid it open to suspicion. *Dives*

respect from the physical object to what it represents troubled many. A broad cultural distrust about how well and how certainly this process worked was focused in Lollard opinion on the subject, which, as the brief sermon excerpt below shows, urged Christians to renounce the physical sign in favor of spiritual truth: "And now men shulden be more gostly and take lesse hede to siche sensible signes. . . . For oure lord god dwellis by grace in gode mennes soulis."[10] Jones cites an anonymous English author of the period who "stressed the priority of the intangible and abstract in the Christian hierarchy of values: 'For we schulden knowe bi resoun that thingis that ben unsensible passen in goodnesse thingis that ben sensible, as helpe that we may not se passith feelinge thingis, and lyf that we may not feele passith feelinge bodies, so god that we may not se passith worldi thingis'" (34). The debate about images was driven by and suffered the same kinds of oppositions as did late medieval discussions of the senses, to which it was clearly related. Both spring from a common anxiety about human psychology. The argument in favor of images was often adduced on the grounds that images are woven into the very fabric of creation in natural signs, and that the apprehension of images is part of the function of the human mind, which literally depends on images to work. This dependence on mental images, by implication, justified created images.

But in the late fourteenth century the very idea that cognition depended on images was increasingly problematic. Clifford Davidson identifies changing ideas about cognition as a fundamental issue in late medieval iconoclasm.[11] Davidson locates a shift between medieval and Renaissance thinking about the nature and function of the sense of sight as an anxiety that produced a "shift from approval of the seeing eye to the hearing ear as the principal source of religious illumination. . . . Instead of originating in the sense of sight, therefore, any religious

---

and Pauper made plain that images were 'venerable and worshipful,' and therefore nobody should 'despise them nor defile them, burn them nor break them.' At the same time Pauper placed limits on the worship of images which in the early fifteenth century . . . could be read as challenging" (178–79). Walter Hilton understood that the attack on images would destroy the Church (179).

On Hilton's defense of images see Joy M. Russell-Smith's "Walter Hilton and a Tract in Defence of the Veneration of Images," *Dominican Studies* 7 (1954): 180–214.

10. G. R. Owst, *Literature and Pulpit in Medieval England* (Cambridge: Cambridge University Press, 1933), 144.

11. "The Anti-visual Prejudice," in *Iconoclasm vs. Art and Drama*, Medieval Institute Publications, Early Drama, Art and Music Monographs Series, 11 (Kalamazoo Mich., 1989), 32–34.

experience involving the imagination must have its origin in the experience of the Word, the Scriptures, principally as these sacred writings are pre-digested in sermons and heard by those in attendance" (35–36). Davidson distinguishes sixteenth-century attitudes toward images and representation from late medieval attitudes: orthodox late medieval thinking about images was predicated on the idea of the

> viewer's identification with the event witnessed or in the special relationship established by him with the figure who is depicted. Through imagination, the events can be made *as if* present before the eyes of the viewer, or the image can be a conduit to the saint represented therein. . . . The image or picture, therefore, participates in the reality of the event or of the saint, and indeed in practice the visual depiction is more than a merely didactic presentation to teach church doctrine to the unlearned. (38)

"To see a thing," he says, "is thus to participate in it somehow, since the eye's rays must extend outward to take it in — and this is the case whether or not the thing is felt to send forth rays which penetrate the eyes [intromission]. To touch something beneficial, such as a holy statue, with one's sight would be a good thing, but if that statue were to be redefined as an idolatrous, superstitious, and therefore dangerous image the act of touching it with one's sight would surely be a very bad thing indeed" (39).

The Protestant reformers of the sixteenth century had no doubt that the eye, attracted to "false images," "becomes in this view a servant of idols" (Davidson, "Anti-visual Prejudice," 41).[12] Susan Hagen finds the same idea expressed a hundred years before the Protestant Reformation. She describes a radical and arresting illustration accompanying the text of the *Pilgrimage of the Life of Man* at lines 6234–58:

One of the rare illustrations of this episode in the poem captures the relationship among seeing, hearing, and understanding with pictorial

---

12. On the antivisual prejudice inherent in early and medieval Christianity Davidson points out that the Reformation attack "on *things seen,* is not, of course, unconnected from the thoughts and prejudices of the previous one thousand years and more of Christianity. The desacralizing of images and their desecration were evidences of extreme attitudes, but such acts were a matter of degree rather than of kind. . . . [T]he sense of sight was commonly regarded paradoxically from the time of the Church Fathers to the Renaissance as at once a metaphor for illumination and knowledge on the one hand and on the other a sign of illusion and danger" ("Anti-visual Prejudice," 41–42).

accuracy. In figure 22, Grace Dieu removes the heretofore unseen scrip and staff from a chest and gives them to the pilgrim, who waits to receive them with hands open. He had no eyes drawn in his face, rather a large eye peers out from his left ear. (*Allegorical Remembrance,* 49)

Hagen says that the poem counsels that the "inner eye of understanding sees more reliably through hearing than it does through the bodily eye. Neither useless nor always deceptive, sight can, nevertheless, be misleading, so it is prudent to turn to hearing for counsel" (48).

This cultural distrust of sight and the gradual shift away from privileging sight as the most important of the bodily senses in respect to gaining true understanding, forms an important element in the context of cultural concern that Chaucer draws on in his version of the Physician's tale, a story of Virginia who is an image of goodness, a story about the mistakes and sorrow attendant on Apius's not being able to see her for what she is. The issue on which the debate about images turned, an issue of how the human mind deals with the idea of representation, how reliably it can move from the sight of something symbolic — the image — to understanding that the physical sight exists to evoke a nexus of ideas that exist independently and apart from the image, is an implicit topic in Chaucer's unique version of the well-known medieval story of Virginia.

Virginia as Image: The Discourse of the Debate

One of the first things an educated late-fourteenth-century audience would notice about this story is that Chaucer, through the Physician, rewrites an ancient and familiar tale. Chaucer removed what was historically the heart of the story. Even though he pays a great deal of particular attention to the proper medieval English forms of court proceedings (6.160–90), he does not stress the legal corruption of these proceedings, a theme, for example, that the *Romance of the Rose* version begins with — literally how Apius feeds his own lust through his power as a judge (5589–5794). Neither does he follow the story from Livy, clearly about corruption within a class system, a story that turns on Virginius's rights and status and on the control of justice within the public life of ancient Rome. Gower's version in the seventh book of the *Confessio Amantis,* almost contemporaneous with Chaucer's, also continues the tradition and preserves the political focus of the story, although he, like Chaucer, pays particular attention to Virginia in the beginning.

At Rome whan that Apius,
Whos other name is Claudius,
Was governour of the cite,
Ther fell a wonder thing to se
Touchende a gentil Maide, as thus,
Whom Livius Virginius
Begeten hadde upon his wif:
Men seiden that so fair a lif
As sche was noght in al the toun.
This fame, which goth up and doun,
To Claudius cam in his Ere,
Whereof his thoght anon was there,
Which al his herte hath set afyre,
That he began the flour desire
Which longeth unto maydenhede,
And sende, if that he myhte spede
The blinde lustes of his wille.[13]

Chaucer's version differs significantly from all these others not only in lacking the traditional political focus, but in beginning with and concentrating attention on an extended description of Virginia, remarkable for its length, its rhetorical flare, and its centrality in the plot. Chaucer's version alone originates the action of the tale at the moment when Apius *sees* Virginia. (Gower's story opens with Apius's hearing of her.) This change invites the reader to look closely at the description Chaucer has created, to ask how it functions in the tale, and to ask how it might have been understood by Chaucer's audience.

The description of Virginia is usually situated within a long pedigree drawn from the high intellectual tradition of medieval thought, especially the *Romance of the Rose*. But there may be another, closer context— Riffaterre's *sociolect*—in which to understand these lines. It is obvious

---

13. John Gower, *Confessio Amantis*, 7.5131–47. Just as Apius first learned of Virginia by hearsay, so the public becomes aware of Apius's "prive tricherie" by "Ere; / And that broghte in the comun feere, / That every man the peril dradde / Of him that so hem overladde" (5287–92). Gower draws two morals from all this: first that "thus stant every mannes lif / In jeupartie for his wif / Or for his dowhter, if thei be / Passende an other of beaute" (5273–76); and second, because the populace, outraged, deposed Apius, he suggests that this story is a cautionary tale, "Whereof thei myhte ben avised / That scholden afterward governe, / And be this evidence lerne, / Hou it is good a king eschuie / The lust of vice and vertu sui" (5302–6).

that the passage, whatever its origins, is here uniquely and carefully structured by verbs of painting, forming, counterfeiting, and artistic creation.[14] Where his sources merely refer to the fact of her existence or indicate her beauty, Chaucer has the Physician introduce Virginia extensively and particularly, as a work of art, Nature's masterpiece:

> Fair was this mayde in excellent beautee
> Aboven every wight that man may see;
> For Nature hath with sovereyn diligence
> Yformed hire in so greet excellence,
> As though she wolde seyn, "Lo! I, Nature,
> Thus kan I forme and peynte a creature,
> Whan that me list; who kan me countrefete?"
>
> (6.7–13)

Nature continues, emphasizing the unequal relationship between nature and human art, and concluding with the purpose to which Virginia and all exquisite creatures are created. In answer to her rhetorical question of who can imitate her works, Nature is imagined to reply,

> "Pigmalion noght, though he ay forge and bete,
> Or grave, or peynte; for I dar wel seyn
> Apelles, Zanzis, sholde werche in veyn
> Outher to grave, or peynte, or forge, or bete,
> If they presumed me to countrefete.
> For He that is the formere principal
> Hath maked me his vicaire general,
> To forme and peynten erthely creaturis
> Right as me list, and ech thyng in my cure is
> Under the moone, that may wane and waxe,
> And for my werk right no thyng wol I axe;
> My lord and I been ful of oon accord.
> I made hire to the worshipe of my lord;
> So do I alle myne othere creatures,
> What colour than they han or what figures."
> Thus seemeth me that Nature wolde seye.
>
> (6.14–29)

---

14. Corsa's note on this passage illustrates the extent to which it has been read within a Neoplatonic context that opposes nature and art, rather than a context that explores nature as artist (*Physician's Tale*, 91–99).

A notable part of the description, a speech for which the *Romance of the Rose,* 16005–248, is the most likely identified source, is the recurrent use of and stress on the word *peynte.* This passage has traditionally been read within a Neoplatonic context suggesting the falseness of artistic creation, the potential for self-delusion and the hubris attendant on mimetic creation.[15] But the issue in the passage is not the duplicity or the hubris of human art. Rather the passage contrasts one kind of art — nature's — with human art.[16] And, while at first glance the language may suggest a topos of deceit based on the recurrence of the terms *peynte* and *countrefete,* a consideration of how the words are used and their primary meanings during the period underscores a concern not with the falseness of art, but with Nature's unique ability to create with God's sanction and for God's praise. While for modern readers the word *peynte* may at first evoke the modern sense of forming by color, the word in Middle English is a richer, more diverse term. We can understand its range of significa-tion if we notice how it is paired in the passage with the verb *forme:* "Thus kan I forme and peynte a creature" (12), and, at line 21, "To forme and peynten erthely creaturis." Nature refers to her ability to bring to life, to create a specific form out of an ideal. In the *Middle English Dictionary* the basic meaning of the word *peynte* is to portray someone or something. What's more, this primary sense, like the basic meaning of the word *countrefete,* carries no pejorative sense. While *countrefete* can mean to pretend, to make a false imitation, its basic, root

---

15. In *Ovid and the Canterbury Tales* Richard Hoffman discusses the reference to Pygmalion in the tale:

> The Middle Ages understood this myth, quite reasonably, as an example of moral rather than physical metamorphosis; they realized, that is, that the 'change' had oc-curred not in the statue but in Pygmalion himself — a classic type of the foolish lover who translates a phantasm of beauty into a tangible image, which then becomes the object of his irrational and idolatrous passion. . . .
>
> The brief allusion to Pygmalion at the beginning of the *Physician's Tale* serves much this same purpose, for Virginia — more beautiful than even Pygmalion's perfect ivory maiden — is, to the lecherous eye of Apius, the embodiment of a phantasm of beauty, an idol created by his own lust. (180)

16. In the *Romance of the Rose,* 16005–248, the section from which Chaucer appears to have drawn a good deal of this passage, Jean de Meun contrasts human art with nature's powers and then passes on to a discussion of alchemy as a human attempt to recover the secret that nature possesses, that is, literally, how to transmute matter from one form to another. The burden of the discussion is clear: the forms that matter takes are transient appearances; nature and art are similar because both can create images, but only nature knows the full extent of affinities underlying matter.

meanings are to follow the example of, to emulate, to imitate. In lines 15 and 17 Nature's ability is opposed to the work of human artists who are also able to "grave, or peynte, or forge, or bete." The two usages render subtle but real distinctions between the creation of beauty and ideal form and the mere production of it by mechanical, albeit artistic means. The burden of the passage is its assertion that Nature is the ultimate artist, capable of creating, forming, bringing to life perfectly what art can never achieve—a creature made to the worship of God. What's more, Nature performs this feat of creation as part of God's providential scheme in the universe. She has the sole right, in the mutable, sublunar world, to create to the "worshipe of" her Lord. No one, no matter how skilled, has this commission, has this power, or has this intention of creating to the greater glory of God. Virginia is thus an image who functions as religious images were supposed to, to steer men's hearts to God.

In conveying the description of Virginia by a rhetoric centered in how Nature's *peyntyng* and *forming* differs from human artists' creations, Chaucer's poetry draws on and contributes to a discourse of late-fourteenth-century sermons and popular religious debates about two points: first the dangers inherent in the appealing beauty of visual images, second the existence in nature of true images that can lead to God, as opposed to false ones created by human art.[17] We do not need to understand the passage in terms of the high philosophical tradition—although it may be there that Chaucer found his first inspiration; we can look to a more popular and, I would argue, a more resonant discourse addressing the same issues, one closer to Chaucer and to the court audience that would have heard this tale. Aware of the power of images to stimulate the human mind to meditation and through meditation to understanding of divine truth, late-fourteenth-century English people were also aware that images, once in the mind, might not function as true signs, but be valued in and for themselves. This dual potential of images fueled debates about their role in religion; fearing that the image could be mistaken for the idea it represented and fearing that images too

---

17. To modern readers of the texts of this period discussions of images may appear as fundamentally linked to Lollard thinking; in fact the debate over images was a more broadly based phenomenon. As Margaret Aston makes clear in *Lollards and Reformers,* during this period it was part of a radical disjunction between religious feeling and intellectual certitude. The role and function of visual images are questions that recur, for example, in mystical literature from this period, as questions of how an image can aid meditation.

beautifully created could occupy the mind with delight in artifice, scholastics and ecclesiastics waged a lively and prolific discussion about the nature and role of images in Christian worship. Interest in the topic also extended beyond religious circles, as Margaret Aston points out.

> Thanks to the activity of the Lollards, images came to the fore as a topic of academic controversy in the last decade of the fourteenth century. . . . In the 1390s . . . the question assumed new urgency and there were masters in both universities who turned their attention to the justification of images and image-worship. The considerable number of surviving manuscripts reflects the liveliness of this debate. . . .
> Images were of absorbing interest both inside and outside university circles, and lay opinion (and laymen's errors) reflected back on learned discussions. (*Lollards and Reformers*, 180)

Most of the discussion of images, based on biblical injunctions against idolatry, specifically the First Commandment, centered in three issues: that true images of God are to be found in humanity; that true veneration of these images of God can be demonstrated through feeding the hungry, caring for the poor, and ministering to the sick; that this appropriate behavior is often obscured or ignored in favor of the attention specific images receive as objects of pilgrimage and as centers of cults located in overly or "untruly decorated" graven images. Here is an excerpt (from a longer passage cited subsequently) showing the Wycliffite concern with attention paid to images rather than to people:

> And ʒit men eren foul in þis crucifixe makyng, for þei peynten it wiþ greet cost, and hangen myche siluer and gold and precious cloþis and stones þeronne and aboute it, and suffren pore men, bouʒte wiþ Cristis precious blode, to be by hem nakyd, hungry, thursty and in strong preson boundun, þat shulden be holpyn by Cristis lawe wiþ þis ilke tresour þat is þus veynnely wastid on þes dede ymagis.[18]

Images were a subject of debate because there was a really debatable issue at stake: how far and in what ways were Christians, members of the living body of Christ, himself both man and God, free from the Old Testament injunction against the creation of graven images given to a

---

18. *Selections from English Wycliffite Writings*, ed. Anne Hudson (Cambridge: Cambridge University Press, 1978), 83.

people who had never experienced the Incarnation. The Incarnation, it was said, endorsed the material world. Because God in Christ clothed himself in matter and presented an image of himself to men, it could be argued — and was — that henceforth his followers could use matter to remind themselves of this integration of the divine and the human. But by the late fourteenth century the issue was not so much whether images should be created, as, once created, how they should be "used" by individual minds. Here is a Middle English version of the *Rosarium Theologie,* a compendium of "Lollard" positions on ecclesiastical and spiritual issues intended for use by preachers.

> Ymagez of representyng 'may be done als welle as yuel: wele for to exercise, for to make liȝt & for to kyndele þe myndez of trew men þat þai worschepe more deuoutely þer God; and yuel þat be occasion of ymagez it be erred fro þe soþefastenes of feiþ, þat þat ymage be worschipid ouþer wiþ *latria* or wiþ *dulia,* or elles þat "he" be delited noȝt dewly in [fayrenes], in preciouste or in affeccion off vnpertinent circumstance.[19]

The description of Virginia from the tale, in its assertion that Nature creates creatures to the worship of God and through God's decree, with its stress on the word *peynte* not only evokes the thematic issues of the image debate — questions about the good and evil images can produce — it also literally echoes the discourse used in debates about the creation of images, in which the term *peynte* recurs with regular frequency. Here is an extended passage on the same subject, the painting of images, from BL MS Additional 24202, folios 26–28v, an early-fifteenth-century manuscript. Recurrent instances of the word *peynte* structure this passage, much as they do the passage of Nature's speech in the tale. It is also notable that the passage does not address the falseness of portrayal, rather the power of images to lead people into error:

---

19. *The Middle English Translation of the Rosarium Theologie,* ed. Christina von Nolcken (Heidelberg: Carl Winter, 1979), 99. This passage also occurs in Wycliffe's *Tractatus de Mandatis Divinis* (1375–76). It is not clear whether Wycliffe's writing was the source for this passage or both passages had a common source. Wycliffe writes, "Et patet quod ymagines tam bene quam male possunt fieri: bene ad excitandum, facilitandum and accendendum mentes fidelium, ut colant devocius Deum suum; et male ut occasione ymaginum a veritate fidei aberretur, ut ymago illa vel latria vel dulia adoretur" (*Johannes Wyclif Tractatus de Mandatis Divinis,* ed. J. Loserth and F. D. Matthew [London: Wyclif Society, 1922], 156; quoted in Aston, *Lollards and Reformers,* 138).

Almyʒty God saue þi puple fro erryng in ymagis þat longe haþ durit in rude wittis of many, forgetyng þe meruelouse and precious werkis þat han ben done by þee, and by þi dere holy seyntis thorowe þi large graunt vnto hem, fully traystyng þat ymagis han done þe werkis of grace and not ʒee. For first men erren in makyng of ymagis whanne þei maken ymagis of þe Godhed, as of þe Trinite, peyntyng þe Fadir as an olde man, and þe Son as a ʒong man on a crosse, and þe Holy Gost comyng furþe of þe Fadur mowþe to þe Son as white dowfe. For in þe olde testament God comaundid þat no man shulde make ony ymage or lickenesse of hym, nowþer in lickenesse of þingis in heuene, ne in erþe ny in water; and þis biddyng of God stondis euermore in stidde wiþouten chaungynge or dispensyng. But syþen Crist was makid man, it is suffrid for lewid men to haue a pore crusifix, by þe cause to haue mynde on þe harde passioun and bittere deþ þat Crist suffrid wilfully for þe synne of man. And ʒit men erren foul in þis crucifixe makyng, for þei peynten it wiþ greet cost, and hangen myche siluer and gold and precious cloþis and stones þeronne and aboute it, and suffren pore men, bouʒte wiþ Cristis precious blode, to be by hem nakyd, hungry, thursty and in strong preson boundun, þat shulden be holpyn by Cristis lawe wiþ þis ilke tresour þat is þus veynnely wastid on þes dede ymagis. And siþ þes ymages ben bokis of lewid men to sture þem on þe mynde of Cristis passion, and techen by her peyntur, veyn glorie þat is hangid on hem [is] an opyn errour aʒenus Cristis gospel. Þei ben worþi to be brent or exilid, as bokis shulden be ʒif þei maden mencion and tauʒten þat Crist was naylid on þe crosse wiþ þus myche gold and siluer and precious cloþis, as a breeche of gold endentid wiþ perry, and schoon of siluer and a croune frettid ful of precious iewelis; and also þat Ion Baptist was cloþid wiþ a mantil of gold and golden heer as sum men peynten hym. And so of ymagis of pore apostlis of Crist, and oþer seyntis þat lyueden in pouert and gret penaunse, and dispiseden in worde and in dede þe foul pride and vanyte of þis karful lif, for þei ben peyntid as þoghe þei hadde lyued in welþe of þis world and lustus of þeire fleyshe as large as euere dide erþely man. But þus don false men þat lyuen now in þer lustis to colour wiþ þer owne cursid lif by þis false peyntyngis; and herfore þei lyen on seyntis, turnyng þer lif to þe contrarie to counfort men in worldly pride and vanyte and lykyng of her wombe and eʒen and oþer lustus. And by þis falsnesse

sclaunderen þei Crist and his seyntis, and bryngen þe symple puple
in errour of Cristis lif and his apostelis and oþer seyntis, and in
errour of bileue, and to waste temperal godis and leeue dedis of
charite to her pore neyeboris þat ben nedy and mysese, made to þe
ymage and lickenesse of God, and so make þe puple to breke þe
heestis of God for her owne wynnyngis. Neþeles in Salamons temple
weren ymagis made by þe comaundement of God þat weren figure
of many trwþis þat ben now endid. But in þe lawe of grace Crist
comaundis not to make siche ymagis, ny he ʒaf þerto ensaumple
nouþer by hymsilf ny by hise apostelis. And now men shulden be
more gostly and take lesse hede to siche sensible signes, as dyden þe
apostlis of Crist þat, by schort tyme and rewlis of Goddis hestis and
charite, ledden men to heuene wiþouten siche newe peyntyngis
schewid by manus craft, for oure lord God dwellis by grace in gode
mennus soulis, and wiþoute comparesoun bettere þan all ymagis
made of man in erþe, and better þan alle bodies of seyntis, be þe
bones of hem neuer so gloriously shreynyd in gold.

Also men erren myche in offrynge to þes ymagis. For to þe gayest and
most rychely arayed ymage raþeest wil þe puple offur, and nouʒt to
no pore ymage stondyng in a symple kirk or chapel, but ʒif it stonde
ryaly tabernaclid wiþ keruyng and peyntid wiþ gold and precious
iewelis as byfor is seyd, and ʒit wiþinne a mynstre or a greet abbey,
where litil nede is, or noon, to help by siche offeryng. And, ʒif þes
makers of ymagis þat stiren men to offer at hem seyen þat it is bettere
to þe puple for to offur her godis to þes ymagis þen to visit and help
here pore neʒeboris wiþ hor almes, þei ben exprestly aʒen Crist and
oute of cristen bileue, and bryngen þe symple puple in heresie.[20]

The thematic and verbal similarity between this passage and the beginning part of the description of Virginia, especially their mutual reliance
on the word *peynte* to mean both the putting paint on wood or stone and

---

20. In Hudson, *English Wycliffite Writings*, 83–84. The excessive length of this citation
is necessary in order to give a sense of how the anti-image rhetoric of the period creates a
semantic context for the language of Chaucer's description of Virginia.

On painting images the *Rosarium Theologie* says, "It is ane forsoþ for to worschepe
peyntorie, anoþer for to lere wat is to be worschiped by þe story of peynture. Forwy þat
Scripture is to þam þat redeþ, þat giffeþ peyntorye to ydiotes seyng it, for þai, ignorant or
vnknowyng, seeþ in it wat þam ow to folow. . . . If any man will make ymages, forbede
hym noʒt; for to worschepe forsoþe ymages, in al maner vtterly forbedde it" (101).

to suggest the formative imagination, comprise the kind of shared cultural context that locates the description as much within late-fourteenth-century image debates as the high medieval literary tradition. Read against the Wycliffite passage, the lines "I made hire to the worshipe of my lord; / So do I alle myne othere creatures" stand out in sharp contrast to the venial motivation and the focus on gain that the Wycliffite passage attributes to medieval image makers and image keepers. Not surprisingly, the strong implication of such passages is that the image is neutral; the human heart, mind, and will determine the use to which it will be put. This is what Chaucer explores in this story as he brings the false judge face to face, as it were, with an overpowering image. Chaucer does not turn the tale into a Wycliffite diatribe against images but uses language that would at the time be recognizable as the discourse of the debate. At the same time, he broadens the topic of both the tale and the image debate—this tale is not about corruption. Rather, a new topos emerges. How and where the human heart goes astray in response to the beautiful, a subtopic of much Lollard concern with the physical attractiveness of images, is Chaucer's concern as he tells the tale of innocence betrayed in Apius's lust for Virginia.

The argument that Virginia is presented to the reader/hearer as a "true" image, one made to the glory of God and in the image of God, finds support in the rest of the description, based in large part on Saint Ambrose's praise of the Virgin Mary in particular and the virgin life in general in *De Virginibus*.[21] The two dimensions of Virginia's description reinforce the idea that she is an image, that her beautiful exterior signifies an interior equally valuable, one that Apius, attracted by the beauty of her exterior, cannot or does not even suspect. As we have seen, she is beautiful.

This mayde of age twelve yeer was and tweye,
In which that Nature hadde swich delit.
For right as she kan peynte a lilie whit,
And reed a rose, right with swich peynture
She peynted hath this noble creature,
Er she were born, upon hir lymes fre,
Where as by right swiche colours sholde be;

---

21. On the analogues of this passage, see Corsa, *Physician's Tale,* 97; and W. F. Bryan and Germaine Dempster, *Sources and Analogues of Chaucer's Canterbury Tales* (1941; rpt. Atlantic Highlands, N.J.: Humanities Press, 1958).

And Phebus dyed hath hire tresses grete
Lyk to the stremes of his burned heete.

(6.30–38)

But her true beauty is inward, rooted in virtue and debonaire deportment:

And if that excellent was hire beautee,
A thousand foold moore vertuous was she.
In hire ne lakked no condicioun
That is to preyse, as by discrecioun.
As wel in goost as body chast was she,
For which she floured in virginitee
With alle humylitee and abstinence,
With alle attemperaunce and pacience,
With mesure eek of beryng and array.
Discreet she was in answeryng alway;
Though she were wis as Pallas, dar I seyn,
Hir facound eek ful wommanly and pleyn,
No countrefeted termes hadde she
To seme wys, but after hir degree
She spak, and alle hire wordes, moore and lesse,
Sownynge in vertu and in gentillesse.
Shamefast she was in maydens shamefastnesse,
Constant in herte, and evere in bisynesse
To dryve hire out of ydel slogardye.
Bacus hadde of hir mouth right no maistrie;
For wyn and youthe dooth Venus encresse,
As men in fyr wol casten oille or greesse.
And of hir owene vertu, unconstreyned,
She hath ful ofte tyme syk hire feyned,
For that she wolde fleen the compaignye
Where likly was to treten of folye,
As is at feestes, revels, and at daunces,
That been occasions of daliaunces.

(6.39–66)

Given criticism of highly decorated images as untrue to the nature of the saints and the God they are supposed to represent, this stress upon the appropriateness of Virginia's beauty, its being, in Wycliffite terms, "trew" rather than "false" beauty, inherent in her very nature, is significant. Significant, too, is the strong implication that her virtue lies to a great extent in her treating her body as a temple of God, another Wycliffite exhortation. She is thus both a perfect being and a perfect creation, an image of what God intended for humanity. And, like all good images, according to the Christian tradition and to Lollard acceptance of the idea that images can be the books of the unlearned, in her one might read the lesson of virtuous living, "As in a book, every good word or dede / That longeth to a mayden vertuous" (6.108–9).

The action of the tale arises from Virginia's attractive perfection. Upon going into town one day, to a temple with her mother, she is seen by a "justice in that toun, / That governour was of that regioun." Apius, the governor, is thrice denominated—he is a justice, a governor, and in line 123 a "juge":

Now was ther thanne a justice in that toun,
That governour was of that regioun.
And so bifel this juge his eyen caste
Upon this mayde, avysynge hym ful faste,
As she cam forby ther as this juge stood.
Anon his herte chaunged and his mood,
So was he caught with beautee of this mayde,
And to hymself ful pryvely he sayde,
'This mayde shal be myn, for any man!'

(6.121–29)

The tale allows no doubt that the fatal action of the plot follows from his seeing Virginia and her effect on his mind. The image of Virginia transmitted by sight becomes a *phantasm* in Apius's brain, a *phantasm* whose intentions he cannot properly judge because his will is fixated on her external, physical beauty. This is what Chaucer and Gower mean by being "blind with lust"—the eye of the mind that can see truth is obscured by an image of an image. Moreover, his misjudgment concerning her is linked directly to the distortion of his judgment in other areas. He is a judge whose sense of justice—of basic right and wrong—has disappeared. He becomes a monster. The tale underscores his function, the corruption it suffers, and the corruption his power spreads, by constantly referring to him as "this false juge":

This false juge, that highte Apius,
(So was his name, for this is no fable,
But knowen for historial thyng notable;
The sentence of it sooth is, out of doute),
This false juge gooth now faste aboute
To hasten his delit al that he may.
And so bifel soone after, on a day,
This false juge, as telleth us the storie,
As he was wont, sat in his consistorie,
And yaf his doomes upon sondry cas.

(6.154–63)

As he is about to kill his daughter, Virginius reiterates the point the
narrator makes, stressing the fact that all their woe has stemmed from
the fact that Apius saw Virginia, a theme present in none of the sources
or analogues:

O doghter, which that art my laste wo,
And in my lyf my laste joye also,
O gemme of chastitee, in pacience
Take thou thy deeth, for this is my sentence.
For love, and nat for hate, thou most be deed;
My pitous hand moot smyten of thyn heed.
Allas, that evere Apius the say!
Thus hath he falsly jugged the to-day.

(6.221–28)

Apius's seeing Virginia is directly linked to his false judgment, both in
his own self-"avysing" and in his role as a civil authority. Uncontrolled,
without the exercise of the will to temper the mind's reaction to the
external world, vision is a dangerous sense, both for the viewer and, by
implication in this tale, for the wider social and political web the individual helps to shape. After all, Virginia is an innocent victim; Apius is a
judge. His misjudgment leads to the terrible social and emotional inver-
sion of making a father into an executioner. Virginia's life, her goodness, and her potential fecundity are all destroyed. Moreover, in his
false judgment and his inability to understand who and what Virginia is,
Apius enacts a pattern of response to beauty predicted by many Wycliffite and Lollard thinkers. As Ritchie D. Kendall points out, much of

the Lollard objection to the world of images, signs, and even drama was an objection founded on the fear that it was easy to "enter the artist's world and never exit; so easy for the signs that seemed transparent and permeable to become opaque and impenetrable; so easy for the fictional to be mistaken for the historical. In this world, man is all too likely 'to forȝet himself.'"[22]

"The Pardoner's Tale" and the Beauty of Gold

"The Pardoner's Tale" provides a companion piece to this story, especially because it is an avowed exemplum, a hortatory story designed to warn people from the errors of sin, particularly drunkenness and gambling.[23] Throughout the tale these sins are linked to loss of mental faculties, especially judgment. This connection ties the tale thematically to "The Physician's Tale" and to the sight-vision-understanding topos in the *Tales.* In describing himself, the Pardoner describes both his appeal to his "audience" to look at, to see, his relics and their miraculous effect, and his ability to fool people in the face of their actual visual examination. In effect he proclaims his ability to render their judgment, based on the sense of sight, useless:

First I pronounce whennes that I come,
And thanne my bulles shewe I, alle and some.

---

22. *Drama of Dissent: The Radical Poetics of Nonconformity, 1380–1590* (Chapel Hill: University of North Carolina Press, 1986), 54.

23. "The Pardoner's Tale" has tended to generate criticism focusing on two aspects of its plot, the "Old Man" and the ending. For years the ending was read, following Kittredge, as an extension of a complex psychological portrait of the "one lost soul" on the pilgrimage. Some critics, like Edmund Reiss in "The Final Irony of the Pardoner's Tale," *College English* 25 (1964): 260–66, have argued a more sympathetic, or at least ambiguous view, of the Pardoner; see, too, Monica McAlpine's "The Pardoner's Homosexuality and How It Matters," *PMLA* 95 (1980): 8–22; and James Rhodes's "Motivation in Chaucer's *Pardoner's Tale:* Winner Take Nothing," *Chaucer Review* 17 (1982): 40–61. Derek Pearsall's "Chaucer's Pardoner: The Death of a Salesman," *Chaucer Review* 17 (1983): 358–65, argues against the long-standing critical tradition of probing the complex inner psychology of a character about whose inner life, Pearsall points out, we know nothing from the text. Carolyn Dinshaw's "Eunuch Hermeneutics," *English Literary History* 55 (1988): 27–51, uses theoretical strategies to develop a reading of the Pardoner correlating his fragmented rhetoric to his sexual incapacity; on the unity of the fragment she says, "The Pardoner follows the Physician's redaction of this tale as if to explain the sordid world of the *Physician's Tale:* it's an unjust world, a world cut off from natural justice, natural love — a castrated world" (30). Eugene Vance in "Chaucer's Pardoner: Relics, Discourse, and Frames of Propriety," *New Literary History* 20 (1989): 723–45, also reads the Pardoner as inseparable from the substance and quality of his diction and discourse.

Our lige lordes seel on my patente,
That shewe I first, my body to warente,
That no man be so boold, ne preest ne clerk,
Me to destourbe of Cristes hooly werk.
And after that thanne telle I forth my tales;
Bulles of popes and of cardynales,
Of patriarkes and bishopes I shewe,
And in Latyn I speke a wordes fewe,
To saffron with my predicacioun,
And for to stire hem to devocioun.
Thanne shewe I forth my longe cristal stones,
Ycrammed ful of cloutes and of bones —
Relikes been they, as wenen they echoon.

(6.335–49)

As a self-proclaimed hypocrite and con artist, the Pardoner assumes that people can be duped, particularly through evidence offered to their sense of sight. He depends on his audience's vision and mental expectations to help him dupe them. We have seen how suggestible and deceptible vision was thought to be in this period. The Pardoner preys on that characteristic of vision as he practices an act composed largely of "shewing" signs of authority — the bulls of "popes and of cardynales," "our lige lordes seel," and his "longe cristal stones" of which he says, "Relikes been they, as wenen they echoon." The Pardoner relies on his audience's predisposed readiness to accept his relics and images as real within the context in which he presents them. Neither does he allow people to reflect on the real meaning of what they have seen. He presents images of authority that people are prepared to respect; his success depends on the fact that people hearing him and seeing his warrants and "relics" wil not take the next step beyond initial vision, the move toward reasoning about their symbolic function or intrinsic value.

In fact the ability to judge, to make a shrewd assessment based on information received through the senses, occupies him as a topic through the exhortatory preamble to the actual exemplum in his tale. Lot, he tells us, acted "unkyndely" with his daughters, "unwityngly" through the effects of drunkenness (6.485–86). Seneca warned that there is no difference between "a man that is out of his mynde / And a man which that is dronkelewe" (6.494–95). The exercise of judgment is closely connected to the exercise of will in responding to desire. We can see this coupling at work in the Pardoner's discussion of gluttony; the Pardoner tells of Adam and his sin with Eve, suggesting through his conclusion that if Adam had exercised his will, that is, the control of his judgment, rather than giving in to *affeccioun,* humans would still be in Paradise: "O, wiste a man how manye maladyes / Folwen of excesse and of glotonyes, / He wolde been the moore mesurable / Of his diete, sittynge at his table" (6.513–16). Later on he announces, "For dronkenesse is verray sepulture / Of mannes wit and his discrecioun. / In whom that drynke hath dominacioun / He kan no conseil kepe; it is no drede" (6.558–61). Even "hasardrye" and "othes false and grete" lead to surrendering control:

> Hasard is verray mooder of lesynges,
> And of deceite, and cursed forswerynges,
> Blaspheme of Crist, manslaughtre, and wast also
> Of catel and of tyme.
>
> (6.591–94)

> This fruyt cometh of the bicched bones two,
> Forswerying, ire, falsnesse, homycide.
>
> (6.656–57)

In the actual exemplum, the three rioters commit all the sins mentioned in the prefatory section of the tale. As the tale opens, they are drinking and cursing. Later their desire for the gold is a notable species of gluttony. At the beginning of the tale the Pardoner opposes the unnamed youth's deliberate explanation of how their "felawe" died to the rioters' reckless and thoughtless quest, showing reason and appropriate understanding on the one hand and drunken, destructive unreason on the other:

> "Sire," quod this boy, "it nedeth never-a-deel;
> It was me toold er ye cam heer two houres.
> He was, pardee, an old felawe of youres,
> And sodeynly he was yslayn to-nyght,
> Fordronke, as he sat on his bench upright.
> Ther cam a privee theef men clepeth Deeth,
> That in this contree al the peple sleeth,
> And with his spere he smoot his herte atwo,

And wente his wey withouten wordes mo.
He hath a thousand slayn this pestilence.
And, maister, er ye come in his presence,
Me thynketh that it were necessarie
For to be war of swich an adversarie.
Beth redy for to meete hym everemoore;
Thus taughte me my dame; I sey namoore."

(6.670–84)

This prudent speech is met with this rejoinder:

"Ye, Goddes armes!" quod this riotour,
"Is it swich peril with hym for to meete?
I shal hym seke by wey and eek by strete,
I make avow to Goddes digne bones!
Herkneth, felawes, we thre been al ones;
Lat ech of us holde up his hand til oother,
And ech of us bicomen otheres brother,
And we wol sleen this false traytour Deeth.
He shal be slayn, he that so manye sleeth,
By Goddess dignitee, er it be nyght!"

(6.692–701)

In the midst of their quest to find and slay death they meet a mysterious old man who directs them up the crooked way to the oak tree where, he assures them, they will find death. The old man, arguably the most enigmatic figure in the tale, presents a clear instance of a sign, a visual representation that the three questors might well stop and think about. Instead they read him mistakenly, unaware of or unable to grasp the *intentiones* he announces to them. The three rioters never see beyond the obvious, that this is an old man. The inferences they draw are confused and mistaken, having originated in the uncertain premise that age necessarily implies hostility to youth: "For soothly thou art oon of his assent / To sleen us yonge folk, thou false theef!" (6.758–59). In response to their rudeness the old man offers them one more chance, directing them toward death, clearly and specifically:

"Now, sires," quod he, "if that yow be so leef
To fynde Deeth, turne up this croked wey,

For in that grove I lafte hym, by my fey,
Under a tree, and there he wole abyde;
Noght for youre boost he wole him no thyng hyde.
Se ye that ook? Right there ye shal hym fynde.
God save yow, that boghte agayn mankynde."

(6.760–66)

But the three are so far from being able to understand the warnings implicit in this speech, that, with characteristic lack of judgment, "everich of thise riotoures ran" to the tree, where they found

Of floryns fyne of gold ycoyned rounde
Wel ny an eighte busshels, as hem thoughte.
No lenger thanne after Deeth they soughte,
But ech of hem so glad was of that sighte,
For that the floryns been so faire and brighte,
That doun they sette hem by this precious hoord.
The worste of hem, he spak the firste word.

(6.770–76)

Obviously this passage marks a critical point in this story. Before they come into the grove where the oak tree is, their drunken folly seems amorphously charged. They have a vague, hubristic, goal — to slay death. In the moment of seeing the florins, something changes.[24] The oak here is a sign based on Scripture and on scriptural exegesis widely disseminated by Chaucer's time, a sign recalling the Old Testament passages where the Israelites are called upon to choose, under oak trees, on a number of occasions, between false gods and the one true God. Chaucer's audience, knowing this scriptural tradition, would see this moment as a moment of choice, too, between salvation wished on them by the old man, who says, "Se ye that ook? Right there ye shal hym [death] fynde. / God save yow, that boghte agayn mankynde, / And yow amende!" (6.765–67), and the death represented by the obsessive love of money. This moment of sight is the turning point in the story. The

---

24. On the changing verbal dynamics of the tale in general and this section, see Stephen Knight, "Chaucer's Pardoner in Performance," *Sydney Studies in English* 9 (1983–84), 27; Knight notes the careful modulation of voice and movement in the tale. On the oak tree, see Collette, "*Ubi Peccaverant Ibi Punirentur:* The Oak Tree and the Pardoner's Tale," *Chaucer Review* 19 (1984): 39–45.

headlong rush of the three rioters, the sudden decision to seek death, the mysterious meeting with the old man, the run up the hill—all that haste is traded for a moment of comparative stasis: "No lenger thanne after Deeth they soughte, / But ech of hem so glad was of that sighte, / For that the floryns been so faire and brighte, / That doun they sette hem by this precious hoord" (6.772–75). No one says anything, the moment is given over to seeing, to the immediate effect of seeing—joy, gladness—and then to the secondary effect of sight—the apparently reasonable, but actually distorted, thinking of the "worste of hem." Close examination of his speech reveals a total change in tone and verbal structure from the earlier speech quoted above, punctuated as it was with oaths and promises to "sleen this false traytour Deeth." This speech, in contrast, seems reasonable, calm, thoughtful:

> "Bretheren," quod he, "taak kep what that I seye;
> My wit is greet, though that I bourde and pleye.
> This tresor hath Fortune unto us yiven,
> In myrthe and joliftee oure lyf to lyven,
> And lightly as it comth, so wol we spende.
> Ey, Goddes precious dignitee! Who wende
> To-day that we sholde han so fair a grace?
> But myghte this gold be caried fro this place
> Hoom to myn hous, or elles unto youres—
> For wel ye woot that al this gold is oures—
> Thanne were we in heigh felicitee.
> But trewely, by daye it may nat bee.
> Men wolde seyn that we were theves stronge,
> And for oure owene tresor doon us honge.
> This tresor moste ycaried be by nyghte
> As wisely and as slyly as it myghte.
> Wherfore I rede that cut among us alle
> Be drawe, and lat se wher the cut wol falle;
> And he that hath the cut with herte blithe
> Shal renne to the town, and that ful swithe,
>
> (6.777–96)

The allusion to working "wisely," the assertion that his "wit is greet," the light, easy phrasing—"This tresor hath Fortune unto us yiven, / In myrthe and joliftee oure lyf to lyven," the generously phrased "Hoom to myn hous, or elles unto youres," all combine to suggest judgment and reflection. The passage exudes calm control and thoughtful planning. It is, of course, a monstrous illusion designed to cloak another plan, whose later explanation and phrasing belie its honeyed tones. As with Apius and his desire to possess Virginia in "The Physician's Tale," the three rioters hatch two plots to allow unrestricted possession of the source of the *phantasms* that so occupy their minds. As soon as the youngest draws the cut and heads to town, the speaker of the passage above speaks again and reveals how the sight of the florins and their image in his mind has destabilized his already shaky reasoning ability:

Thow knowest wel thou art my sworen brother;
Thy profit wol I telle thee anon.
Thou woost wel that oure felawe is agon.
And heere is gold, and that ful greet plentee,
That shal departed been among us thre.
But nathelees, if I kan shape it so
That it departed were among us two,
Hadde I nat doon a freendes torn to thee?

(6.808–15)

The plan is devised, and the happy tone of the first speech resumes: "And thanne shal al this gold departed be, / My deere freend, bitwixen me and thee. / Thanne may we bothe oure lustes all fulfille, / And pleye at dees right at oure owene wille" (6.831–34). While it is clear that the speaker is fooling himself about the clarity of his thought, we are left wondering about the reasoning power and the understanding of the "middle" rioter—how can he think that the "worste of hem" will stop at one killing? What's happened to his judgment? He assents to the plan.

In the meanwhile, the youngest of the three, on the way to town, is captive to his imagination, as "Ful ofte in herte he rolleth up and doun / The beautee of thise floryns newe and brighte" (6.838–39). The sight of the florins has similarly inspired him to do some thinking, and he, too, has a plan, inspired in turn by "the feend, oure enemy." In both his case and the case of his companions back in the grove, the sight of the florins has further disturbed an already displaced sense of judgment. The result, as the Old Man has forecast, is death, in fact a particularly awful death, by murder, all for desire aroused by the image of money and the pleasures money can buy.

At the conclusion of the tale the Pardoner, in what must surely be a Chaucerian parody of the corruption of the concept of pardons, urges the pilgrims to buy his pardons "Al newe and fressh at every miles ende" (6.928); he then goes on to assert that it is a lucky thing he is on the pilgrimage, for, in case of fatal accident, he can "assoille" all "Whan that the soule shal fro the body passe" (6.940), an outright lie. At this point he turns to Harry Bailly to offer him the chance to be first, to "kisse the relikes everychon" (6.944). In a moment of rare acuity Harry Bailly penetrates to the heart of the problem of the Pardoner, the invisibility of what he offers, the deceit of his "powerful" objects of religious *vertu*. When he says, "Thou woldest make me kisse thyn olde breech, / And swere it were a relyk of a seint, / Though it were with thy fundement depeint!" (6.948–50), he calls attention to the fact that the Pardoner deals in control, including control of people's senses. His false relics are not apparently false to the naked eye. Here the tale comes full circle, returning to the opening theme of the Pardoner's Prologue. The problem is how to discern what the relics the Pardoner carries truly are, how to judge whether they are symbols and images warranting respect because they can truly connect one to the larger forces of creation, or whether they are what they seem, *stikkes and stones and ded mens bones.* The Pardoner's job is to deny people's ability to trust their senses; he makes his money from those who disbelieve the evidence of their senses, affirming that bits of rag and bone are natural signs of divine presence. When Harry Bailly refuses the Pardoner's offer of relics, he enacts a clear instance of judgment based on vision. He can see the supposed relics are worthless.

But the two tales of the fragment pose a more complex problem: how to respond to what is potentially quite valuable. Ever since Kittredge deemed him the one lost soul on the pilgrimage, most discussions of psychology in "The Pardoner's Tale" have focused on the Pardoner. But the sheer number of critical discussions of the Pardoner's complicated interiority, of his inability to believe in the faith he corrupts, as of his sexuality, have tended to mask the fact that within the tale, as within the fragment, Chaucer presents other complex psychologies, delineated within the framework of his own culture's questions about, and understanding of, how the human mind works, especially in response to vision. A woman's beauty and the beauty of money are essentially neutral, neither good nor evil in themselves; they become so only in the way they are viewed and desired, transformed by vision and imagination. In the end Fragment VI of *The Canterbury Tales,* so long dominated by questions of the Pardoner as a character, seems to be an inquiry into much more abstract and intellectual subjects than we have so far recognized.

5

Nature Obeying the Thoughts and Desires of the Soul: Alchemy and Vision in "The Second Nun's Tale" and "The Canon's Yeoman's Tale"

The twin medieval fascinations with hagiography and alchemy that domi-nate the eighth fragment of *The Canterbury Tales* seem at first to have very little to do with the psychology of vision. To most readers the two tales of the fragment seem to reflect mutually exclusive philosophies. Although they are linked by patterns of language and verbal themes, it has been generally assumed that the tales are separate and oppositional, and that while a common topos of alchemical language links them, they comprise a whole composed of oppositional halves in which Christianity is contrasted to alchemy. But reading late medieval alchemical texts leads to the conclusion that if the two tales are oppositional, it is not because Christianity is opposed to the "falseness" of alchemy, but be-cause in the two tales Chaucer contrasts "real" alchemy—an intellectual and spiritual search dependent on preparation of the senses and training of the mind—to a kind of dull, mechanical alchemy that, lacking a spiritual, philosophical foundation, depends on deception of the senses, particularly sight.[1]

---

1. Criticism seems to have expunged the idea of philosophy from alchemy, preferring to deal with its material, experimental aspects. In the mid–twentieth century Pauline Aiken, "Vincent of Beauvais and Chaucer's Knowledge of Alchemy," *Studies in Philology* 41 (1944): 371–89; and Edgar Duncan, "The Yeoman's Canon's 'Silver Citrinacioun,'" *Modern Philology* 37 (1940): 241–62, and "The Literature of Alchemy and Chaucer's Canon's Yeoman's Tale: Framework, Theme, and Characters," *Speculum* 43 (1968): 633–56, working from the list of material and processes in part 1 of the tale, argued that Chaucer clearly knew the major works of alchemy available in the West during his time and relied especially on Arnold of Villanova. Joseph E. Grennen, in a series of articles written in the 1960s, explicated the range and breadth of Chaucer's knowledge of alchemy, all the while consistently maintaining, as he puts it in "The Canon's Yeoman's Alchemical

It is hard to see the connection between alchemy and the idea of realizing the full potential of the human body because today the term *alchemy* popularly connotes a kind of rudimentary chemistry nourished by human greed. In the late Middle Ages, however, alchemy was a much more serious proposition, a subject that in its highest form approached what we today might call a grand unification theory. In Chaucer's time alchemy wore two faces. In one guise it constituted a system of philosophy that could explain the secret unity of all matter, a secret whose practice was often compared to the mystery of the Mass where the matter of bread and wine became the body of Christ. At its heart philosophic alchemy was a system of thinking about the nature of things.

What occurred in the Hermetic vase or crucible was a microcosm of the striving of man and of matter toward God—perfection—the Philosopher's Gold. The chemical process was a symbol of the life

---

Mass," *Studies in Philology* 62 (1965): 546–60, that Chaucer was "a superb ironist who was obviously never taken in for a moment by any of the alchemical clap-trap he heard or read" (547). Grennen argued that Chaucer's knowledge of alchemical literature was "extensive if not deep, and his response to it was as much a response to the verbal miasm in which the alchemists worked as to the theoretical positions they took or to the futile experiments they conducted" (547). In "Saint Cecilia's 'Chemical Wedding': The Unity of the *Canterbury Tales,* Fragment VIII," *JEGP* 65 (1966): 466–81, he maintained that "The Second Nun's Tale" is designed to "stand against the 'confusioun of alchemy'" in the "Canon's Yeoman's Tale" (481), and that "The mystical fancies of the 'philosophers' and their emphasis on the *one*-ness of the alchemical *opus* did not prevent Chaucer from seeing that the alchemists were (in their own terms) 'multipliers'—but multipliers of words, treatises, recipes, ingredients, anything, in short, but the gold, health, or virtue which they imagined themselves to be seeking" (472).

A persistent school has maintained the essential unity of the fragment through contrast—alchemy to religion, sight to blindness, reason to revelation. Bruce Rosenberg's "The Contrary Tales of the Second Nun and the Canon's Yeoman," *Chaucer Review* 2 (1968); 278–91, argues that the two tales are linked through the theme of alchemy, but that alchemy is a test case; he maintains that a "philosophical polarity" dominates the fragment, a polarity that locates "one of the most debated intellectual problems of the Middle Ages: reason and revelation" (289). Glending Olson has noted the "conceptual coherence and extensive verbal cross-reference" between the two tales ("Chaucer, Dante, and the Structure of Fragment VIII (G) of the *Canterbury Tales, Chaucer Review* 16 [1981]: 225); and Peter Brown, arguing the apocryphal nature of "The Canon's Yeoman's Tale," outlines the frequent argument that it is linked to "The Second Nun's Tale" by a web of language and theme in "Is the 'Canon's Yeoman's Tale' Apocryphal?" *English Studies* 6 (1983): 481–90. The most recent exemplar of this school seems to be Robert M. Longsworth, who, in "Privileged Knowledge: St. Cecilia and the Alchemist in the *Canterbury Tales,*" *Chaucer Review* 27 (1992): 87–96, places insight and wisdom at the heart of both tales in the fragment: "For Chaucer, at any rate, these two narratives display the linkage between the epistemology of faith and the epistemology of art" (95).

process. . . . The opus naturally lent itself to religion; the death of the metallic seed and its rebirth as the *lapis* was similar to the death and resurrection of Jesus.[2]

Alchemy's protean discourse signified the deep cosmic secret at its heart. Sheila Delany points out that:

> the progressive sub-text of alchemy was framed in the language of an archaic myth-system: the theory of correspondences or cosmic similitudes that constituted its intellectual structure. . . . The *New Pearl of Great Price,* an Italian text of the fourteenth century, teaches that the creation of an embryo from menstrual blood, of a chicken from an egg, or of gold from sulphur and mercury are analogous processes. Alchemy sees nature as constantly in flux. . . . Moreover the telos of this change is perfection.[3]

Bruce Rosenberg similarly describes the basic principle of medieval alchemy as the striving of all nature toward perfection and purification: "Medieval alchemists felt, with Aristotle, that the seven known metals, like all things else in nature, were striving toward perfection. As with man, all matter was composed of a body and a spirit and it was the task of the alchemists to perfect the spirit, or seed, of metals by speeding up their slow evolution toward perfection" ("Swindling Alchemist," 566–67). As the author of an anonymous late medieval alchemical text put it, "Yett lesse World and greate World is all but One / Thus still we keep an Unyon." The locus of union and the center of perfection was blood, figuring the fecundity and unity of all matter:

> Whatsoever itt is that is alive,
> Without Blood they may not thrive.
> Sperme is Generacion of each thing,
> Of what kinde soever itt bene;
> Blood is Sperme be itt White or Redd,
> For without Blood each thing is dead:

---

2. Bruce Rosenberg, "Swindling Alchemist, Antichrist," *Centennial Review* 6 (1962): 567.

3. Sheila Delany, "Run Silent, Run Deep: Heresy and Alchemy as Medieval Versions of Utopia," in *Medieval Literary Politics: Shapes of Ideology,* ed. Sheila Delany (Manchester: Manchester University Press, 1990), 11.

Blood conteineith the three things I have told,
And in his Tincture hath nature of Gold . . .
Without Blood noe Body hath bene fitt of light:
Thus doth the greate and lesse World still,
Hold the Union according to Gods will.[4]

Alchemy of the late Middle Ages was a philosophic system highly metaphoric in its discourse, seeing analogy and correspondence throughout creation, seeking to achieve its ultimate goal of perfecting matter under the skilled and learned guidance of a philosopher-alchemist. It is typical of alchemical discourse to incorporate the discourse of other fields into its analogies and explanations; in fact this is one of the obvious causes of its semantic instability and semiotic richness. The term *multiplication*, with which Chaucer was clearly familiar, is a good example. An anonymous late medieval alchemical text defines *multiplication* as the generating of forms, drawing for analogy on the optical metaphor of multiplication of *species*. Writing of how alchemy is accomplished, trying to explain the unexplainable, the author turns to theories of vision for an appropriate analogy:

The Species of all things both more and lesse each one,
Are mainteyned by reason of Multiplication;
Then if they be not Multiplyed they decay,
. . . .
Soe likewise our *Stone* must needs Multiply,
Or elce the Species of that *Stone* will dye.
                    (*Theatrum Chemicum Britannicum*, 412)

Here multiplication of *species* and multiplication of forms are treated as deriving from the same life impulse — implying yet one more metaphor inherent here, that of multiplication as generation of life. Alchemy and the processes of vision alike were explained through organic metaphors of generation and decay, both centered in the most basic forces of nature.[5]

---

4. *Theatrum Chemicum Britannicum, Containing Severall Poeticall Pieces of our Famous English Philosophers, who have written the Hermetique Mysteries in their owne Ancient Language Faithfully Collected into one Volume with Annotations thereon by Elias Ashmole, Esq.* (London, 1652; rpt., with introduction by Allen G. Debus, New York: Johnson Reprint Corporation, 1967), 405.

5. Pearl Kibre, writing of the *De Occultis Naturae* (a fifteenth-century MS in the British Library), attributed to Albertus Magnus, locates the same analogy in a passage that also

By the later Middle Ages serious alchemy had accrued a large body of interpretive literature that linked the success of alchemical attempts to find the essential secrets of matter to the state of mind of the alchemist and his ability to refine his senses in their response to the world of matter. In a number of texts that have survived from this period the alchemist's orientation toward matter is expressed in the trope of vision as understanding. The alchemist's ability to "see" was both physical and allegorical; it was an ability to understand what happened in invisible physical reactions by looking for visible results.

In contrast to this elevated and overarching system of correspondences seeking to touch the very heart of life, a much more narrowly focused aspect of alchemy also flourished. Various unscrupulous or obsessed people became caught up in the material aspects of alchemy, concentrating not on the philosophy of the subject, but on one of its practical aspects, the transformation of base metal into gold. Unable to identify, much less command the philosophic principles that would enable alchemists to release the secret power of all matter, they labored in stinking chambers with explosive, unstable combinations of elements, constantly failing in their attempts. The frustration these failures produced was addictive; to continue their experiments, these "puffers," as they were called, often resorted to defrauding the unwary, pretending to share the receipt for transmuting base matter into silver or gold — for a price. Chaucer presents these two faces of alchemy in the eighth fragment of the *Tales;* "The Second Nun's Tale" is a tale of true alchemical transformation of the body expressed in the conventions of hagiography. "The Canon's Yeoman's Tale" is a tale of obsession and bafflement. Both stories are tales of alchemy. Both rely on a common discourse of

---

incorporates other elements of the physical world into its attempt to explain how the stone works. She describes the contents this way:

> It discusses the analogies between the multiplication of species in the animal kingdom and the production of mineral substances. . . . It further draws analogies between the production of the alchemical stone and the sowing of grain, the planting and fructifying of trees. . . . In short, the "De occultis naturae" contains a very large proportion of the curious alchemical devices and phrases characteristically found in alchemical treatises of the fourteenth century. (*"De Occultis Naturae* Attributed to Albertus Magnus," in *Studies in Medieval Science: Alchemy, Astrology, Mathematics and Medicine,* ed. Pearl Kibre [London: Hambledon Press, 1984], 34)

The same principle that enables vision sustains life and alchemy. Today this broad esoteric dimension of medieval alchemy seems to be overshadowed by our attention to how the practical experimental dimension led to fraud.

sight-blindness, perception-deception, purity-corruption, a discourse giving rise to major metaphoric patterns in the tales derived from the alchemical literature of Chaucer's time.

Alchemy in Chaucer's World

Chaucer's exact relationship to the "science" of alchemy is not clear. The most common assumption has been that Chaucer was far too intelligent to get involved in such nonsense; the next most common assumption has been that Chaucer was once the dupe of an alchemical trickster. A vocal but minority chorus has also consistently insisted that Chaucer's descriptions and references to alchemical terms and processes suggests he knew the literature of the subject quite well. Early in the twentieth century Pauline Aiken and Edgar Duncan established that Chaucer knew of the major works of alchemy available in the West during his time.[6] During the middle years of the century, critics like Joseph Grennen tended to construe indications that Chaucer had more than a passing knowledge of alchemy as an index of his disapproval of the "science." A more fruitful approach is to ask how alchemy figured in late-fourteenth- and early-fifteenth-century English culture.

Alchemy entered the West during the twelfth century, bringing with it the classical principle that all matter is animate and that man as a microcosm is a reflection of the divinely created universe, the macrocosm.[7] Apparently medieval authorities treated alchemy seriously, if ambivalently. On the one hand they sought to restrain its practice because of the economic disruption its abuse produced; on the other they sought to control it by appropriating it to their own uses. Over the course of the

---

6. In the first half of the twentieth century, Pauline Aiken wrote a series of articles about the influence of Chaucer's knowledge of Vincent of Beauvais on various of the *Canterbury Tales*. She maintained that Chaucer's knowledge of alchemy is part of a larger pattern of scientific knowledge woven into the fabric of the *Tales:* "Vincent of Beauvais and Dame Pertelote's Knowledge of Medicine," *Speculum* 10 (1935): 281–87; "Arcite's Illness and Vincent of Beauvais," *PMLA* 51 (1936): 361–69; "Vincent of Beauvais and Chaucer's Knowledge of Alchemy," *Studies in Philology* 41 (1944): 371–89; "Vincent of Beauvais and the 'Houres' of Chaucer's Physician," *Studies in Philology* 53 (1956): 22–24.

7. Will H. L. Ogrinc, "Western Society and Alchemy from 1200 to 1500," *Journal of Medieval History* 6 (1980): 103. See also Stanislas Klossowski De Rola, *Alchemy: The Secret Art* (London: Thames and Hudson, 1973); and Stanton J. Linden, *Darke Hieroglyphicks: Alchemy in English Literature from Chaucer to the Restoration* (Lexington: University Press of Kentucky, 1996), on alchemy in Europe and England.

fourteenth century a growing opposition to alchemy developed, not so much on moral or theoretical grounds as on economic grounds, because its enthusiastic practitioners began to interfere with the money supply. The papal bull of Pope John XXII, *Spondent quas non exhibent,* of 1317 sought to curtail the practice of those who, pretending to be alchemists, were in fact counterfeiters (Ogrinc, 114). What is most interesting from the point of view of trying to place "The Canon's Yeoman's Tale" in an intellectual context is that alchemy flourished in the several royal courts of the fourteenth century, in England among other places, partially because it promised a way out of financial difficulties. As Will H. L. Ogrinc's research into the history of alchemy in England discovered,

> Many documents in the Public Record Office in London attest to the interest of King Edward III in alchemy. The king kept various alchemists at his court and repeatedly intervened to protect them against the public. . . . Richard II seems to have shown a similar interest . . . but Henry IV issued a prohibition of alchemy in 1403/4 in order to stop the production of counterfeit money. . . . During the Hundred Years' War there is a noticeable quickening of interest in alchemy. . . . Henry VI issued four decrees after 1436 addressed to the nobility, the clerical order, the professors and the medical doctors in his kingdom, enjoining them to contribute their talent to the replenishment of the treasury and to the needs of the kingdom. He made a special overture to the priests for whom, as he said, it should be easy to change *(transubstantiare)* base metal into precious since they daily changed bread and wine into the body and blood of Christ. (118–19)[8]

In 1452 Henry VI created a commission of "three persons to arrest those who practised alchemy without a royal charter" (120).

Ogrinc identifies the fourteenth century as a crucial period in the evolution of alchemy, for in the fourteenth century alchemy moved from the province of the learned clergy into the secular world. An increased skepticism attended this popularization, however, because of the charlatanism alchemy spawned as it grew more popular. Moreover, alchemical deception often centered in counterfeiting money, a practice that attracted royal attention:

---

8. On the authority of a 1670 text; see Ogrinc, "Western Society and Alchemy," 131.

An often repeated complaint about the alchemist was that he counter-
feited money. . . . And this is the crucial point: most rulers — and not
only rulers — believed in transmutation but were not capable of distinguishing between the true alchemist and the cunning fake. This incapacity explains the policy of the secular authorities toward alchemy;
they tried to contain it with every possible means, prohibitions on the
one hand and licenses with offers of protection on the other. ("Western Society and Alchemy," 125–26)

Ogrinc's research reveals a pattern of ambivalence about alchemy: alchemy is real, but many practitioners are frauds; its secret, though real,
is highly elusive. As it happened, even the failures of alchemy might be
put to good use. Some partially "successful" alchemical processes could
indeed make base metal look like gold by creating a surface change; as a
result it was possible to use this counterfeit coin with a thin veneer of
goldlike metal to debase an enemy's currency (Duncan, "Silver Citrinacioun," 249–50). This debasing was actually used by English and
French against each other during the Hundred Years' War to destabilize
the enemy's money supply (Ogrinc, 120).

Considering such a history, it is reasonable to infer that alchemy, its
potential and its abuse, were familiar topics in the circle in which Chaucer lived and wrote. Viewed within a literary context, Chaucer's writing
about alchemy in "The Canon's Yeoman's Tale" — the lists of materials,
the story of the trick, the emphasis on failure, poverty, the need for
money, the hope that alchemy is real, but not easily accomplished — was
more conventional than original, even though no apparent source or
close analogue for the tale has yet been identified. The same themes and
elements appear in Gower's writings and later in Lydgate's. The textual
evidence suggests that alchemy was a popular topic among Chaucer's
circle and literary heirs.

This conventionality may account for the fact that historically, that
is, until the modern period, Chaucer's interest in alchemy was understood as part of a venerable intellectual tradition. Elias Ashmole's seven-
teenth-century *Theatrum Chemicum Britannicum* treats Chaucer as part
of a learned tradition, describing him as an adept in the science, and as a
pupil of Gower: "Now as Concerning Chaucer (the Author of this Tale)
he is ranked amongst the *Hermetick Philosophers,* and his *Master* in this
Science was Sir *John Gower,* whose familiar and neere acquaintance

began at the *Inner Temple* upon *Chaucer's* returne into *England,* for the Troubles of the *Times* towards the latter end of Rich: *the second's Raign* had caused him to retire out of their *Danger* into *Holland, Zeland, and France"* (470). Whatever the historical truth of this explanation, it seems reasonable to infer that Renaissance scholars interested in alchemy saw Chaucer as part of a native English literary tradition that reflected both knowledge and acceptance of alchemy as a legitimate area of study and inquiry; that, as Ashmole says, "he that Reads the latter part of the *Chanon's Yeoman's Tale,* will easily perceive him to be a *Iudicious Philosopher,* and one that fully knew the Mistery" (470).[9]

Knowledge of alchemy, as the following passage from Gower's *Confessio Amantis* shows, was knowledge of how the world worked. In this system of thinking the transmutation of matter lay at the heart of alchemy—both literally and allegorically. Because gold was the most perfect form of mineral, it was understood to be the apogee of that kind of matter, the end toward which all transformation of metals strove. But other principles besides transmutation claimed importance in medieval alchemy. A major principle, which Rosenberg alluded to in the quotation above, the idea that what happens in the crucible was a "microcosm of the striving of man and of matter toward God," was based on the idea that alchemy reenacted the very processes of life and of material creation.

In describing what the philosopher's stone is in *Confessio Amantis,* book 4, 2557–2632, Gower concentrates on how it can perfect and

---

9. The tradition that Chaucer was knowledgeable about alchemy dates back at least to the sixteenth century. Francis Thynne's *Animadversions Upon Speght's First (1598) Edition of Chaucer's Works,* ed. G. H. Kingsley, Early English Text Society, 9 (London, 1875) contains a passage correcting Speght's term *resagor,* saying, "This worde shold rather be 'resalgar'; wherefore I will shewe you what Resalgar ys in that abstruce scyence whiche Chawcer knewe full well, althoughe he enveye againste the sophisticall abuse thereo [sic] in the chanon's yeoman's tale" (36). Gabriel Harvey's *Marginalia,* ed. G. C. Moore-Smith (Stratford upon Avon, 1913) observes, "Other [sic] commend Chawcer, & Lidgate for their witt, pleasant veine, varietie of poetical discourse, & all humanitie: I specially note their Astronomie, philosophie, & other parts of profound or cunning art. Wherein few of their time were more exactly learned. It is not sufficient for poets, to be superficial humanists: but they must be exquisite artists, & curious vniuersal schollers" (160–61).

The tradition of Chaucer as a philosopher of the art was apparently maintained by alchemists in the period between the seventeenth and twentieth centuries. In her *Hermetic Philosophy and Alchemy: A Suggestive Inquiry into "The Hermetic Mystery" with a Dissertation of the More Celebrated of the Alchemical Philosophers* (1850), rev. ed. (New York: Julian Press, 1960), 51, Mary Anne Atwood cites the tale as an example of Chaucer's exposing not the falsity of alchemy (which she defends), but the deceit that some of its followers visit on the gullible.

cleanse matter. His description leaves no doubt that the "stone" is, as Ogrinc says, an *agens,* that is, a force that works on matter. In fact, in Gower's alchemy, the philosopher's "stone" is actually triune; three "stones" comprise it: the animal, the vegetable, and the mineral — what we know as the stone that multiplies gold. In Gower's explication, cited below from the *Theatrum Chemicum,* the mineral stone is but one aspect of the triune power of the philosopher's elixir. The vegetable stone, equally important, possesses the "proper vertue" "mans heale for to serve, / As for to keepe, and to preserve, / The body fro sicknes all, / Til death of kinde upon hym fall" (370). The second stone, the "*Lapis Animalis* hote," has the virtue of perfecting the senses:

> For Eare and Eye, Nose and Mouth;
> Wherof a man may here, and see,
> And smell and tast, in his degree,
> And for to feele and for to goe,
> Itt helpeth a man of both two:
> The witts five he underfongeth
> To keepe, as it to hym belongeth.
>
> (370–71)

The third stone, the mineral, works to purify metals, allowing them to realize their potential:

> Attempreth, till that thei ben fyne;
> And pureth hem by such a wey,
> That all the vice goth awey,
> Of Rust, of Stynke, and of Hardnes:
> And when they ben of such clennes,
> This minerall so as I fynde,
> Transformeth all the fyrst kynde,
> And maketh hem able to conceive,
> Through his vertue and receive
> Both in substance and in figure,
> Of Gold and Silver the nature.
> For thei two ben the extremitees,
> To which after the propertees,
> Hath every mettall his desire,
> With helpe and comforte of the fyre.
>
> (371)

Two of the three dimensions of the philosopher's stone enable the human body to reach its full potential—they preserve the body, support and perfect the senses, and purify matter so it can reach its apogee. The strong implication of alchemy so explained is that it is a principle of human empowerment—that it can improve the state of the body and the senses.[10]

Gower, like Chaucer, stresses the potential for fraud inherent in both the science and its processes:

> But now it stant all otherwise:
> Thei speken fast of thilke *Stone,*
> But how to make it now wote none.
> After the sooth Experience,
> And nathles greate diligence,
> Thei setten up thilke dede,
> And spillen more then thei spede;
> For alwey thei fynde a lette,
> Which bringeth in povetee and Dette;
> To hem that rich were to fore,
> The Losse is had the Lucre is lore:
> To gette a pound thei spenden five,
> I not how such a Craft shall thrive:
> In the manner as it is used,
> It were better be refused,
> Then for to worchen upon wene,
> In thinge which stant not as thei wene:

---

10. In light of the prevailing religious discourse of purification from sin and transformation of the soul, which after death and at the Last Judgment will be brought into its full potential, it is hard to read the description of the third stone's ability to purify metal as isolated from the discourse of how sin may be purged and the human soul cleansed, brought to its full aureate potential, and saved. One sign system evokes the other in a cross-fertilization of metaphor and idea. Rosenberg notes that "Ripley, canon of Bridlington, thought that the alchemical fire was the Holy Ghost who united the Father with the Son, the Father presumably being mercury and the Son, sulphur" ("Swindling Alchemist," 572). He also remarks, "I have already mentioned that the *lapis* assumed in the minds of many alchemists a sacred, even a religious dimension. Just to what degree alchemy had become involved with religion is patent in the suggestion of Nicolao Melchiore, who in his *Adam Et Processum* at the beginning of the sixteenth century expounded the alchemical process in the form of the Mass. Elsewhere, Melchiore compared the black state of the experiment to the death on Calvary, and the red state to Easter" (573).

But not for thy who that it knew,
The Science of himselfe is trew.
        (*Theatrum Chemicum Britannicum,* 371–72)

This passage introduces an important correlative issue in both Gower's and Chaucer's discussions of alchemy, their shared sense that the secret of alchemy is real, but, for various reasons, hidden in the modern world. Modern (i.e., medieval) practitioners find themselves unable to understand the writings of the ancient practitioners because the words have lost their referents, their meaning; they "knowen litle that they mene, / It is not one to wite and wene, / In forme of words thei it trete" (*Theatrum Chemicum Britannicum,* 373).[11] Nevertheless, Gower asserts that the science "grounded is upon nature" (373). The lost knowledge of the science is actually lost truth. The conceptual umbrage in which alchemists work signifies an impoverished world. As in Chaucer's poem "The Former Age," a sense of a long-past golden age pervades discussions of alchemy. This characteristic hallmark of alchemical texts of this period suggests a sense of radical dissociation from the secrets of the universe, a sense of being cut off from them and ultimately from God who is their source. The constant refrain of late medieval English alchemical texts is the sense of lost secrets, known formerly, but now hidden from humans in unstable language.[12]

---

11. Several critics have discussed "The Canon's Yeoman's Tale" as a tale about language, not a surprising approach because of the dynamic potential of the discourse of alchemy. Alchemy grafts to itself whole sign systems that then become interchangeable in signification and discourse. But in late medieval and early modern texts, this interweaving of discourses and metaphors is deemed useful and appropriate. Contemporary criticism has deemed it unstable and problematic. On this topic, see Jane Hilberry, "'And in Oure Madnesse Everemoore We Rave': Technical Language in the *Canon's Yeoman's Tale,*" *Chaucer Review* 21 (1987): 435–43; Lee Patterson, "Perpetual Motion: Alchemy and the Technology of the Self," *Studies in the Age of Chaucer* 15 (1993): 25–57; Grennen, "Saint Cecilia's 'Chemical Wedding.'" Both Judith Herz, "The Canon's Yeoman's Prologue and Tale," *Modern Philology* 58 (1961): 231–37; and Olson, "Chaucer, Dante," maintain that Chaucer experiments with narrative voice, types of discourse, and their relationship to moral issues (Olson, 232) and to self understanding (Herz, 236) in the fragment.

12. Lydgate's alchemical text, *The Translation of the Second Epistle that King Alexander sent to his Master Aristotle,* reiterates the same lament that Chaucer, Gower, and others make: this is a secret craft, never widely known, now known to even fewer. Lydgate connects this lament to the familiar theme of the dangers of alchemy. People who start to practice alchemy often find themselves obsessed by their desire to discover its secret, and impoverished by their inability to understand the lost art. Thus it is certainly no craft for poor men, because it devours money, time, and spirit and can lead to obsession:

Alchemy and Vision

Alchemy required keen vision, both literal and figurative. Reading alchemical literature of the late Middle Ages, one is struck by frequent references to the assumption that alchemy works on and through the human body, particularly the sense of sight and the imaginative dimension of the mind. The very study of alchemy was thought to maintain and improve human vision. Gower's writing on alchemy shows that the animal dimension of the philosopher's stone helps perfect the human senses. George Ripley's preface to *Medulla* (1476) describes the three virtues of the philosopher's stone as helping to achieve and sustain youthful vigor:

> To cure all things their vertue is,
> In every cause what soe befall,
> Mankinde in health preserve they shall:
> Reneweth Youth and keepeth it sound,
> As trew by proofe the same is found.
>
> (*Theatrum Chemicum Britannicum*, 390)

At the same time that alchemical texts of the period assume that the evidence of alchemy is sensual and that the senses, especially sight, will be able to validate the evidence of invisible processes having actually been at work, they also uniformly warn that clever tricksters work their

---

> It is no Crafft poore men t'assayle,
> It causeth Coffers and Chestys to be bare,
> Marryth wytts, and braynes doth affray;
> Yit by wryting this booke doth declare,
> And be Resons lyst not for to spare,
> Wyth Golden Resouns in taast moost lykerous.
> Thyng *per Ignotum* prevyd *per Ignocius.*
>
> (*Theatrum Chemicum Britannicum*, 401)

Warning of the dangers of attempting this practice lightly, Lydgate says,

> For he that lyst putte in Experience,
> Forboode secrees I hold hym but a foole,
> Lyke hym that temptyth of wylfull neglygence,
> To stonde up ryght on a three foote stoole,
> Or sparyth a stewe, or fyssheth in a bareyn poole.
> Whan all is doon, he get noon othir grace,
> Men wyl skorne hym and mokke hys foltish [*sic*] face.
>
> (401)

frauds by deceiving the senses, particularly sight. Norton's *Ordinal of Alchemy* begins its *Prohemium* with the caveat, repeated throughout the work, to beware of "fals illusions" of fakers who will try to trick the unknowing by tricking their senses:

> Nethirles clerkis grete secretis here may leere,
> But al lay-men shal fynde here cause to feere,
> And to be ware of fals Illusions
> which multipliers worch with theyr conclusyons.[13]

Norton goes on to stress the dangers laymen may encounter in the search for true alchemy, that is, true understanding, repeatedly using a discourse structured by the polarities of truth and falsehood, vision and deception. In a series of passages that echo the situation and the setting of the "Canon's Yeoman's Tale," he warns,

> Fals colorid metalle nevir to counterfett;
> As thei that seche blanchers or citrinacions
> which will not abyde alle examynacions,
> where-with fals plate þei make as thei can,
> Or monay to begile som good trew man.

(Ll. 112–16)

He urges his readers to beware

> The fals man walkith fro towne to towne,
> For the moste parte with a thredbare gowne,
> Euyr serching with diligent a-wayte
> To wyn his pray with som fals disceyte.
> Of swering and lesyng such wil not cese,
> To say how thei can siluer plate encrese;
> And euyr thei rayle with periurye,
> Sayng how thei can multiplye
> Gold and siluer, and in suche wise
> with promyse thei please the covetyse,
> And causith his mynde to be on hym sett;
> Then falshode and couetyse be fully mett,

---

13. *Thomas Norton's Ordinal of Alchemy,* ed. John Reidy, Early English Text Society, 272 (Oxford: Oxford University Press, 1975), ll. 9–12.

But afterwarde, within a litille while,
The multiplier doth hym begyle.
With his faire promyse and with his fals othis
The covetise is broght to thredbare clothis,
But if he can hasteli be welle ware
Of the multipliere & of his cheffare,
Of whose deceptis moche can y reporte,
But I darre not, lest I gife comforte
To such as be disposide to tregedie,
For so moche hurte myght growe therbye

(Ll. 323–44)

The method of deception is typically a deception of the eyes, because
the evidence of alchemy is a change in the perceptible form:

For the properties of euery thynge
Be perceyvide bi his worchynge,
As bi colours in vrynys we be bolde
To geve sentence of hete and colde.

(Ll. 1489–92)

The change itself is invisible, yet the senses, primarily sight (but also
smell and taste, for good odor signifies good work), can testify to the
invisible processes' having worked:

When the iiij elementis wisely ioyned be,
And euerych of them sett in his degre,
Then of dyuers degrees & of diuers digestion
Colours wil a-ryse toward perfeccion.
For then worchith inward hete naturalle,
which in oure substance is but intellectuall;
To sight vnknow, hand may not it feld
His worching is know of few men & seld.
And when this hete naturall movid be shall
Bi oure outward hete artificiall,
Then nature excitid to labour will not cese
Many diuersitees of degrees to encrece;
which is one cause bi reson ye may see
whi in oure werkis so many colours bee.

(Ll. 1689–1702)

Near the end of the text Norton repeats his theme, that sight is the chief test of alchemy:

> Who can be sure to fynde his trewe degre,
> Magister magnus in igne shall he be;
> It is the hardyr to know trewly his myght,
> There is no triall for it but our Eye sygth.

(Ll. 3041–44)

Alchemy's relationship to the senses is said to depend on the proper preparation of the body and mind, to precede, not to follow from alchemy. As Ann S. Haskell notes,

> The spiritual preparation of the practitioner's soul was as important as the practical preparation of the materials for the work, and cleanness, or chastity, was a part of the preparation. In the *Aurora Consurgens,* for example, a quotation from Alphidius advises, "Know, that thou canst not have this science, unless thou shalt purify thy mind before God, that is, wipe away all corruption from thy heart. . . ." Since the relative purity of the alchemical practitioner was directly operable on the purification of the metal—variously described as "impure," "sick," "sinful," or "dirty"—which needed to be cleansed, purified, made unsinful or healthy to become gold, the clean spiritual state specified for the alchemist is frequently compared to physical health. Conversely, physical disease or deformity was symbolic of spiritual disease.[14]

In a number of alchemical works from the late Middle Ages and Renaissance the alchemist is like a mystic. First, it is assumed that the alchemist will prepare himself physically; that no one whose body is not perfect will attempt the great work. The frequently cited *Sum of Perfection, or of the Perfect Magistery,* attributed to Geber, contains an early chapter that discusses the impediments to alchemical work "from the Part of the Body of the Artificer" and remarks that

> if any *Man* have not his *Organs compleat,* he cannot by himself come to the *Compleatment* of this *Work;* no more than if he were *Blind* or

---

14. Ann S. Haskell, "The Saint Gile's Oath in the *Canon's Yeoman's Tale,*" *Chaucer Review* 7 (1973): 222–23.

wanted his *Limbs;* because he is not helped by the *Members:* by meditation of which, as ministering to *Nature,* this Art is perfected.[15]

A pure, young, and whole body is only half the requirement; the practitioner must have a pure soul and a mind free from fantasy:

> Therefore, we say, he that hath not a *Natural Ingenuity,* and *Soul,* searching and subtily scrutinizing *Natural Principles,* the *Fundamentals of Nature,* and *Artifices* which can follow *Nature,* in the properties of her *Action,* cannot find the true *Radix* of this most precious *Science.* As there are many who have a stiff *Neck,* void of *Ingenuity* in every perscrutation; and who can scarcely understand *Common Speech,* and likewise with difficulty learn *Works* vulgarly Common. Besides these, we also find many who have a *Soul* easily opinionating every *Phantasie;* but what they believe they have found true, is all *Phantastick,* deviating from *Reason,* full of *Error,* and remote from Natural *Principles;* Because their *Brain,* repleat with many *Fumosities,* cannot receive the true *Intention* of *Natural Things.* (27)

This fundamental idea appears in the 1597 *The Mirror of Alchimy composed by the Thrice-Famous and Learned Fryer, Roger Bacon:*

> For Nature (as *Avicen* teacheth, in the foresayde places) obeyeth the thoughts, and vehement desires of the Soule; yea, there should be no operation at all in men, if the naturall vertue in the members did not subject it selfe to the thoughts and desires of the soule. For (as *Avicen* teacheth in the thirde of the *Metaphysickes*) the first moover is a thought, and the next a desire conformable to the thought: And last of all, the vertue of the Soule in the members, which yeeldeth obedience to the desire and thought, and that both in evill and good. Whereupon when these thinges are to bee seene in a man, a good complexion, health of bodie, youth, beautie, comly proportion of the members, and a Soule free from sinne, an earnest thought and vehement desire to some worke, then whatsoever may be effected by the kinde and vertue of man, by the spirits and naturall heate, it must of

---

15. *The Works of Gerber, Englished by Richard Russell, 1678,* ed. E. J. Holmyard (London: J. M. Dent, 1928), 26.

necessitie be more forcibly and throughly wrought by these & such like Spirites, Vapours, and influences, then if anie of these were wanting, especially if there bee an earnest desire and forcible intention."[16]

The end of such preparation of body, mind, and will was both to achieve an alchemical transformation and to reach the level of understanding superseding the normal level of sensual, rational understanding attained by most humans.

Alchemy and Vision in the Two Tales

The two tales of Fragment VIII reflect both aspects of the alchemical tradition: purification, preparation, and expansion of the ordinary senses, especially sight, as well as the dead end of focusing on the merely material aspects of the science without attention to the philosophic preparation that alone could enable the alchemist to change matter. Chaucer united the two tales in their common dependency on oppositions of bodily purity and impurity, sight and insight, penetration and blindness. The result is a fragment that questions how human senses help humans understand the true nature of the created world, yet holds out hope of approaching God's deepest secrets through careful preparation of the sensory portals of the body.

"The Second Nun's Tale" opens with a Prologue that opposes the life of the flesh, *ydelnesse,* to *feithful bisynesse. Ydelnesse,* "that porter of the gate is of delices" (8.3), lies in wait with "his thousand cordes slye" (8.8) to entrap humans in a life of sleeping, eating, and drinking (8.17–29). *Feithful Bisynesse,* the life of the mind, in contrast, seeks to "translate" the story of Saint Cecilia, to transfer it from one form of existence to another. The following "Invocacio ad Mariam" is on the one hand a totally conventional invocation of the spiritual purity of the Virgin Mary as a model for human purity of body and mind, and a faithful echo of much alchemical literature about the necessity of approaching the science with a clean spirit in order to free oneself from the contagion of matter. The lines exemplify a crossover of discourse, an interpenetration that places both alchemy and religion in a different light. The narrator prays to Mary,

---

16. *The Mirror of Alchimy Composed by the Thrice-Famous and Learned Fryer, Roger Bacon,* ed. Stanton J. Linden (New York: Garland, 1992), 54–55.

And of thy light my soule in prison lighte,
That troubled is by the contagioun
Of my body, and also by the wighte
Of erthely lust and fals affeccioun;
O havene of refut, O salvacioun
Of hem that been in sorwe and in distresse,
Now help, for to my werk I wol me dresse

(8.71–77)

The recurrent stress on the ideal of purity manifest in brightness, itself a sign of light, dominates much of the tale. It radiates from the Virgin Mary, just as it features prominently in the explication of the saint's name, for the word *Cecile* signifies "hir grete light / Of sapience and for hire thewes cleere" (8.100–101). Similarly the word *brighte* describes Cecile throughout the next twenty lines; the narrator speaks of "this maydens name bright" (8.102), of her works "brighte of excellence" (8.112), and of the fact that she was "brennynge evere in charite ful brighte" (8.118). The term is all the more significant because it stands in opposition to the "derke fantasyes" that have dominated the mental landscape of so many of the other tales we have discussed. "The Second Nun's Tale" promises a way out of self-reflexive, self-created, self-limiting habits of mind, a way to transcend the human weakness associated with the uncontrolled imagination.[17]

Not surprisingly, Cecile, the spiritual alchemist, is in full control of herself throughout the tale. We first meet her at her own wedding feast, to which she has worn an invisible hair shirt. Outwardly splendid, in-

---

17. On the relationship of the story of Saint Cecilia to alchemy in the fourteenth century, see Thomas Connolly, *Mourning into Joy: Music, Raphael, and Saint Cecilia* (New Haven: Yale University Press, 1994), 178–85; Connolly points out that the story was already associated with transformation motifs in continental versions, and that "It would have been hard . . . not to think alchemical thoughts while reading Cecilia's answer to the officers sent by Almachius to induce her to sacrifice to Jove" (181). See also Russell Peck, "The Ideas of 'Entente' and Translation in Chaucer's *Second Nun's Tale*," *Annuale Mediaevale* 8 (1967): 17–37, on the language and themes; Carolyn P. Collette, "A Closer Look at Seint Cecile's Special Vision," *Chaucer Review* 10 (1976): 337–74, on vision in the tale within a Neoplatonic context; V. A. Kolve's "Chaucer's *Second Nun's Tale* and the Iconography of Saint Cecilia," in *New Perspectives in Chaucer Criticism*, ed. Donald M. Rose (Norman, Okla.: Pilgrim Books, 1981), 137–74. Kolve argues that the tale must be read and understood by itself and rejects any simple identification of the marriage of Cecilia and Valerian with the alchemical metaphor of the marriage of mercury and sulphur, although he sees the topical similarity.

wardly penitential, she emblematizes the theme of disjunction between appearance and reality that pervades the two tales. At the feast she sits praying to God to keep her body "Unwemmed, lest that I confounded be" (8.137). For her, physical love, even married love, is equivalent to "vileynye" (8.156), as she warns her husband not to touch her or to love her physically. Instead she offers him a greater love, from God who will "yow loven as me, for youre clennesse, / And shewen yow his joye and his brightnesse" (8.160–61). Any lingering doubt about the source of brightness is now gone; it is an attribute of God and as such must flow from him as the source throughout the tale.

Cecile offers Valerian a love and an experience of love that both overwhelms and transcends his senses. When warned not to embrace his wife, for fear that the angel who protects her will kill him, Valerian responds, "Lat me that aungel se and hym biholde; / And if that it a verray angel bee, / Thanne wol I doon as thou hast prayed me" (8.164–66). Valerian asks to validate her assertions with his sense of sight. Cecile complies, assuring him that he can see the angel — signifying that physical sight is a step on the way to full understanding of the divine. At the same time, though, she puts the stress — as has the narrator in the Prologue — on physical preparation for such sight. Like the true alchemist, Valerian must prepare himself for the sight, must purge the dross of his fleshly life, must prepare his spirit to receive and to invite the true vision he is promised. He must go to the Via Apia, among the poor, and tell them that Cecile has sent him:

Telle hem that I, Cecile, yow to hem sente
To shewen yow the goode Urban the olde,
For secree nedes and for good entente.
And whan that ye Seint Urban han biholde,
Telle hym the wordes which I to yow tolde;
And whan that he hath purged yow fro synne,
Thanne shul ye se that angel, er ye twynne.

(8.176–82)

Valerian's visit to Urban in turn produces Urban's thanksgiving at Valerian's transformation, his translation, as it were, from one state of being to another: "thilke spouse that she took but now / Ful lyk a fiers leoun, she sendeth heere, / As meke as evere was any lomb, to yow!" (8.197–99). Urban presents Valerian a creed and asks him to swear that he believes it to be true. The passage seems odd because it is grammatically unconventional — there is no verb in the creed; it is essentially a series of noun phrases and modifiers: "O Lord, o feith, o God, withouten mo, / O Cristendom, and Fader of alle also, / Aboven alle and over alle everywhere" (8.207–9). The pure nominalism of this passage signifies perfect comprehension unmediated by action in time. The creed is a corollary to the psychological state Valerian will enter after he swears his belief in it — a state in which he will see the angel who will present him and Cecile with the two crowns from paradise which, unlike crowns of flowers on earth, "nevere mo ne shal they roten bee, / Ne lese hir soote savour" (8.228–29). These crowns are invisible to the outward eye of anyone who is impure, who does not see with spiritual insight, but visible to everyone who possesses spiritual insight.

Valerian is so overcome by having entered a world without time, a world of everlasting freshness and beauty, that he prays to the angel to allow his brother Tiburce a similar conversion. Tiburce arrives and, with the angel acting as an intermediary, smells the "soote savour" of the lilies and the roses, an unaccountable odor, given the time of the year. His response enacts another instance in which human sense offers an entry to wider comprehension, but remains an entry only. He immediately subordinates his experience of the miraculous flowers to his ordinary worldly experience, specifically to his life in the world of time. His reference to the "tyme of the yeer" coming in the first line of this speech signifies his living in the sublunar world of mutability and of corruption, a world he seems ready to forget by the end of his speech: "The sweete smel that in myn herte I fynde / Hath chaunged me al in another kynde" (8.251–52).

Valerian assures him of the reality of the crowns though his "eyen han no myght to see" them as yet, but says that "If it so be thou wolt, withouten slouthe, / Bileve aright and knowen verray trouthe" (8.255, 258–59), he will see them. Tiburce answers, "Seistow this to me / In soothnesse, or in dreem," and Valerian replies with one of the central affirmations of the tale: "In dremes . . . han we be / Unto this tyme, brother myn, ywis, / But now at erst in trouthe oure dwellyng is" (8.260–64). Once again the purity theme is underscored as Valerian assures Tiburce that he will see the angel who has brought the crowns "if that thou wolt reneye / The ydoles and be clene" (8.268–69).

In this tale a discourse of seeing and showing betokens understanding. Once Tiburce has cleansed himself of impurity, prepared himself, he gains true understanding of the nature of matter and its relation to the divine:

Tho shewed hym Cecile al open and pleyn
That alle ydoles nys but a thyng in veyn,
For they been dombe, and therto they been deve,
And charged hym his ydoles for to leve.

(8.284–87)

The tale plays the dead senses of the stone idols and those who revere them against the heightened senses of the converts and Cecile herself. The message is not so much transcendence of the senses but, as in the alchemical enterprise, fulfillment of them, challenging them to their fullest capacity, allowing them to help the purified soul to ascend to ever greater joy. Cecile offers insight and a richer experience of this world through suprasensual and supersensate experience, urging Tiburce to go with his brother "and thee baptise, / And make thee clene, so that thou mowe biholde / The angels face of which thy brother tolde" (8.299–301).

Foreshadowing Cecile's martyrdom at the end of the tale and underscoring the alchemical-transformation theme of the plot, the next passage in which Tiburce inquires about Urban, who "is so ofte dampned to be deed" (8.310), concludes with his expectation that "Algate ybrend in this world shul we be!" (8.318). Like the good alchemist who oversees the shedding of dross, Cecile, who has effected all these transformations — and more to come — assures Tiburce that what he will lose from this world is of no value and certainly nothing in comparison to what awaits him in the life to come:

Men myghten dreden wel and skilfully
This lyf to lese, myn owene deere brother,
If this were lyvynge oonly and noon oother.

But there is bettre lif in oother place,
That nevere shal be lost, ne drede thee noght.

(8.320–24)

Tiburce's reward for faith and for despising the flesh's natural fear of death is to see "every day . . . in tyme and space / The aungel of God" (8.355–56). Chaucer affirms the physical reality of Tiburce's vision — it is in time and space — as well as its spiritual nature. The action here is not mere transcendence of the senses but their ultimate purification, much like work of the alchemist who seeks to reclaim gold from the dross corruption of material, and who therefore does not eschew or scorn the matter that is potential gold.

Cecile's faith converts even the Roman soldiers sent to arrest the Christians, particularly their officer Maximus, who, witnessing the martyrdom of "Cristes owene knyghtes leeve and deere" (383), sees "hir soules . . . to hevene glyde / With aungels ful of cleernesse and of light" (402–3) and is beaten for his faith by Almachius, the Roman prefect, with a "whippe of leed" (406). The detail of the leaden whip may function primarily as an indication of the brutal affliction visited upon the Christians, but it also simultaneously helps to construct the oppositional topos of corruption/cleanness, darkness/brightness, a central topos in the initial martyrdom scene that invokes the Second Epistle to Timothy 4:7–8 and the Epistle to the Romans 13:12:

> Cast alle awey the werkes of derknesse,
> And armeth yow in armure of brightnesse.
> Ye han for sothe ydoon a greet bataille,
> Youre cours is doon, your feith han ye conserved.
>
> (8.384–87)

Understanding is linked to light, light to true vision, true vision to ultimate understanding throughout the tale. These verbal links create a constellation of associations in which Chaucer explores the possibilities of knowledge, the limits of human senses, and their miraculous transformation of human psychology through deep spirituality, the kind of alchemy Cecile practices. By infusing it with alchemical discourse, he transforms this saint's story.

Almachius, hearing of these disturbances, orders Cecile brought before him "that he myghte hire see, / And alderfirst, lo, this was his axynge. / 'What maner womman artow. . . ?'" (8.422–24). For him the sight of Cecile is not enough to explain or to provide understanding. The ensuing debate between the prefect and the saint is a debate over philosophy, over how far and in what ways matter can embody or convey a sense of the divine. He repeatedly threatens Cecile with the power of the Roman Empire, the power their "myghty princes free" (8.444) have invested in him to kill those who will not sacrifice.

Han noght oure myghty princes to me yiven,
Ye, bothe power and auctoritee
To maken folk to dyen or to lyven?

(8.470–72)

Cecile offers to explain, to "shewe al openly," the error of his statement.
His power is only to end life, not to give it. In this limitation he stands in
sharp contrast to Cecile, who throughout the tale has the power, from
God, to lead the way to new life, both in this world and in the world to
come. Almachius's gods have no such power, being, as she charges,
merely stone. His faith is misplaced and blind; he cannot use his sight to
see through matter to its creator, to understand her showings. Using his
physical senses only, he sees a rock and calls it god:

Ther lakketh no thyng to thyne outter yen
That thou n'art blynd; for thyng that we seen alle
That it is stoon — that men may wel espyen —
That ilke stoon a god thow wolt it calle.
I rede thee, lat thyn hand upon it falle
And taste it wel, and stoon thou shalt it fynde,
Syn that thou seest nat with thyne eyen blynde.

It is a shame that the peple shal
So scorne thee and laughe at thy folye,
For communly men woot it wel overal
That myghty God is in his hevenes hye;
And thise ymages, wel thou mayst espye,
To thee ne to hemself mowen noght profite,
For in effect they been nat worth a myte.

(8.498–511)

With these charges Cecile effectively denies Almachius's claim to be a
"philosophre" (8.489–90). Certainly he is not a philosopher in the sense
of the alchemical philosopher who can see in base matter the potential
realization of gold, for he never asks to look beyond the surface appearance of matter. Almachius perseveres, however, in what may be called an
alchemical attempt to rid himself of Cecile. He orders her killed by being
burned in a bath — an obviously alchemical symbol. But because he is
truly no philosopher, his perverse alchemy does not work — he cannot

transform her from living to dead. She, the true alchemist of the tale, lives for three days, with her head half struck off, "And nevere cessed hem the feith to teche / That she hadde fostred; hem she gan to preche" (8.538–39). She asks God to grant her three days of life, she disposes of her goods, and in her final act of transformation, she prays that she "myghte do werche / Heere of myn hous perpetuelly a cherche" (8.545–46). In her martyrdom Cecile triumphs over the flesh even while her flesh itself — pure, spotless — triumphs over the laws of physical matter. She is both the symbol of, and the worker of, alchemy.

"The Canon's Yeoman's Tale" seems to stand in direct contrast to "The Second Nun's Tale." Where the one stresses brightness, cleanliness, and spiritual insight, the other dwells on filth, material corruption, deception, and the inability of physical sight to discern the essential truths of creation in matter. Cecile preaches, converts, teaches, and finally establishes her home as a permanent, stable heritage for those who seek truth. She creates the kinds of transformation medieval alchemy sought to achieve. In contrast "The Canon's Yeoman's Tale" exemplifies the other face of alchemy. The canon in the tale works by deception and lives a life of instability, explosion, flight, and brinksmanship. Cecile shows the way to true understanding and to eternal unity with God. The Canon's Yeoman repeatedly fails of his goal. His story ends with defeat, hers in victory, but he, like Cecile, holds on to the goal of unity with God. In fact, his conclusion virtually exhorts the audience to follow Cecile's example of spiritual insight that leads to understanding, using both the blindness and stone motifs of "The Second Nun's Tale":

> Ye been as boold as is Bayard the blynde,
> That blondreth forth and peril casteth noon.
> He is as boold to renne agayn a stoon
> As for to goon bisides in the weye.
> So faren ye that multiplie, I seye.
> If that youre eyen kan nat seen aright,
> Looke that your mynde lakke noght his sight.
> For though ye looken never so brode and stare,
> Ye shul nothyng wynne on that chaffare,
>
> (8.1413–21)

He urges, "Lat no man bisye hym this art for to seche" unless he "th'entencioun and speche / Of philosophres understonde kan," for to do so otherwise is folly: "For this science and this konnyng . . . Is of the secree of secretes, pardee" (8.1442–47). He concludes with this final warning, "For unto Christ it is so lief and deere / That he wol not that it discovered bee, / But where it liketh to his deitee" (8.1467–69). The secret exists, it rests with God, it may be found, but the way to it is not through matter or through the experiential application of the senses (to look, to see, to touch, to feel). Rather, it is to be gained through the mind, by preparing the soul to see with its inner eye. The secret comes from Christ, the great alchemist who unites matter and divinity, who is himself the cause and the subject of the transformation of the Mass. The world of matter in and of itself holds no answers to the mystery; it is merely the channel through which the mystery works.[18]

Chaucer's brilliance in "The Canon's Yeoman's Tale" has been to affirm through the character of his yeoman that alchemy is real and simultaneously to delineate the life of "puffers" by showing obsession as the root of deception, not mere cozening or cunning. The tale does not contest the validity of alchemy so much as outline the effect of alchemical obsession in those who have not developed a spiritual/philosophical approach to it. It is plain that both the Canon's Yeoman and the Canon

---

18. On the theme of sight and nonexperiential knowledge in the fragment, the subject of much of the following discussion, see Rosenberg, "The Contrary Tales." Bruce L. Greenberg in "The *Canon's Yeoman's Tale:* Boethian Wisdom and the Alchemists," *Chaucer Review* 1 (1966): 37–54, recognizes the importance of the sight theme in the tale: "The love of earthly things, certainly the primary characteristic of the canons, darkens or beclouds, says Boethius, the eyes of man. And, pertinent to this development, Fortune, the object of earthly ambition, is described by Boethius as being 'cloudy.' It seems likely that Chaucer's great familiarity with Boethius gave him, in this instance, the very imagery with which to describe the cupidity of the false alchemists" (46). Edgar Duncan in "The Literature of Alchemy" notes the same theme of sight and blindness and its alchemical roots: "The emphasis upon the priest's blindness, an obvious image of course for the yeoman to use (we recall that his own eyes are 'blered' as a result of his seven years' blowing upon his master's fires), could have received added impetus from the treatises. Both Geber and Arnald use the term. Geber warns, for instance, that if an artificer 'have not his organs complete he cannot by himself come to the completion of his work, as if he were blind or wanted his limbs.' And others fail from mental blindness: 'because their brain replete with many fumosities cannot receive the true intention of natural things.' Both he and Arnald in the *Rosary* refer to an alchemical fact so obvious that even a one-eyed man (*monoculus*) may see it. And in the *Rosary* Arnald uses twice an image I have already quoted from him. The artificer who attempts practice before he has mastered theory, he writes, proceeds 'blind' *(cecus)* as an ass to a banquet" (651).

in the tale are obsessed with their goal. Unlike the Pardoner, they do not seek money for its own sake, but as a means to obtain the material and equipment they believe necessary to help them penetrate to the heart of the alchemical mystery. This tale, far from being Chaucer's rejection of alchemy or a bitter reflection on his own deception by a charlatan, is his exploration of how people obsessively and mistakenly seek shortcuts to understanding and knowledge of the central mysteries of creation. The ultimate message of this tale, like "The Second Nun's Tale," is about realizing the potential inherent in the human body by using, and then moving beyond, sense perception: Look with the eye of the mind, prepare yourself to see, and you will receive insight and vision that so far surpass physical sight alone as to be incomparable.

Expecting parallels rather than oppositions between the two tales, one finds a number of interesting echoes. "The Canon's Yeoman's Tale" begins with a visual puzzle that echoes "The Second Nun's Tale" both verbally and thematically. In "The Second Nun's Tale" Almachius's blind adherence to the stone gods of his philosophy replicates on a spiritual level his inability to see matter for what it is, or to move beyond the physical to suprasensual understanding. When Cecile appears before him, he asks the question, "What maner womman artow?" The Prologue to "The Canon's Yeoman's Tale" echoes this motif because so much of its activity is directed to answering the same question asked of the yeoman — what kind of man are you? In the Prologue to this tale we are immersed in a world of sign-readers. But while Almachius was a very poor reader of signs, both the narrator and the host are able to gain a degree of understanding from their physical sight. Here is the narrator on the yeoman's appearance:

And in myn herte wondren I bigan
What that he was til that I understood
How that his cloke was sowed to his hood,
For which, what I hadde longe avysed me,
I demed hym som chanoun for to be.

(8.569–73)

Harry Bailly is even more astute, when in response to the Yeoman's evasive and inconsistent answers about his Canon, he displays a Holmesian ability to read visual signs as clues to reality:

This thyng is wonder merveillous to me,
Syn that thy lord is of so heigh prudence,
By cause of which men sholde hym reverence,
That of his worshipe rekketh he so lite.
He overslope nys nat worth a myte,
As in effect, to hym, so moot I go,
It is al baudy and totore also.
Why is thy lord so sluttissh, I the preye,
And is of power bettre clooth to beye,
If that his ded accorde with thy speche?
Telle me that, and that I thee biseche?

                                                    (8.629–39)

When Harry Bailly asks the yeoman, "Why artow so discoloured of thy face?" (8.664), the Second Nun's emphasis on the spotless purity of Cecile comes to mind. In the Yeoman's description of his living with his canon, the reader is reminded of Saint Urban hiding in the catacombs in order to advance God's work on earth, to receive and to baptize the newly converted.

In the suburbes of a toun . . .
Lurkynge in hernes and in lanes blynde,
Whereas thise robbours and thise theves by kynde
Holden hir pryvee fereful residence,
As they that dar nat shewen hir presence;
So faren we, if I shal seye the sothe.

                                                    (8.657–62)

The tale goes on to describe how the insatiable appetite of alchemy devours matter: "For so helpe me God, therby shal he nat wynne, / But empte his purs and make his wittes thynne" (8.740–41); "lost is al oure labour and travaille" (8.781); "He shal no good han that hym may suffise, / For al the good he spendeth theraboute / He lese shal" (8.831–33); "They kan nat stynte til no thyng be laft" (8.883). At the end of this section, the narrator summarizes his description and points its moral, the difficulty of discerning truth in this world:

we concluden everemoore amys.
We faille of that which that we wolden have,

And in oure madnesse everemoore we rave.
And whan we been togidres everichoon,
Every man semeth a Salomon.
But al thyng which that shineth as the gold
Nis nat gold, as that I have herd told;
Ne every appul that is fair at eye
Ne is nat good, what so men clappe or crye.
Right so, lo, fareth it amonges us:
He that semeth the wiseste, by Jhesus,
Is moost fool, whan it cometh to the preef;
And he that semeth trewest is a theef.

(8.957–69)

The second part of the tale describes what would today be called the "sting," the deception of a foolish priest. The priest is introduced to us as a "plesaunt" and "servysable" (8.1014) *annueleer,* whose presence in his lodging is so gratifying to the goodwife who runs it that she will accept no payment from him in return for his board (8.1015–17). As a result, "spendying silver hadde he right ynow" (8.1018). The canon dupes the priest under the guise of borrowing money from him and assuring him of repayment. In thanks for the favor of a loan, he offers to share his knowledge of a great secret. Given the late medieval connection between clerics and alchemy and the connection between alchemy and the Mass, a degree of irony surely inheres in the idea of a priest searching for such a secret:

I wol yow shewe, and if yow list to leere,
I wol you teche pleynly the manere
How I kan werken in philosophie.
Taketh good heede; ye shul wel seen at ye
That I wol doon a maistrie er I go.

(8.1056–60)

The narrator rarely leaves the center stage of his tale. Once he has introduced the priest and set up the sting, he editorializes on the "false dissymulynge" (8.1073) of the canon, and on the "sely preest . . . sely innocent" who "With coveitise anon . . . shalt be blent!" (8.1076–77). He apostrophizes the priest, underscoring the blindness theme, "O gracelees, ful blynde is thy conceite, / No thyng ne artow war of the deceite / Which that the fox yshapen hath to thee!" (8.1078–80).

The canon's trick evolves through a litany of exhortations to look, to see, to trust sight, all consonant with alchemy's dependence on sight, yet all instances of how deceptible sight can be. The canon assures the priest, "For ye shul seen heer, by experience" (8.1125); he refers to his "konnyng, which that I yow shewen shal" (8.1135). His purpose, the narrator says, is "to blynde with this preest" (8.1151). In one of the verbal paradoxes of the tale, he exhorts the priest to "Loke what ther is; put in thyn hand and grope" (8.1236). The priest does find silver, "and glad in every veyne / Was this preest, when he saugh it was so" (8.1241–42). Later on, in a repeat "proof" that the process works, he is urged to "Putte in your hand, and looketh what is theer" (8.1329). The priest thinks he is buying a secret, a great *soutiltee* (8.1371). His excitement is so great that on first "seeing" the transformation he exclaims,

> "Goddes blessyng, and his moodres also,
> And alle halwes, have ye, sire chanoun,"
> Seyde the preest, "and I hir malisoun,
> But, and ye vouche-sauf to techen me
> This noble craft and this subtilitee,
> I wol be youre in al that evere I may."
>
> (8.1243–48)

His blessing, in its breadth, suggests the scope of what he thinks he is purchasing, for alchemy touches forces at the heart of the universe. The priest pays the forty pounds, gains the recipe, and finds it does not work. The canon "wente his wey, and never the preest hym sy" (8.1381) after that. The Yeoman concludes this exemplum with a lengthy discussion of the cause of such episodes, the debate between men and gold, identifying the reason the secret is lost as human greed manifested in fixation on one small part of the science:

> Considereth, sires, how that, in ech estaat,
> Bitwixe men and gold ther is debaat
> So ferforth that unnethes is ther noon.
> This multiplying blent so many oon
> That in good feith I trowe that it bee

The cause grettest of swich scarsetee.
Philosophres speken so mystily
In this craft that men kan nat come therby,
For any wit that men han now-a-dayes.
They mowe wel chiteren as doon jayes,
And in hir termes sette hir lust and peyne,
But to hir purpos shul they nevere atteyne.
A man may lightly lerne, if he have aught,
To multiplie, and brynge his good to naught!

(8.1388–1401)

The secret so many seek is the "secree of the secretes" (8.1447), known
to Plato and the other philosophers, who "sworn were everychoon /
That they sholden discovere it unto noon, / Ne in no book it write in no
manere" (8.1464–66). The attempt to discover the secret is an attempt
to set oneself in opposition to God,

Thanne conclude I thus, sith that God of hevene
Ne wil nat that the philosophres nevene
How that a man shal come unto this stoon,
I rede, as for the beste, lete it goon.
For whoso maketh God his adversarie,
As for to werken any thyng in contrarie
Of his wil, certes, never shal he thryve,
Thogh that he multiplie terme of his lyve.
And there a poynt, for ended is my tale.
God sende every trewe man boote of his bale!

(8.1472–81)

The tales of the fragment conclude with two very similar messages out
of very different premises. Both tales direct attention to how the senses
work to grasp the essential truths of creation. "The Second Nun's Tale"
affirms the capacity of the senses to apprehend the suprasensual, but it
does so as an eerie foreshadowing of the surrender of those senses in
martyrdom. In the tale everyone who has gained true *understanding*
dies. In a saint's life such an ending may be said to be exemplary, but as a
guide for living it has little appeal for most people. "The Canon's Yeoman's Tale" takes a different route to a correlative conclusion: by themselves, the senses, particularly sight, are highly deceptible. Vulnerable

to human fantasies, obsession and fixation, they cannot penetrate to truths beyond appearance. Moreover, the tale warns implicitly that physical sight is liable to lead one astray from other available channels of deeper understanding. The priest, duped by the canon into "seeing" what is not real, in the very moment of his fall, ironically calls forth blessings from Christ and the saints, the true alchemists. Ultimately, the created world of matter will not yield its secrets except to those whom, having prepared body and mind as true alchemists, God chooses.

The heart of "The Second Nun's Tale" lies in Cecile's instructing the other characters in alchemy of the highest kind, in ways of realizing the potential inherent in the body that God has created, freeing the mind and the imagination to realize and to embrace the potential of the created world, and the reality of God's presence in it. Her miraculous martyrdom is but one instance — along with the invisible but real crowns of roses and lilies — of how mind can overcome ordinary physical limitations. Both her tale and the Canon's Yeoman's assert the validity of spiritual insight — imagination attuned to the creative *imaginatio* of God — greater than physical sight by itself. A common warning in the two tales and the body of alchemical literature quoted above cautions against mistaking physical evidence available to the senses, particularly through sight, as sure signs of the operation of the invisible. In "The Second Nun's Tale" Chaucer draws on the alchemical tradition outlined above, but alters its conventions, combining it with a conventional saint's story. Doing so, he asserts in this fragment that deep insight and spiritual gnosis come through physical vision working with a receptive psyche. These tales are played out against a background of alchemy that argues gnosis is possible, but only in terms of "The Second Nun's Tale," through realization of the potential of the senses, rather than a repudiation of them. Using the senses to transcend the merely sensual is a complicated but typically Chaucerian "spin" on conventional wisdom and conventional oppositions.

"The Second Nun's Tale" does not oppose alchemy but subsumes it into its action, merging alchemy, hagiography, and human psychology. Late medieval theories of alchemy strove to achieve just the kinds of transformation Cecile achieves in the tale. True alchemy required purification of the senses and rewarded the alchemist with simultaneous sensual and suprasensual experience — knowledge that alchemical transformation has indeed occurred by careful observation of attendant signs and by careful alignment of the soul through study of hermetic philosophy.

Just as the senses are important in alchemy, so in both these tales the senses, and in particular the sense of sight, figure prominently as the portals to alchemical knowledge and wisdom. In "The Second Nun's Tale" the senses lead to higher levels of understanding; in "The Canon's Yeoman's Tale" they are misled. What the fragment says is not so much about the folly of alchemy but about the mistakes made by humans who think that the physical world is only what it appears to be and who believe that the physical senses are sufficient to grasp reality. It also suggests that ironically, in this limited conceptualization of the senses and of reality, they remain ignorant of the true potential of human sensory knowledge when it is channeled to, and by, more spiritual ends.

6

Understondyng: "The Parson's Tale"

"The Parson's Tale" may seem an unlikely subject for the last chapter of a book on vision and medieval theories of psychology. There is nothing very visual about it and very little in it to feed the imagination.[1] Rather, "The Parson's Tale" is replete with authority and structured by repeated injunctions, exhortations, and expressions of hope that its audience will *understonde* its messages. But, paradoxically, this very emphasis on its audience's *understanding* is what ties the tale to the larger topic. In medieval psychology the end of vision was understanding, a level of comprehension that built on vision, reason, and judgment but transcended all these ways of knowing and judging, reaching its apogee in comprehension of God. In this last tale of *The Canterbury Tales* Chaucer sets out to create a text that communicates *understanding* without invoking the imaging function of the mind, an attempt at undistorted communication such as Lollard sympathizers hoped for in direct, plain speech. When one considers the language patterns Chaucer chooses for his Parson's final tale, the conclusion that Chaucer used this tale and its teller to experiment with literalism and direct communication is inescapable.

In the eighth fragment of the *Tales* true understanding, equated there with Christian faith, arose out of the senses. In "The Second Nun's Tale" Tiburce and Valerian's religious conversion initially uses sensory evidence as validation of internal, invisible processes, finally culminating in a kind of faith that supersedes sensual experience. "The Parson's Tale" aims to convey important religious truths so that an audience will understand them, but it follows a different route; beginning with a different

---

1. Of course there is figurative language in the tale in conventional references to ashes, the sun and clouds, and in the arboreal metaphor that structures much of the presentation. Arguably the most memorable figurative image comes from ll. 420–25, where Chaucer compares the view of men's bodies in the new fashion to the "hyndre part of a she-ape in the fulle of the moone." Such figurative language as appears is generic and largely confined to the discussion of the Seven Deadly Sins.

premise, it offers almost nothing of sensual origin to the imagination. Instead, it employs didactic explication and citations of authority. As a correlative result, the tale turns away from the kind of communication that depends on metaphor, specific detail, and verbal images, all of which feed the receiving imagination and encourage it to participate in creating — and, it might be said, distorting — the author's intended text.

This is an unorthodox way of approaching the tale. Most Chaucerians think of "The Parson's Tale" as an example of an instructional devotional treatise, a tale that by its very nature cannot represent the essence of Chaucerian art — a carefully nuanced, poetic narrative.[2] Recent work by Thomas Bestul and Lee Patterson, building on work done earlier in this century by Pfander, has shown that the tale shares with other late medieval English devotional and instructional manuals the same contents and the same transitions — or apparent lack thereof — among its several parts.[3]

---

2. For a discussion of the tale in respect to language and morality, see Thomas H. Bestul, "Chaucer's Parson's Tale and the Late Medieval Tradition of Religious Meditation," *Speculum* 64 (1989): 600–619. His argument provides important support for the argument of this chapter, for it points out that the tale is a meditation that draws on contemporary meditative literature for various elements and that it eschews literary style and fiction as it searches for a way to communicate. Bestul maintains that "there is good evidence that Chaucer in compiling the tale from his sources was consciously doing so at least in part with the formal and thematic requirements of devotional prose in mind and that certain sections of the Parson's Tale were directly influenced by the tradition of meditative literature, in Latin and the vernacular, to a degree not heretofore recognized" (601). The purpose of meditation was to stimulate the emotions to move beyond "fear of God's judgment and love for Christ toward systematic self-examination as a prelude to penance" (604).

Bestul observes that the meditative tradition resembles poetry in that "both depend for their effects on the arousal of the emotions of the reader" (614). But whereas poetry can divert the emotions from virtue, meditation leads them toward a better end:

> medieval poetry depends on figures and images for its effect. Kolve's book demonstrates the centrality of visual images in Chaucer's poetic art. As Kolve notes, concrete visual imagery belongs to devotional literature as well, but the final goal was to transcend it. In the devotional tradition, visual images produced by the faculty of the imagination are esteemed but regarded as a concession to human weakness: in the passage from Richard of St. Victor cited above, imagination is given the lowest place, and Richard elsewhere explained the relative value of images and the place of the imagination in respect to the other faculties. . . .
>
> Visual images are valuable for beginners because they place us in contact with the beauty of God, but the ultimate desire is to meditate or to contemplate without relying on them, to perceive the essence of God through pure intellect, unmarred by any shadow of corporeal substances. (616–17)

3. While the tale is even now commonly referred to as a "sermon," over the last seventy years its ties to the devotional, penitential manual have been clearly established.

In general, the critical discussion the tale has engendered analyzes its sources or alternatively its narrative style, which, most critics agree, is not highly engaging. In Helen Cooper's assessment, "The Treatise is written in the plain style appropriate to exposition, where understanding is more important than persuasion. In keeping with the emphasis on sin as the subordination of reason, the appeal is to the intellect, not the emotions."[4] This view seems to characterize the most generous critical attitudes

---

See Bestul, "Chaucer's Parson's Tale"; Lee W. Patterson, "The 'Parson's Tale' and the Quitting of the 'Canterbury Tales,'" *Traditio* 34 (1978): 331–80; H. G. Pfander, "Some Medieval Manuals of Religious Instructions," *JEGP* 35 (1936): 243–58; Beryl Rowland, "Sermon and Penitential in *The Parson's Tale* and Their Effect on Style," *Florilegium* 9 (1987): 125–45. Siegfried Wenzel has published the fruits of his extensive research into the tale's sources in the following articles: "The Source for the 'Remedia' of the Parson's Tale," *Traditio* 27 (1971): 433–53; "The Source of Chaucer's Seven Deadly Sins," *Traditio* 30 (1974): 351–78; "Notes on the *Parson's Tale,*" *Chaucer Review* 16 (1981): 237–56.

4. Helen Cooper, *The Canterbury Tales,* Oxford Guides to Chaucer (Oxford: Oxford University Press, 1989), 408. It has generally been felt that the tale's style betrays some element of the narrator's personality, either deadly dull earnestness or sanctimonious self-approbation, or that the author felt himself distanced from the narrator; see, for example, Laurie A. Finke, " 'To Knytte up all this Feeste': The Parson's Rhetoric and the Ending of the *Canterbury Tales,*" *Leeds Studies in English* 15 (1984): 95–108: "The Parson's limitation is inherent in his language, at once familiar and self-congratulatory. He reduces a complex work of art, reflecting a variety of human experience, to a straight forward admonitory discourse" (96). Judson Boyce Allen maintained that the tale is ironic and that Chaucer didn't "wholly agree with his Parson's recommendation of penance" ("The Old Way and the Parson's Way: An Ironic Reading of the Parson's Tale," *Journal of Medieval and Renaissance Studies* 3 [1973]: 256).

In a more positive vein Chauncey Wood reads the tale as "A Bok for Engelondes sake," contending that Chaucer, like Gower in the *Confessio Amantis,* intended his art to work through individuals to help change society: "In its location at the outskirts of England's spiritual capital, in its open concern for sin and the remedies of sin, in its clear indebtedness to the literary tradition of the penitential manual, in asking the reader to stand upon the ways and to choose the right way, Chaucer's 'Parson's Tale' is arguably his most Gowerian tale" ("Chaucer's Most 'Gowerian Tale,'" in *Chaucer and Gower: Difference, Mutuality, Exchange,* ed. R. F. Yeager [Victoria, B.C.: University of Victoria Press, 1991], 81). Rodney Delasanta in "Penance and Poetry in the *Canterbury Tales,*" *PMLA* 93 (1978): 240–47 reads the tale against the eschatological symbolism of its introduction and position; Jesus had promised an hour coming "'when I will no more speak to you in parables, but will show you plainly of the Father' (John xvi: 25). Like his Master, whose doctrine he teaches without gloss, the Parson knows that the pilgrims have arrived at their moment of truth. The time for parables has ceased. The time for plain speaking is ahead" (245). Paul Beekman Taylor in "The Parson's Amyable Tongue," *English Studies* 64 (1983): 401–9, notes that the Parson ties together thought, word, and deed: "In philosophical terms, the Parson's discussion of words in his treatise has as its purpose a reconstitution of linguistic Realism. The tales, by and large, as well as the interchanges between pilgrims, exhibit a kind of nominalistic skepticism. They display words as *flatus vocis,* without any real referents" (403). The Parson, in contrast, deems all words "*sentence* in the expression of the soul" (404).

toward the text. But the Chaucer who could imbue the narrative of a saint's life with implicit references to the philosophy of alchemy could also choose to infuse a penitential manual's dry style with a subtext implicitly calling attention to its own an-imagistic style.

When asked to tell a tale, the Parson agrees by disagreeing, framing his contribution as an opposition to the agreed-upon pattern of tale telling, because he scorns tales as fables. He replies, "Thou getest fable noon ytoold for me, / For Paul, that writeth unto Thymothee, / Repreveth hem that weyven soothfastnesse / And tellen fables and swich wrecchednesse" (10.31–34). According to the *Middle English Dictionary,* the term he scorns, *fable,* referred to "fictitious or imaginative narrative or statement," or secondarily meant a "false statement intended to deceive."[5] The *Riverside Chaucer* identifies the Parson's reference here as 1 Timothy 1:4, "Neither give heed to fables and endless genealogies, which minister questions, rather than godly edifying which is in faith," and 1 Timothy 4:7, "But refuse profane and old wives' fables, and exercise thyself rather unto godliness."[6] But fables, imaginative or potentially false narratives, are the subject of other passages from the epistles to Timothy that indicate fables are suspect not only because they are fictions, but because they open the way for uncontrolled reception. These other passages that might just as well be adduced to gloss the Parson's reference include, "But shun profane and vain babblings: for they will increase unto more ungodliness. And their word will eat as doth a canker" (2 Tim. 2:16–17) and 2 Timothy 4:2–4, "Preach the word; be instant in season, out of season; reprove, rebuke,

---

5. The word *fable* in the Prologue likely evoked topical associations during this period, because of frequent Lollard criticism of fables and tales. While the very fact that the Parson is on a pilgrimage argues against understanding him as a Lollard, he apparently shares with Lollards a distrust of fables for the same reasons that the Lollard tract *Rosarium Theologie* expresses. The citation of Lollard ideas here and later in the chapter does not suggest an argument about Chaucer's interest in or adherence to Lollard ideas so much as argue that a discourse of popular writing and preaching that addressed some of the same topics Chaucer addresses and that highlighted some of the same words Chaucer seems to emphasize was part of the semantic field in which Chaucer's work was received. For a different perspective on the diction of "The Parson's Tale" than the one developed here see Douglas J. Wurtele, "The Anti-Lollardry of Chaucer's Parson," *Mediaevalia* 11 (1985): 151–68.

6. Citations here are to the King James translation of the Bible; the word *fable* also appears in the Wycliffe translation of these passages. See *The Holy Bible, Containing the Old and New Testaments, with the Apocryphal Books, in the Earliest English Versions Made From the Latin Vulgate by John Wycliffe and His Followers,* ed. Josiah Forshall and Frederic Madden, 4 vols. (Oxford: Oxford University Press, 1850).

exhort with all long-suffering and doctrine. For the time will come when they will not endure sound doctrine; but after their own lusts shall they heap to themselves teachers, having itching ears; And they shall turn away their ears from the truth and shall be turned unto fables." These passages are important in creating a fuller context for the word *fable* than the passages usually cited because they situate the telling of fables within a dynamic of teller and tale, assuming what we would call "reader reception" as part of the dynamic. People take pleasure *(lust)* in fables that encourage them to "Heap to themselves teachers" of a fictional sort. In refusing to tell a fable, the Parson signals his desire to control the terms in which his speech will be received, stored, and remembered by his audience.

This anxiety about fables as opposed to edifying texts was not new at the end of the fourteenth century, but it was a matter of current interest in Chaucer's world. The same anxiety about fables that the Parson expresses also characterizes Lollard texts, reflecting a late medieval current of distrust about the effect and purpose of what today we call literature. The *Rosarium Theologie* equates and condemns fables and poetry, precisely because they can stir individual imaginations to "entysyng of lusts": "'þerefor [forsoþ] is a Cristen man forbed for to red figmentis of feynyngz of poetez, for be delityngz of fablez þei stirre to mich the mynde [to] entysyng of lustez.' Þerfor seiþ þe apostel, I. *Chor.* 15., 'Iuel spechez corrumpeþ gode manerez'" (73). Aware of the warning of both the epistles cited above and the kind of thinking that lay behind the *Rosarium,* Chaucer creates speech for his Parson that will edify and instruct. He does so against a cultural background of suspicion about the power of mental images to cloud as well as assist clear comprehension of the material world and of its creator. Insofar as poetry/fable creates mental images, poetry is language out of control, legitimate authority usurped. At the end of *The Canterbury Tales* both *fable* and *ymaginacioun* are equivocal terms, not so much because they represent fiction, but because they stimulate the human mind in some of its least stable activities.

In concluding the *Canterbury Tales* with a tale that deliberately sets out not to appeal to imagination, Chaucer seems to turn away from his own extended interest in the poetic imagination recorded in his other works. In "Chaucer and the Imagination" Russell Peck writes about the central role of imagination in Chaucer's art, expressed in the Prologue to the *Legend of Good Women:* "The daisy poetic is a poetic of imagination, where ideas are perceived through images and expressed through images, where the image-making faculty, rather than being a hindrance or a deceptive fantasy that interferes with reason, enables the intellect and memory to interact through perceptual likenesses."[7] But in fact Chaucer had historically shown interest in different kinds of communication, both the "poetic of imagination" Peck identifies here and a kind of knowing that builds on and transcends the senses. As Peck shows in another article on *The Legend of Good Women,* evidence of Chaucer's interest in both coexists in that comparatively early work. Chaucer was also interested in the possibility of a different kind of textual communication, one that transcended images,

> one of experience to be sure, but of an experience beyond the outward senses. The allusion to Bernard [*Legend of Good Women,* G 14–16] anticipates subsequent allusions to the Virgin Mary and the Annunciation, and functions, along with other such casual references as the "Etik" and "Agaton," as part of his demonstration of the limitations of the physical senses and the possibilities of suprasensory vision.[8]

Set within the context of Chaucer's previous interest in kinds of communication, "The Parson's Tale" assumes a significant position both within the *Tales* and within the body of Chaucer's work. In its spareness and its position at the end of a series of tales that have delineated human psychology as highly individualistic, often enclosed, self-referential systems of fantasy and reasoning built on imagination, this tale, deliberately moving away from both a poetic of imagination and a psychology of mental images, picks up the experiment Peck recognized in *The Legend of Good Women.* It is one more instance of Chaucer's exploration of the dynamics of language both in utterance and in reception. In fashioning "The Parson's Tale" as he does, Chaucer creates a text seeking to construct its own reception, to limit its interpretation and so avoid misunderstanding. For this reason, the tale, a text that if it existed anywhere outside *The Canterbury Tales* would not merit a great deal of consider-

---

7. Russell Peck, "Chaucer and the Imagination," *Studies in the Age of Chaucer,* Proceedings 2 (1986): 41.

8. "Chaucerian Poetics and the Prologue to the *Legend of Good Women,*" in *Chaucer in the Eighties,* ed. Julian N. Wasserman and Robert J. Blanch (Syracuse: Syracuse University Press, 1986), 49–50.

ation, becomes an important artistic text. The Parson's tale's interest lies in its oppositional relationship to the rest of the poetic tales. In eschewing poetry and fable, it attempts to control the creation and arousal of *phantasms* in the process of its reception, attempts to bypass imagination and appeal directly to understanding.

The Tale

The exposition of the substance of the tale depends on a metaphor of vision as both awareness and comprehension. Sermons from the period indicate that the sight/blindness topos was a frequently invoked motif useful in expressing comprehension or ignorance of religious truth. Chaucer employs this metaphor of seeing as comprehension in a verbal pattern that recurs regularly throughout the tale. His use of the metaphor of sight as comprehension of ideas seems to direct attention away from the sense of vision as focused on material reality. For example, he uses *see* to suggest being aware of, rather than as a way of apprehending images, as in these passages:

Loo, heere may ye seen that Job preyde respit a while. (10.175–80)

"The derkness of deeth" been the synnes that the wrecched man hath doon, which that destourben hym to see the face of God, right as dooth a derk clowde bitwixe us and the sonne. (10.180–85)

For ther been two manere of consentynges: that oon of hem is cleped consentynge of affeccioun, whan a man is moeved to do synne, and deliteth hym longe for to thynke on that synne; and his reson aperceyveth it wel that it is synne agayns the lawe of God, and yet his resoun refreyneth nat his foul delit or talent, though he se wel apertly that it is agayns the reverence of God. (10.290–95)

Seeing can also mean a species of comprehension, as in passages like these:

There may ye seen that deedly synne hath, first . . . (10.330–35)

Thus may ye seen that the gilt disserveth thraldom. (10.755–60)

Heere may ye seen that nat ooonly the dede . . . (10.845)

Right so shal your light lighten bifore men, that they may see your goode werkes. (10.1035–40)

For alle the creatures in hevene, in erthe, and in helle shullen seen apertly al that they hyden in this world. (10.1060–65)

Chaucer also employs the word *looke* to direct the mind's attention, not to the material world, but to show that an idea warrants attention and consideration, as in these passages:

Looke that in th'estaat of innocence, whan Adam and Eve naked weren in Paradys . . . (10.320–25)

If a man love God in swich manere that al that evere he dooth is in the love of God and for the love of God verraily, for he brenneth in the love of God, / looke how muche that a drope of water that falleth in a fourneys ful of fyr . . . (10.380–85)

Looke how that fir of smale gleedes . . . (10.545–50)

Looke eek what Seint Peter seith, *Actuum quarto, Non est aliud nomen sub celo.* (10.595–600)

Looke forther, in the same gospel, the joye and the feeste . . . (10.700–705)

Looke eek what seith Seint Paul of Glotonye. (10.815–20)

Thanne shal man looke and considere that if he wole maken a trewe and a profitable confessioun, ther moste be foure condiciouns. (10.980–85)

In neither the case of *see* nor *looke* does he suggest that either is a transitive verb — except in the one instance of 180–85, "to see the face of God." Rather, the idiom of the tale strongly appeals to an internal sense of insight whose comprehension is intellectual, functioning without visual images.

The discourse of vision as comprehension that appears throughout "The Parson's Tale" complements the central importance of the word *understonde* in the structure and argument of the tale. The word *understonde* occurs on average once every twenty-five lines, at least forty-two times in a tale 1,080 lines long.[9] Once the reader notices it, subsequent appearances of this word seem to leap from the page. In most instances in "The Parson's Tale" the word *understonde* clearly signifies the idea of mental comprehension

And now, sith I have declared yow what thyng is Penitence, now shul ye understonde that ther been three acciouns of Penitence. (10.90–95)

In this Penitence or Contricioun man shal understonde foure thynges. (10.125–30)

And ye shul understonde that in mannes synne is every manere of ordre or ordinaunce turned up-so-doun. (10.255–60)

And forther over, it is necessarie to understonde whennes the synnes spryngen, and how they encreessen, and whiche they been. (10.320–25)

And thogh so be that no man kan outrely telle the nombre of the twigges and of the harmes that cometh of Pride, yet wol I shewe a partie of hem, as ye shul understonde. (10.390–95)

And therefore understoond that bothe he that selleth and he that beyeth thynges espirituels been cleped symonyals (10.780–85)

---

9. *A Concordance to the Complete Works of Geoffrey Chaucer and to the Romaunt of the Rose,* ed. John S. P. Tatlock and Arthur G. Kennedy (Washington, D.C.: Carnegie Institution of Washington, 1927), lists at least forty-five occurrences of the word in the tale, of which at least twenty-two occur in the beginning sentences of what are paragraphs in the Riverside edition: 95–100, 105–10, 125–30, 290–300, 305–10, 315–20 (2), 350–55, 380–85, 390–95, 475–80, 515–20, 535–40 (2), 760–70, 800–805, 915–20, 1045–50 (2), 1050–55, 1055–60, 1075–80. The pattern of frequency of appearance and the function of the word in structuring the flow of the tale indicate how central the term is to the conception as well as the discourse of the tale. It is interesting to note that the word recurs frequently at the beginning of five paragraphs in the last thirty-five lines of the tale. Such a clustering seems to suggest a degree of urgency and a concentration of effort to communicate.

> And ye shul understonde that orisouns or preyeres is for to seyn a pitous wyl of herte. (10.1035–40)

> And thou shalt understanden eek that God ordeyned fastynge, and to fastynge appertenen foure thinges. (10.1045–50)

Sometimes the sense of "being aware of" implicit in the idea of comprehension is closer to the surface. This sense, too, appears throughout the tale:

> Now is it good to understonde the circumstances that agreggen muchel every synne. (10.955–60)

> Thanne shaltow understonde whiche thynges destourben penaunce. (10.1055–60)

At other times, as in the following passages, the term emphasizes the interpretive dimension of understanding, appearing after a citation of authority and clearly suggesting that understanding is a "correct" interpretation of the words cited:

> And thereof seith God by the mouth of Ezechiel, that "if the rightful man returne agayn from his rightwisnesse and werke wikkednesse, shal he lyve?" / Nay, for alle the goode werkes that he hath wroght ne shul nevere been in remembraunce, for he shal dyen in his synne. / And upon thilke chapitre seith Seint Gregorie thus: that "we shulle understonde this principally; / that whan we doon deedly synne, it is for noght thanne to rehercen or drawen into memorie the goode werkes that we han wroght biforen." (10.235–40)

> And truste wel that in the name of thy neighebor thou shalt understonde the name of thy brother. (10.515–20)

> Understoond eek that in the name of neighebor is comprehended his enemy. (10.520–25)

And forther over, ther as the lawe seith that temporeel goodes of boonde-folk been the goodes of hir lordshipes, ye, that is for to understonde, the goodes of the emperour, to deffenden hem in hir right, but nat for to roben hem ne reven hem. (10.755–60)

Now shaltow understonde that matrimoyne is leeful assemblynge of man and of womman. (10.915–20)

This consistency of usage across the sections of a tale thought to be a compilation, almost a palimpsest of borrowings from a wide variety of sources, marks the shaping influence of Chaucer's style and intention in this pattern of language centered in vision and understanding. The sheer density of this language indicates a kind of urgency supported by the fact that in virtually all instances where the word *understonde* appears it does so in combination with the second-person pronoun or as an imperative, creating both the well-recognized didactic tone of the treatise as well as a particular urgency focused on the reader. Judging from his language, understanding is an urgent, important action centered in the audience's reception of the Parson's text.

Verbal Contexts

Because the word *understonde* appears with such frequency in this text, it is useful to ask how the word was used in Chaucer's world and in his writings, in order to comprehend what he understood it to mean. One answer, of course, is that the term is a common one, to be found in all sorts of religious as well as instructional texts in Middle English. While the word naturally occurs in other devotional and penitential texts in English from this period, it does not appear with such regularity as it does in "The Parson's Tale." Neither the potential sources and analogues Germaine Dempster and Wenzel have identified, nor the edited texts that comprise the devotional, meditative literary corpus of this period, use the same verbal structure.[10] Close attention to sources is

---

10. For example, John Myrc's *Instructions for Parish Priests,* ed. Edward Peacock, Early English Text Society, 31 (London, 1902), relies on the term *teche* to structure its explication; the *Speculum Christiani,* ed. Gustaf Holmstedt, Early English Text Society, 182 (London, 1933), uses *techyng* and *cunnyng;* the *Lay Folks Catechism,* ed. Thomas Frederick Simmons and Henry Edward Nolloth, Early English Text Society, 118 (London, 1901) relies on the word *know* in its attempt to instruct; the *Memoriale Credencium,* ed. J. H. L. Kengen (1979) relies on no one of these common terms.

always useful, but in this case the known sources of the tale are multiple and in both Latin and French. Because there is no one consistent source to match with Chaucer's tale, there is no way of knowing if he found a single word or phrase in Latin or French that he translated as *understanding* in his English adaptation. Rather, his consistent use of metonymy centered in vision and of the word *understondyng* throughout the tale argues that this rhetoric is his addition to the various sources he drew on for the tale. The multiplicity of identifiable sources that he may have drawn upon for different sections of the tale makes it all the more reasonable to consider the tale's diction and literal metaphors within the context of late-fourteenth-century English, to search, as with "The Physician's Tale," for comparable language used comparably in order to determine the semantic field in which Chaucer's terms would have been received by a late medieval audience.

Both the Parson's words in the Prologue, scorning fables, and the exchange between the Host and the Parson in the Epilogue to "The Man of Law's Tale" (2.1173, 1177) tie the Parson to Lollardy, in respect to his attitude toward language. It follows, then, that if Chaucer intentionally connected the Parson with some of the hallmarks of Lollard sympathies, that one useful context to consider for the language of the tale is the discourse associated with Lollardy. Texts broadly sympathetic to subjects like inward contemplation, direct reception of Scripture, individual spirituality — all loosely termed "Lollard" issues — often rely heavily on the same terms and, doing so, provide a useful *sociolect* in which to place Chaucer's own use of the word in "The Parson's Tale."

Such "Lollard" texts provide a natural starting point for trying to discover the semantic valence of the word *understonde* and its variants in Chaucer's world, because one of the central principles of the ideas that we loosely term Lollard in this period was the individual reception of meaning from Scripture, an internalization of that meaning into one's mind, closely correlated with action in the world. Hence we might expect the term *understonde* to be linked both to intellectual comprehension and to practical action in Lollard texts. The word *understonde* recurs as part of the discourse of preaching in the sermons collected in Anne Hudson's *English Wycliffite Sermons*.[11] It also appears with some regularity within a cycle of fifty-four sermons on Sunday Gospels as a

---

11. Anne Hudson, ed., *English Wycliffite Sermons*, vol. 1 (Oxford: Oxford University Press, 1983).

topic in its own right. Sermon 18, on the text *Accesserunt ad Iesum pharisei audientes* (Matt. 22), addresses the topic of understanding as part of an explication of the First Commandment; in it human understanding and its reflection in daily life becomes an analogy of the Trinity: "For vndyrstondyng in a man and acte of hym þat is his lyf and reflexioun of lif, þat is muynde and wille of sowle, bytookneþ to cristene men her God þat is þe Trinnite" (293). Understanding also becomes a topic in Sermon 30 *(Vidit Iohannes Iesum uenientem ad se)*, where after a discussion of how signs betokening God function, the text urges plain, direct speech to facilitate understanding and condemns argument of "fooles" and "sophistres." This passage shows that the term *understonde* helped to express contemporary anxiety about meaning and language:

In þis mote men vndirstonde diuersite in wordis and to what entent þes wordes ben vndirstondene. And þus by auctorite of þe lawe of God schulde men speke her wordis as Godis lawe spekiþ, and straunge not in speche from vndirstondyng of þe peple, and algates be war þat þe puple vndirstonde wel, and so vse comun speche in þer owne persone; and, ʒif þei spekon in Cristes persone wordis of his lawe, loke þat þei declaren hem for drede of pryue errour. And scorne we þe argumentis þat fooles maken here þat by þe same skyle schulde we speke þus, for God spekiþ þus in wordus of his lawe; sich apis liknessis passen bestis foly, for þei wolden brynge by þis þat eche man were God. And so ʒyue we God leue to spekon as hym lykuþ al ʒif we speke not ay so by þe same auctorite. Þese wordus þat God spekiþ schulde we algatys graunte, and declaren hem to trewe vndyrstondyng. And recke we not of argumentis þat sophistres maken, þat we ben redarguede grauntynge þat we denyen; for we graunte þe sentence and not only þe wordys, for þe wordis passen awey anoon whan we han spoken hem. (347–48)

The word also appears frequently in the anonymous "Mirror of Sinners" (Oxford, University College MS 97), an early-fifteenth-century manuscript (1400–1410?), with a possible Lollard provenance.[12] The

---

12. I am grateful to Dr. Jill C. Havens of Baylor University, who shared her research on this text with me. All line citations of the "Mirror of Sinners" are to her 1995 Oxford University doctoral thesis, "Instruction, Devotion, Meditation, Sermon: A Critical Edition of Selected English Religious texts in Oxford, University College MS 97 with a Codicological Examination of Some Related Manuscripts."

"Mirror of Sinners" is a meditation on sin, salvation, and the life to come. In its 367 lines, the word *understonde* appears twenty times, approximately every eighteen lines; this frequency makes it structurally similar in its discursive function to the Parson's use of the same term. "The Mirror of Sinners" takes as its text a passage from Deuteronomy, "Vtinam saperent, et intelligerent, ac nouissima prouiderent" (32:29), which it translates as "Wolde God þat men sauouredyn and vnderstoden and purueieden for the laste thynges." The verb in this text signifies mental comprehension that will lead to some direct result, usually an implied action. Throughout the "Mirror's" 367 lines, the writer addresses the reader as "deere brother." He urges the reader to pay particular and close attention to this "sentence": "My deere brother, I prey þee vnderstond wel what þow redist, for the bisy vnderstondyng of this sentence is distruccion of pruyde, quenchyng of enuye, medicyne of malice, dryuyng awey of licherie, voidyng of boost" (ll. 23–28). It is clear from the context of this letter that "vnderstondyng" follows reflection—men are urged to *sanour,* to *vnderstonde,* and then to *purueie;* in line 94f. the author makes this point explicitly: "Biholde, brother, thre thynges been set bifore þe in this myrour; sauoury knowyng, vnderstondyng, and purueaunce. For God wole that þow sauoure þat þou knowest, þat þow vnderstonde, and þat be of good purueaunce" (ll. 94–99).[13] The text then proceeds to explicate these three mental virtues, explaining what comprises each. Knowing lies in being aware "þat thys lyf is passyng, al bilapped in wrecchednesse, soiet to alle maner of vanytee, defouled with filthes of synne, corrupt with couetise, and þat it schal perisshe withynne schort tyme" (99–105); understanding consists in comprehending the individual's place in this world:

> Vnderstond, þerefore, how wooful is þin entree, how chaungeable is thy lyuynge heere, and how feerful is thy passyng awey. Ande / passyng al this vnderstonde, I prey þee, that in this vaale of weepyng, þow art bothe seeke and an outlawe, ful poore in vertues, ful vnstable

---

13. Chaucer's use of the term *understonde* is quite abstract in comparison to the way it is used in Lollard texts. Even though Chaucer uses it in an instructional treatise aimed at changing behavior, the word seems cut off from worldly action in the grammatical patterns in which it appears. The tale is generally oddly undirective; only the remedies for Envy and Lechery involve direct advice about what to do and what not to do; the other descriptions of the sins and their remedies, for example, are largely descriptive rather than prescriptive.

in thy lyuyng, and happily thow schalt not abide til tomorwe. (Ll. 115–23)

Purveyance for what will come lies in praying that God will make known "the noumbre of my dayes, that I may knowe what me fayleth" (ll. 144–45). Contemplation of the inevitable day of death and planning to meet that day with a clear conscience comprise the best manner of purveying for the future (ll. 225–35). Such mental activity in turn leads to confession: "In this manner of thenkynge the soule conceyueth forthenkynge, forthenkyng bryngeth forth confessioun, and confession norisscheth amendynge and ful assseth makyng, and alle thise togidere engendryn in a man verrey hope strecchyng into God" (ll. 233–38). Understanding follows knowing and precedes action.

The term also appears prominently in yet a third Lollard text, the Prologue to the *Wycliffe Bible,* which contains an extensive inquiry into how to read Scripture. Not surprisingly, this inquiry turns on the ways in which Scripture can be understood. In the process of explicating the nature and role of the abundant use of figurative language in Scripture, and explaining the fourfold series of interpretations Scripture can support, the text makes a number of points about understanding that help to contextualize Chaucer's usage of that term. Chapter 12 of the Prologue warns to seek the sentence, to be careful of keeping the literal and the figurative separate; in doing so it relies on the word *understonde,* which, as in Chaucer's text and the Lollard examples above, recurs frequently:

It is to be war in the bigynnyng, that we take not to the lettre a figuratif speche, for thanne, as Poul seith, the lettre sleeth, but the spirit, that is, goostly vndirstonding, qwykeneth; for whanne a thing which is seid figuratifly is taken so as if it be seid propirly, me vndirstondith fleschly; and noon is clepid more couenably the deth of soule, than whanne vndirstonding, that passith beestis, is maad soget to the fleisch in suynge the lettre.[14]

Later, in chapter 14 the author asserts the primacy of literal understanding, writing, "Natheles all goostly vndirstondinges setten bifore, either requyren, the literal vndirstonding, as the foundement . . ." (53).

---

14. See Forshall and Madden edition of Wycliffe's Bible, 1:44.

Clearly the question of how to understand language, even scriptural language, is a vexing one. The literal level of meaning must be acknowledged as primary, but to be too literal, to understand a thing "seid figuratively . . . so as if it be seid propirly," is to miss the essential message of Scripture. Language is a dangerous as well as a powerful tool. Misunderstanding can lead to "the deth of the soule" when the capacity to understand is "maad soget to the fleisch." All these texts bespeak anxiety about correct or full apprehension of meaning and intention. Each example employs the verb and its noun intensively, suggesting that the idea of *understanding* fully and correctly is of immense importance. Read within the context of Lollard discourse, the Parson's tale appears to share the same desire for direct communication and the same anxiety that his audience might misunderstand either the literal or the spiritual message his language conveys.

Another way of contextualizing Chaucer's use of the term *understandyng* in "The Parson's Tale" is to look at Chaucer's own idiolect, his individual use of the term. The most frequent appearance of the word outside "The Parson's Tale" is in Chaucer's translation of the *Consolation of Philosophy,* where he uses the Middle English *understonde/undirstonde* to translate a variety of Latin verbs that include both the idea of sensual apprehension of knowledge and the abstractive power of intellection.

Chaucer's translation of several Latin verbs into the English term *undirstonde* often diminishes distinctions among intellectual processes the Latin might have suggested. The effect of Chaucer's reliance on the word is to reduce a variety of mental activities to an abstract sense of comprehension. For instance, in a number of places Chaucer employs *undirstonde* to translate the Latin *intelligo,* to understand, to perceive: "By the senses or understanding, to mark, perceive observe, feel; to form an idea or conception, to think, to understand." Here, for example, is Chaucer's translation of book 3, prosa 7, lines 7–8: "Of whiche delices I not what joie mai ben had of here moevynge, but this woot I wel, that whosoevere wol remembren hym of hise luxures, he schal wel undirstonden that the issue of delices ben sorweful and sorye." The Latin original corresponding to this passage is "Quarum motus quid habeat iucunditatis, ignoro. Tristes vero esse voluptatem exitus, quisquis reminisci libidinum suarum volet, intelleget."[15] In book 3, prosa 10, c. line

---

15. All citations of the Latin version of *The Consolation of Philosophy* and all quotations of the modern English translation are from *Boethius: The Consolation of Philosophy,*

190, Chaucer translates the Latin "'Intellego,' inquam, 'quid investigandum proponas, sed quid constituas audire desidero'" (p. 282, ll. 109–11) as "'I undirstonde wel,' quod I, 'what thou purposest to seke, but I desire for to herkne that thow schew it me.'"[16] This passage occurs at a point where Boethius and the Lady Philosophy have already "concluded" a number of points about God and his nature. "Undirstonde" here seems to signify comprehension based in the first case on experience, in the second on a series of verbal instructions. In book 2, prosa 4, c. line 140, Chaucer uses *undirstonde* and *gadere togidere* to translate the Latin *collige*. "And that thow mayst knowe that blisfulnesse ne mai nat standen in thynges that ben fortunous and temporel, now undirstond and gadere it togidre thus" [Atque ut agnoscas in his fortuitis rebus beatitudinem constare non posse, sic collige] (p. 196, ll. 78–79).[17] The Latin word *collige* means to "bring together, collect, assemble"; it also carries the sense "to infer, to conclude." In choosing to translate both aspects of the verb Chaucer makes it clear that *undirstondynge* as he uses it suggests the wider, more abstract notion inherent in *collige*.

In book 2, prosa 5, Philosophy, instructing Boethius says, "Sed quoniam rationum iam in te mearum fomenta descendunt, paulo validioribus utendum puto. Age enim si iam caduca et momentaria fortunae dona non essent, quid in eis est quod aut vestrum umquam fieri queat aut non perspectum consideratumque vilescat?" (p. 198, ll. 1–6). Chaucer renders this: "But for as mochel as the norisschynges of my resouns descenden now into the, I trowe it were tyme to usen a litel strengere medicynes. Now undirstand heere; al were it so that the yiftes of Fortune ne were noght brutel ne transitorie, what is ther in hem that mai be thyn in any tyme, or elles that it nys fowl, yif that it be considered and lookyd parfitely?"[18] Here Chaucer translates *Age* in "*Age enim si iam,*"

---

trans. S. J. Tester, Loeb Classical Library, 74 (Cambridge: Harvard University Press, 1978), p. 256, ll. 6–8. Loeb translation: "What pleasure there is in stirring them up, I do not know; but that these pleasures have a bitter end, anyone will understand who is willing to recall his own lusts" (257).

16. Loeb translation: "'I understand what you are proposing for our investigation,' I said, 'but I long to hear what your conclusion is'" (283).

17. Loeb translation: "Now to see that happiness cannot consist in the fortuitous things of this mortal life, look at it in this way" (197).

18. Loeb translation: "But since you are now well warmed by the poultices of my arguments, I think it is now time to use rather stronger medicines. Come now, suppose that the gifts of fortune were not transient and purely temporary, is there any among them which could ever become truly yours or which on proper examination is not seen to be worthless?" (199).

"to recognize, allow, acknowledge/suppose," by a much stronger phrase, one that loses the sense of contingency the Latin carries, creating instead a sense of urgency and exhortation.

Chaucer's frequent recourse to this one word in situations where a modern reader might expect greater variation of diction may reflect the relative limitations of English as a philosophic language in the late fourteenth century. Chaucer's choices may therefore indicate that for him *undirstonde* was a generic term that he used to signify elevated mental activity. But we can be relatively sure that for him understanding was different from other kinds of mental activity, that something of the notion of abstract intellection inhered in the word, when we look at his use of the word in his translation of a passage in book 4, prosa 6, c. ll. 140, discussing the distinctions between *intellecto* and *ratiocinato*. What Chaucer does with the passage supports the idea that he uses *undirstonde* to signify a kind of abstract intellection as distinct from either imagination or reason. Here he links understanding with broad comprehension, translating the Latin comparison of *intellectum* (a perceiving, perception, sensation; understanding, comprehension) to *ratiocinatio* (a careful and deliberate consideration and conclusion; a reasoning ratiocination, argument, syllogism) by preserving a crucial distinction: "Igitur uti est ad intellectum ratiocinatio, ad id quod est id quod gignitur, ad aeternitatem tempus, ad punctum medium circulus, ita est fati series mobilis ad providentiae stabilem simplicitatem" (p. 362, ll. 78–82). He renders this into "Thanne right swich comparysoun as is of skillynge to undirstondyng, and of thing that ys engendrid to thing that is, and of tyme to eternite, and of the cercle to the centre; right so is the ordre of moevable destyne to the stable symplicite of purveaunce."[19] Chaucer interprets *intellectum* in the widest sense of comprehension, ideation, translating it as *undirstondyng,* and interprets *ratiocinatio* narrowly as close reasoning, implicitly tied to arguments and language; the *Middle English Dictionary* lists the "act of reasoning" as the primary meaning of the term *skillynge* during this period. The participle comes from the verb *skillen,* "to distinguish good from evil, to cause words to differ, to make unique or distinctive." Both the participle and the infinitive strongly convey a sense of mechanical separation, division. By this choice of rendering *ratiocinatio* and *intellectum* different in meaning in English,

---

19. Loeb translation: "Therefore as reasoning is to understanding, as that which becomes is to that which is, as time is to eternity, as the circle is to its centre, so is the moving course of fate to the unmoving simplicity of providence" (363).

Chaucer's translation demonstrates his awareness of the limits of reason and his identification of intellection with understanding.

It is this highest kind of knowing, the knowing of understanding and intelligence that the Parson tries to stir in his tale. We have seen how Chaucer has used the word *undirstonde* as his most frequent term for elevated mental activity in the *Consolation,* where it carries a sense of urgency and abstraction. Understanding is an important concept of this period, as both the mystical and Lollard movements attest; English people were concerned with approaches to God and with ways of knowing. Chaucer's use of the word *undirstonde* wtih the second-person pronoun and with the imperative in the tale and his reliance on it in the translation resembles in many respects how other English people of the time used the term. But there is also a significant difference: in virtually every instance of Chaucer's use of the word and its variants, the focus is on reception and internalization. Chaucer's sense of understanding seems less directed to action than Lollard uses of the term, more toward understanding as an achievement of a level of knowing beyond struggle. In many ways the sacrament of penance entails the same kind of peace. There is every reason to think that he chose the word deliberately to structure the tale and to suggest that the tale's lack of poetic form and material designed to appeal to and to stir the imagination is a deliberate omission.

The Poetic Imagination: Reception and the Retraction

Reading "The Parson's Tale" this way also provides a new perspective on the Retraction.[20] Rosemarie Potz McGerr makes a case for under-

---

20. Recent criticisim of the Retraction that intersects the line of argument here includes James Dean, "Chaucer's Repentance: A Likely Story," *Chaucer Review* 24 (1989): 64–76, in which Dean points out the existence of a fourteenth-century narrative tradition combining the pilgrimage/storytelling/penitence scheme of the *Tales;* James Dean, "Dismantling the Canterbury Book," *PMLA* 100 (1985): 746–62, where Dean argues that the Second Nun's tale, the Canon's Yeoman's, the Manciple's, and the Parson's constitute a "closure group" signaling the "abandonment of important fictions of the *Canterbury Tales* and a later change in the book's design" (746); Russell A. Peck, "St. Paul and the *Canterbury Tales,*" *Mediaevalia* 7 (1981): 91–131, in which Peck notes that the problem of correct interpretation has been an issue throughout the *Tales* (95); Peter Travis, "Deconstructing Chaucer's Retraction," *Exemplaria* 3 (1991): 135–58, in which Travis notes the structural tension within the Retraction, locating it in the transition "Wherefore," which acts as a hinge between "two sets of assertions . . . which are mutually exclusive. Chaucer's opening benediction of his art is totally subverted by his closing malediction of his art and vice versa" (146).

standing the Retraction(s) at the end of the tale within the context of Augustinian thinking about the role of signs in the imagination, and the reception of signs into the individual mind. McGerr notes,

> For Augustine, the first step in communication takes place in the process of memory. The act of thinking — of the mind turning upon itself in memory — results in what Augustine calls "inward speech" or the "unspoken word," of which spoken language is an external sign. In verbal communication, the action of one mind is transferred or recreated in the mind of another by means of the exterior manifestation of the first thought process. . . . The key to this process is that the words conceived by means of images re-create those images in the mind of the hearer as *they* pass through *his* senses. The words, in fact, have replaced the original events.[21]

McGerr makes this point within a reading of the Retraction as part of an Augustinian tradition of authorial "responsibility, before God, to ensure that readers come away from his works with the right ideas" (99). Memory is the storehouse of literary experience from which *phantasms* and images that verbal signs evoke are summoned in the processes of reason and judgment. McGerr's emphasis is on Chaucer's sense — as an heir to the Augustinian epistemological and psychological model — of his own responsibility to make clear his "intent of doctrine" (112–13).

Eugene Vance provides an additional perspective on this topic. Vance calls attention to the individuality of semiotic reception, its dependence on will and *phantasms* within the individual mind. Offering a verbal text for public reception, an author surrenders his control of signs:

> Medieval intellectuals concurred that sensible reality is mediated to consciousness by signs. Verbal signs signify only by convention, and are therefore inherently equivocal. Right understanding is a *discursive* process unfolding within the mind. Thus, a sign is an instrument of the intellect distinct both from the concept that it summons and from the existing thing from which the concept has derived. Stimulated by a sign, the will summons into the intellect some *visio,* some *fantasma* latent in the memory, thereby making it visible to the inner eye. ("Chaucer's Pardoner," 725–26)

---

21. "Retraction and Memory: Retrospective Structure in the *Canterbury Tales,*" *Comparative Literature* 37 (1985): 105.

Vance argues Chaucer's apparent recognition of the implications of such a psychology: in individual reception signs "break down"; that is, conventional meaning dissolves under the pressure of individual experience and its shaping effect on the mind's discursive process operating on verbal patterns offered by texts. Vance sees the development of Chaucer's art as an exploration of semiotic codes, stability, and instability:

> From *The Book of the Duchess* onward, Chaucer's constant concern is to explore ethical suppositions underlying the supposedly neutral conventions of different discourses. Like Wyclif, Chaucer does not imagine ontological continuity between the order of human discourse and the Word. Rather, in *The House of Fame* Chaucer makes it clear that human speech has no center, but is labyrinthine, self-referential, and inflationary. Verbal signs have no inherent power to refer, much less to assign stable meaning to human action. The friction between codes that animates almost all of Chaucer's poetry brings into clear relief the arbitrariness of conventional semantic markings and of the ethical values they imply. (731–32)

In such a world, where the semiotics of signs is dependent on individual memory, it is not surprising to see an artist capable of multiple voices and of styles experimenting with these styles as a way of asking whether and in what circumstances it is possible to control reception and stabilize signs.

Read against this knowledge of the philosophical and literary implications of vision and understanding in relation to language, the Retraction takes on an added dimension. There Chaucer does not so much refute his art, as acknowledge its independence — a recognition that is a far cry from repudiation. It is not his poetic legacy that makes him anxious so much as the independence of signs in reception. The term he uses to denote this uncontrolled process is "sownen":

> Wherefore I biseke yow mekely, for the mercy of God, that ye preye for me that Crist have mercy on me and foryeve me my giltes; / and namely of my translacions and enditynges of wordly vanitees, the whiche I revoke in my retracciouns: / as is the book of Troilus; the book also of Fame; the book of the xxv. Ladies; the book of the Duchesse; the book of Seint Valentynes day of the Parlement of Briddes; the tales of Caunterbury, thilke that sownen into synne; / the

book of the Leoun; and many another book, if they were in my
remembrance, and many a song and many a leccherous lay, that Crist
for his grete mercy foryeve me the synne.

(10.1080–90)

As a transitive verb *sownen* conveys the idea of signification; its intransi-
tive meanings convey the idea of stirring the imagination, as the *Middle
English Dictionary* definition shows: "tend toward, be consonant with."
A reading of the retraction more nearly consonant with the fourteenth-
century denotation of the term Chaucer uses here would be a reading in
which the poet does not repudiate his poetry—as has often been remarked, he did not destroy the works he names—so much as acknowledge for one last time a problem he has acknowledged throughout his art,
the tendency of art, especially poetry, to escape its creator's bounds, what
he refers to as "sownen into synne." In fact the *Middle English Dictionary*
offers a meaning for *sownen* that seems to fit the grammar of this phrase,
for *sownen* could mean of a word or phrase, "capable of being translated
from one language to another." Those tales that "sownen into sin" may
refer to the problem of reception as much as moral or immoral content.
Perhaps Chaucer was aware both of the fallacy of intentionality as a
governing principle in the reception of art, and of the infinite "translatabil-
ity" of signs from one meaning to another. Indeed even before he men-
tions his poems, he addresses the issue of his intention—that he would
have done better if he could, and his worry that readers will misunderstand him and his works' limitations as limitations of choice, not as limitations of ability. At the end of his work, as in its opening in the General
Prologue, the poet calls attention to the mystery of poetry and of verbal
signification in general. In a world where mental images can arise from
the experience of reading texts as much as from the experiences of visual
life, to read a vicious, or as Chaucer says "lecherous," poem is to experience the lechery it describes.

The question of the Retraction's relationship to "The Parson's Tale"
and its structural unity remains open. What we can say for certain,
though, is that at the very end of the *Canterbury Tales* Chaucer raises
issues of meaning, intention, and reception in both the tale and the
Retraction. He shows one path toward full understanding of verbal texts
virtually unmediated by imagination—the nonfictional prose of "The
Parson's Tale." Such a concluding tale does not necessarily imply Chaucer's own repudiation of fables and poetry. It could just as well imply

his fascination with perennially insoluble questions that we still address today, questions about how art and language communicate, questions about authorial intention and reader reception, questions about the nature and function of the human imagination.

What we can also say for certain, too, is that the *Tales* conclude with a meditation about human action, both mental and physical. In this sense the *Tales* conclude where they begin, with the variety of human thoughts and the variety of human beings. The beginning of the pilgrimage in the General Prologue brings together people who ostensibly seek a religious experience at the shrine of Saint Thomas; the conclusion in "The Parson's Tale" calls attention to the way people think and act, implicitly connecting cognition and action, as the Parson's hortatory tone makes explicit. David Benson has described *The Canterbury Tales* as a drama of style, an array and a clash of different kinds of verbal patterns. But it is not just a drama of verbal patterns, it is also a drama of perception, communication, and miscommunication. Vision, imagination, and understanding are at the center of medieval ideas of human action and human psychology. They are also a central subject in Chaucer's last, unfinished, protean work.

Afterword

It may be argued that to read *The Canterbury Tales* as this book has done is to adopt an essentialist approach toward medieval literature, implying that it is possible to read a text "correctly" within a certain limited tradition, if that tradition can be recovered. I would certainly not want to make such an assertion. It is foolish to think that we can recover or re-create any more than a small part of the *mentalité* of late medieval England. The sign systems, the physical experience of the world, the very assumptions about humans and about nature are all too complexly different from our own for us to assert that we have anything more than partial knowledge of the culture. In this book I have tried to show how Chaucer's work builds on one small, but complex principle: the assumption that each individual mind, through active engagement with the physical world, receives and re-creates sensory information about that world in a unique way, governed by a unique pattern of experience and desire. I have argued that this principle of human psychology was commonly available to Chaucer and his audience and that detailed knowledge of how the mind and senses functioned together was so familiar that it entered the discourse of a number of apparently unrelated areas such as theology and alchemy. I have argued that *The Canterbury Tales* as a collection of stories is a uniquely appropriate site in which to explore individual psychology, an opportunity to which Chaucer calls attention in the Retraction. In trying to reconstruct what Chaucer's audience would have taken for granted in the human psychology of the tales I have discussed, I have sketched an outline of a way of thinking about human beings, knowledge of which, I believe, significantly affects how modern readers understand the action and the characters of the tales.

In addition to valuing this knowledge for its own sake, I think that awareness of medieval paradigms of human psychology complement current critical and theoretical interest in the human body as it was constructed in the late Middle Ages. For nearly twenty years critics of medieval culture and literature have discussed medieval attitudes to- ward the body, its gender, its wholeness, its boundaries. Research into ideas of cognition and psychology complements and enlarges this inter- est, for it suggests that late medieval models of human psychology, deeply ambivalent about the fundamental processes of cognition, about the senses on which these processes depended, and about the certainty of knowledge humans might achieve, constitute a source of deep ambiva- lence about the human body and the nature of the self. In medieval models of how the mind and senses work together the boundaries mod- ern readers might think of as normal boundaries between the self and the "outside world" hardly exist. In a world instinct with energy, where objects have the power to replicate their *species* through space, striking the individual eye and entering the imagination, the self is by definition fully integrated into the external world. Late medieval thinking about human psychology posits the individual in a reciprocal relationship with the physical world apprehended by the senses. A gazer exerts some power in the act of gazing, but is acted upon by the object of his or her gaze, as well. Emelye, May, Virginia, even Griselda are never merely objects of male desire or will; each has the power profoundly to affect the men who see her.

This interplay of self as agent, self as object, is one of Chaucer's sub- jects in *The Canterbury Tales,* where the nature of the human body — what its boundaries and limits are — is a recurrent subject. How and in what way are Arcite and Palamon imprisoned? What power does the old hag draw upon in order to appear transformed? Can Griselda's will really be an extension of Walter's will? Why do the images of the rocky coast of Brittany possess Dorigen so? In many of the tales the self is the site of psychological struggle. In repeatedly telling tales in which autonomous subjectivity is complicated by the presence and effect of the external world as mental image, Chaucer draws attention to how easily people can become one another's imaginative creations, how humans are all tied to one another in a process of seeing, imagining, remembering.

Over their course the tales begin to define a recurrent question about how and in what ways humans can achieve certain knowledge, how they can break free of the constant flux of imagination in order to establish a clear, fixed identity. The *Tales* offer two models. One way is the way of Seint Cecile, a path into spiritual gnosis expressed in an alchemical trope. This path, as outlined in "The Second Nun's Tale," is a difficult one in which the senses are fulfilled even as they are denied. In that process of fulfillment, the self is established as fixed in eternity through knowledge of God's love. The difficulty of following that path is clear, for few people are situated like Valerian and Tiburce, with a saint to guide their steps toward spiritual alchemy. Moreover, Cecile's example, the ultimate assertion of a stable, defined self in an act of martyrdom that surrenders the body, seems to suggest that absolute agency and self-definition exist only outside human society.

The Parson offers a second path in his tale, but, like the path of spiritual alchemy, this way to creating a stable self by escaping a mental landscape of self-generated and self-referential imagination is a difficult one, requiring renunciation not only of imagination, but of the free play of association that feeds imagination. This play is more than individual, however; it is rooted in communication and hence in community. At the end of *The Canterbury Tales* the Parson agrees to speak, but breaks the rules Harry Bailly established at the outset of the journey, where he proposed that every pilgrim "telle tales tweye" (1.792) in a social contest. The Parson, when his turn comes, refuses to enter the contest. The *game* and *pley* of the pilgrims as tale-tellers is the play of imagination, of one tale eliciting another, of individuals noticing or imagining slights and insults. The Parson shows the path to "thilke parfit glorious pilgrymage" (10.50) as a narrow and strict one, indeed. To follow that path means turning away from the play of images as fluid signs within the individual mind. It also means moving away from the tale telling within a temporary community that the Canterbury pilgrims have adopted as their purpose. The Parson agrees to participate, but not in the common endeavor of fable and imagination. He will use words differently, to a different purpose.

Although he has the last tale, the Parson does not have the last word. The play of imagination, which connects humans in community, structures Chaucer's last, unfinished work. The way that tales arise one from the other suggests Chaucer's interest in how sensory information can evoke unexpected associations in individuals — the Reeve's response to the Miller is one example, the Clerk's response to the Wife another, perhaps more predictable, example. But the principle is apparent throughout the *Tales* in the fact that Harry Bailly cannot control the tale telling. The human mind seeing, hearing, responding, charts its own paths, creates its own associations. Figures of authority and order may try to control the process, but usually fail. Within the *Tales* the Wife of Bath's reaction to the authority of Church teaching is the most memorable example of the uncontrolled play of signs in reception. She refers to her appropriation of the authorial voices and writings on women, her unique reception and re-creation of them as her *fantasye,* her own way of receiving, processing, and recalling information her senses have received. Her Prologue, with its blend of authority and individual interpretation, reveals Chaucer's awareness of the idiosyncracies of individual reception and their challenge to authority. The very design of *The Canterbury Tales* builds on the play between image and imagination, authority and reception in its fiction of narrators whose tales come out of reaction and association. This play lies at the heart of the work and makes Chaucer's last work his most thought-provoking, for it locates complex issues of human cognition and human psychology squarely within a community of tale-tellers who assume and demonstrate the paradigm of medieval psychology discussed in the preceding chapters. In combining medieval psychology and the social nature of literary creation, *The Canterbury Tales* links communication to individual imagination in a work that reflects Chaucer's awareness of the dynamic creativity of the autonomous human mind.

Bibliography

Aers, David. *Chaucer, Langland, and the Creative Imagination.* London: Routledge and Kegan Paul, 1980.

———. "Chaucer's Representations of Marriage and Sexual Relations." In *Critical Essays on Chaucer's Canterbury Tales,* ed. Malcolm Andrew, 205–13. Toronto: University of Toronto Press, 1991.

Aiken, Pauline. "Arcite's Illness and Vincent of Beauvais." *PMLA* 51 (1936): 361–69.

———. "Vincent of Beauvais and Chaucer's Knowledge of Alchemy." *Studies in Philology* 41 (1944): 371–89.

———. "Vincent of Beauvais and Dame Pertelote's Knowledge of Medicine." *Speculum* 10 (1935): 281–87.

———. "Vincent of Beauvais and the 'Houres' of Chaucer's Physician." *Studies in Philology* 53 (1956): 22–24.

Alford, John A. "The Wife of Bath versus the Clerk of Oxford: What Their Rivalry Means." *Chaucer Review* 21 (1986): 108–32.

Allen, Judson Boyce. "The Old Way and the Parson's Way: An Ironic Reading of the Parson's Tale." *Journal of Medieval and Renaissance Studies* 3 (1973): 255–71.

Allen, Judson Boyce, and Theresa Anne Moritz. *A Distinction of Stories: The Medieval Unity of Chaucer's Fair Chain of Narratives for Canterbury.* Columbus: Ohio State University Press, 1981.

Aston, Margaret. *Lollards and Reformers: Images and Literacy in Late Medieval Religion.* London: Hambledon Press, 1984.

Atwood, Mary Anne. *Hermetic Philosophy and Alchemy: A Suggestive Inquiry into "The Hermetic Mystery" with a Dissertation of the More Celebrated of the Alchemical Philosophers.* 1850. Rev. ed. New York: Julian Press, 1960.

Augustine, Saint. *De Trinitate.* In *A Select Library of Nicene and Post-Nicene Fathers of the Christian Church.* Vol. 3. Ed. Philip Schaff. Grand Rapids: Eerdmans, 1956.

Bachman, W. Bryant Jr. "'To Maken Illusioun': The Philosophy of Magic and the Magic of Philosophy in the *Franklin's Tale.*" *Chaucer Review* 12 (1977): 55–67.

Bacon, Roger. *The Opus Maius of Roger Bacon.* Trans. Robert Belle Burke. 2 vols. Philadelphia: University of Pennsylvania Press, 1928.

———. *Roger Bacon's Philosophy of Nature: A Critical Edition, with English Translation, Introduction, and Notes of* De multiplicatione specierum *and* De speculis comburentibus. Ed. David C. Lindberg. Oxford: Oxford University Press, 1983.

Baker, Denise N. "Chaucer and Moral Philosophy: The Virtuous Women of the *Canterbury Tales.*" *Medium Aevum* 60 (1991): 241–56.

Bennett, J. A. W. *Chaucer at Oxford and at Cambridge.* Toronto: University of Toronto Press, 1974.

Bergan, Brooke. "Surface and Secret in the 'Knight's Tale.'" *Chaucer Review* 26 (1991): 1–16.

Bestul, Thomas H. "Chaucer's Parson's Tale and the Late-Medieval Tradition of Religious Meditation." *Speculum* 64 (1989): 600–619.

Blake, Kathleen A. "Order and the Noble Life in Chaucer's *Knight's Tale?*" *Modern Language Quarterly* 34 (1973): 3–19.

Bloch, R. Howard. "Chaucer's Maiden's Head: 'The Physician's Tale' and the Poetics of Virginity." *Representations* 28 (1989): 113–34.

Boccaccio, Giovanni. *The Book of Theseus: Teseida delle Nozze d'Emilia.* Trans. Bernadette Marie McCoy. New York: Medieval Text Association, 1974.

Boethius. *The Consolation of Philosophy.* Trans. S. J. Tester et al. Loeb Classical Library, 74. Cambridge: Harvard University Press, 1978.

Bonaventure, Saint. *The Journey of the Mind to God.* Trans. Philotheus Boehner. Ed. Stephen F. Brown. Indianapolis: Hacket, 1993.

Brown, Carleton. "The Evolution of the Canterbury 'Marriage Group.'" *PMLA* 48 (1933): 1041–59.

Brown, Peter. "Is the 'Canon's Yeoman's Tale' Apocryphal?" *English Studies* 6 (1983): 481–90.

———. "An Optical Theme in *The Merchant's Tale.*" *Studies in the Age of Chaucer,* proceedings 1 (1984): 231–43.

Brown, Peter, and Andrew Butcher. *The Age of Saturn: Literature and History in the* Canterbury Tales. Oxford: Basil Blackwell, 1991.

Brown, William H. Jr. "Chaucer, Livy, and Bersuire: The Roman Materials in *The Physician's Tale.*" In *On Language: Rhetorica, Phonologica, Syntactica; a Festschrift for Robert P. Stockwell from his Friends and Colleagues,* ed. Caroline Duncan-Rose and Theo Vennemann, 39–51. London: Routledge, 1988.

Bryan, W. F., and Germaine Dempster, eds. *Sources and Analogues of Chaucer's* Canterbury Tales. Atlantic Highlands, N.J.: Humanities Press, 1958.

Bundy, Murray Wright. *The Theory of Imagination in Classical and Medieval Thought.* University of Illinois Studies in Language and Literature, 12. Urbana, 1927.

Burnley, J. D. *Chaucer's Language and the Philosophers' Tradition.* Cambridge: D. S. Brewer, 1979.

Carruthers, Mary. "The Wife of Bath and the Painting of Lions." *PMLA* 94 (1979): 209–22.

———. *The Book of Memory: A Study of Memory in Medieval Culture.* Cambridge: Cambridge University Press, 1990.

Chaucer, Geoffrey. *The Riverside Chaucer.* Gen. ed. Larry D. Benson. Boston: Houghton Mifflin, 1987.

Cigman, Gloria. *Lollard Sermons.* Early English Text Society, 294. Oxford, 1989.

Coleman, Janet. *Ancient and Medieval Memories: Studies in the Reconstruction of the Past.* Cambridge: Cambridge University Press, 1992.

Collette, Carolyn P. "A Closer Look at Seint Cecile's Special Vision." *Chaucer Review* 10 (1976): 337–49.

———. "'Peyntyng with Greet Cost': Virginia as Image in the *Physician's Tale.*" In *Chaucer Yearbook II,* ed. Michael N. Salda and Jean E. Jost, 49–62. Woodbridge: D. S. Brewer, 1995.

———. "Seeing and Believing in the *Franklin's Tale.*" *Chaucer Review* 26 (1992): 395–410.

———. "*Ubi Peccaverant Ibi Punirentur:* The Oak Tree and the *Pardoner's Tale.*" *Chaucer Review* 19 (1984): 39–45.

Connolly, Thomas. *Mourning into Joy: Music, Raphael, and Saint Cecilia.* New Haven: Yale University Press, 1994.

Cooper, Helen. *The Canterbury Tales.* Oxford Guides to Chaucer. Oxford: Oxford University Press, 1989.

Corsa, Helen Storm, ed. *A Variorum Edition of the Works of Geoffrey Chaucer.* Vol. 2, *The Canterbury Tales, Part 17, The Physician's Tale.* Norman: University of Oklahoma Press, 1987.

Courtenay, William. "Nominalism and Late Medieval Religion." In *Pursuit of Holiness in Late Medieval and Renaissance Religion,* ed. Charles Trinkaus and Heiko A. Oberman, 26–59. Leiden: J. S. Brill, 1974.

Dalbey, Marcia A. "The Devil in the Garden: Pluto and Proserpine in Chaucer's *Merchant's Tale.*" *Neuphilologishe Mitteilungen* 75 (1974): 408–15.

David, Alfred. *The Strumpet Muse: Art and Morals in Chaucer's Poetry.* Bloomington: Indiana University Press, 1976.

Davidson, Clifford. "The Anti-Visual Prejudice." In *Iconoclasm vs. Art and Drama,* 33–46. Medieval Institute Publications, Early Drama, Art, and Music Monographs Series. Kalamazoo, Mich., 1989.

———, ed. *A Tretise of Miraclis Pleyinge.* Kalamazoo, Mich.: Medieval Institute Publications, 1993.

Davis, Nicholas. "The *Tretise of Myraclis Pleyinge:* On Milieu and Authorship." *Medieval English Theatre* 12 (1990): 124–51.

Dean James. "Chaucer's Repentance: A Likely Story." *Chaucer Review* 24 (1989): 64–76.

———. "Dismantling the Canterbury Book." *PMLA* 100 (1985): 746–62.

Delany, Sheila. "Run Silent Run Deep: Heresy and Alchemy as Medieval Versions of Utopia." In *Medieval Literary Politics: Shapes of Ideology*, 1–18. Manchester: Manchester University Press, 1990.

Delasanta, Rodney. "Penance and Poetry in the *Canterbury Tales*." *PMLA* 93 (1978): 240–47.

———. "Sacrament and Sacrifice in the *Pardoner's Tale*." *Annuale Mediaevale* 14 (1973): 43–52.

Diamond, Arlyn. "Chaucer's Women and Women's Chaucer." In *The Authority of Experience: Essays in Feminist Criticism*, ed. Arlyn Diamond and Lee Edwards, 60–83. Amherst: University of Massachusetts Press, 1977.

DiMarco, Vincent. "The Dialogue of Science and Magic in Chaucer's *Squire's Tale*." In *Dialogic Structures*, ed. Thomas Kuhn and Ursula Schaefer, 50–68. Tübingen: Gunter Narr, 1996.

Dinshaw, Carolyn. "Eunuch Hermeneutics." *English Literary History* 55 (1988): 27–51.

Dives and Pauper. Ed. Priscilla Heath Barnum. Part 1, Early English Text Society, 275. Oxford: Oxford University Press, 1976.

Duncan, Edgar H. "The Literature of Alchemy and Chaucer's Canon's Yeoman's Tale: Framework, Theme and Characters." *Speculum* 43 (1968): 633–56.

———. "The Yeoman's Canon's 'Silver Citrinacioun.'" *Modern Philology* 37 (1940): 241–62.

Edwards, Robert. "Narration and Doctrine in the Merchant's Tale." *Speculum* 66 (1991): 342–67.

Eldredge, L. M. "Some Medical Evidence on Langland's Imaginatif." *Yearbook of Langland Studies* 3 (1989): 131–36.

Ferster, Judith. *Chaucer on Interpretation*. Cambridge: Cambridge University Press, 1985.

Finke, Laurie A. "'To Knytte Up All This Feeste': The Parson's Rhetoric and the Ending of the *Canterbury Tales*." *Leeds Studies in English*, n.s. 15 (1984): 95–108.

Fleming, John V. *An Introduction to the Franciscan Literature of the Middle Ages*. Chicago: Franciscan Herald Press, 1977.

Fletcher, Alan. "Preaching and the Pardoner." *Studies in the Age of Chaucer* 11 (1989): 15–35.

———. "The Topical Hypocrisy of Chaucer's Pardoner." *Chaucer Review* 25 (1990): 110–26.

Forshall, Josiah, and Frederic Madden, eds. *The Holy Bible, Containing the Old and New Testaments, with the Apocryphal Books, in the Earliest English*

Versions Made From the Latin Vulgate by John Wycliffe and His Followers. 4 vols. Oxford: Oxford University Press, 1850.

Geber. *The Works of Geber, Englished by Richard Russell, 1678.* Ed. E. J. Holmyard. London: J. M. Dent, 1928.

Ginsberg, Warren. "The Lineaments of Desire: Wish-Fulfillment in Chaucer's Marriage Group." *Criticism* 25 (1983): 197–210.

Gower, John. *Confessio Amantis.* Ed. Russell A. Peck. Medieval Academy Reprints for Teaching, 9. Toronto, 1980.

Grant, Edward. "Scientific Thought in Fourteenth-Century Paris: Jean Buridan and Nicole Oresme." In *Machaut's World: Science and Art in the Fourteenth Century,* ed. Madeleine Pelner Cosman and Bruce Chandler, 105–24. Annals of the New York Academy of Sciences, vol. 314. New York, 1978.

———. *Source Book in Medieval Science.* Cambridge: Harvard University Press, 1974.

Green, Donald C. "The Semantics of Power: *Maistrie* and *Soveraynetee* in *The Canterbury Tales.*" *Modern Philology* 84 (1986): 18–23.

Greenberg, Bruce L. "The *Canon's Yeoman's Tale:* Boethian Wisdom and the Alchemists." *Chaucer Review* 1 (1966): 37–54.

Grennen, Joseph E. "Saint Cecilia's 'Chemical Wedding': The Unity of the *Canterbury Tales,* Fragment VIII." *JEGP* 65 (1966): 466–81.

———. "The Canon's Yeoman's Alchemical Mass." *Studies in Philology* 62 (1965): 546–60.

Hagen, Susan K. *Allegorical Remembrance: A Study of the* Pilgrimage of the Life of Man *as a Medieval Treatise on Seeing and Remembering.* Athens: University of Georgia Press, 1990.

Hanning, Robert W. "'The Struggle between Noble Designs and Chaos': The Literary Tradition of Chaucer's Knight." *Literary Review* 23 (1980): 519–41.

Hansen, Elaine Tuttle. *Chaucer and the Fictions of Gender.* Berkeley and Los Angeles: University of California Press, 1992.

Harley, Marta Powell. "Last Things First in Chaucer's Physician's Tale: Final Judgment and the Worm of Conscience." *JEGP* 91 (1992): 1–16.

Harvey, Gabriel. *Marginalia.* Ed. G. C. Moore-Smith. Stratford upon Avon, 1913.

Harvey, Ruth E. *The Inward Wits: Psychological Theory in the Middle Ages and the Renaissance.* London: Warburg Institute, 1975.

Harwood, Britton J. "Imaginative in *Piers Plowman.*" *Medium Aevum* 44 (1975): 249–63.

Haskell, Ann S. "The Saint Gile's Oath in the *Canon's Yeoman's Tale.*" *Chaucer Review* 7 (1973): 221–26.

Havens, Jill C. "Instruction, Devotion, Meditation, Sermon: A Critical Edition of Selected English Religious Texts in Oxford, University College MS 97 with a Codicological Examination of Some Related Manuscripts." Ph.D. diss., Oxford University, 1995.

Heffernan, Carol Falvo. "Tyranny and *Commune Profit* in the *Clerk's Tale.*" *Chaucer Review* 17 (1983): 332–40.

Herz, Judith. "The Canon's Yeoman's Prologue and Tale." *Modern Philology* 58 (1961): 231–37.

Hilberry, Jane. "'And in Oure Madnesse Everemoore We Rave': Technical Language in the *Canon's Yeoman's Tale.*" *Chaucer Review* 21 (1987): 435–43.

Hill, John M. *Chaucerian Belief: The Poetics of Reverence and Delight.* New Haven: Yale University Press, 1991.

Hoffman, Richard L. *Ovid and the Canterbury Tales.* Philadelphia: University of Pennsylvania Press, 1966.

Howard, Donald R. "The Conclusion of the Marriage Group: Chaucer and the Human Condition." *Modern Philology* 57 (1959–60): 223–32.

Hudson, Anne. *The Premature Reformation: Wycliffite Texts and Lollard History.* Oxford: Clarendon Press, 1988.

———, ed. *Selections from English Wycliffite Writings.* Cambridge: Cambridge University Press, 1978.

Hudson, Anne, and Michael Wilks, eds. *From Ockham to Wyclif.* Oxford: Ecclesiastical History Society, Basil Blackwell, 1987.

Irvine, Martin. "Medieval Grammatical Theory and Chaucer's *House of Fame.*" *Speculum* 60 (1985): 850–76.

John of Salisbury. *The Metalogicon of John of Salisbury: A Twelfth-Century Defense of the Verbal and Logical Arts of the Trivium.* Trans. Daniel D. McGarry. Berkeley and Los Angeles: University of California Press, 1955.

Johnson, Lynn Staley. "The Prince and His People: A Study of the Two Covenants in the *Clerk's Tale.*" *Chaucer Review* 10 (1975): 17–29.

Jones, W. R. "Lollards and Images: The Defense of Religious Art in Later Medieval England." *Journal of the History of Ideas* 34 (1973): 27–50.

Julian of Norwich. *A Book of Showings to the Anchoress Julian of Norwich.* Ed. Edmund Colledge and James Walsh. 2 vols. Toronto: Pontifical Institute of Medieval Studies, 1978.

Kaulbach, Ernest N. "The 'Vis Imaginativa secundum Avicennam' and the Naturally Prophetic Powers of Ymaginatif in the B-Text of *Piers Plowman.*" *JEGP* 86 (1987): 496–514.

Kearney, A. M. "Truth and Illusion in *The Franklin's Tale.*" *Essays in Criticism* 19 (1969): 245–53.

Kellogg, Alfred L., and Louis A. Haselmayer. "Chaucer's Satire of the Pardoner." *PMLA* 66 (1951): 251–77.

Kelly, Henry A. *Love and Marriage in the Age of Chaucer.* Ithaca, N.Y.: Cornell University Press, 1975.

Kempton, Daniel. "The *Physician's Tale:* The Doctor of Physic's Diplomatic 'Cure.'" *Chaucer Review* 19 (1984): 24–38.

Kendall, Ritchie D. *The Drama of Dissent: The Radical Poetics of Nonconformity, 1380–1590.* Chapel Hill: University of North Carolina Press, 1986.

Kibre, Pearl. "*De Occultis Naturae* Attributed to Albertus Magnus." In *Studies in Medieval Science: Alchemy, Astrology, Mathematics, and Medicine,* ed. Pearl Kibre. London: Hambledon Press, 1984.

Kirkpatrick, Robin. "The Griselda Story in Boccaccio, Petrarch, and Chaucer." In *Chaucer and the Italian Trecento,* ed. Piero Boitani and Anna Torti, 231–48. Cambridge: Cambridge University Press, 1983.

Kittredge, George Lyman. "Chaucer's Discussion of Marriage." *Modern Philology* 9 (1911–12): 435–67.

Klassen, Norman. *Chaucer on Love, Knowledge, and Sight.* Cambridge: D. S. Brewer, 1995.

Klibansky, Raymond, et al. *Saturn and Melancholy: Studies in the History of Natural Philosophy, Religion, and Art.* London: Thomas Nelson and Sons, 1964.

Klossowski De Rola, Stanislas. *Alchemy: The Secret Art.* London: Thames and Hudson, 1973.

Knight, Stephen. "Chaucer's Pardoner in Performance." *Sydney Studies in English* 9 (1983–84): 21–36.

Kolve, V. A. *Chaucer and the Imagery of Narrative: The First Five Canterbury Tales.* Stanford: Stanford University Press, 1984.

———. "Chaucer's *Second Nun's Tale* and the Iconography of Saint Cecilia." In *New Perspectives in Chaucer Criticism,* ed. Donald M. Rose. Norman, Okla.: Pilgrim Books, 1981.

Kruger, Steven. "Mirrors and the Trajectory of Vision in *Piers Plowman.*" *Speculum* 66 (1991): 74–95.

Kuksewicz, Zdzislaw. "Criticisms of Aristotelian Psychology and the Augustinian-Aristotelian Synthesis." In *The Cambridge History of Later Medieval Philosophy from the Rediscovery of Aristotle to the Disintegration of Scholasticism, 1100–1600,* ed. Norman Kretzmann et al. Cambridge: Cambridge University Press, 1982.

Lay Folks Catechism. Ed. Thomas F. Simmons and Henry E. Nolloth. Early English Text Society, 118. London, 1901.

Lee, Brian L. "The Position and Purpose of the Physician's Tale." *Chaucer Review* 22 (1987): 141–60.

Lindberg, David C., ed. *John Pecham and the Science of Optics: Perspectiva Communis.* Madison: University of Wisconsin Press, 1970.

———. *Theories of Vision from Al-kindi to Kepler.* Chicago: University of Chicago Press, 1976.

Linden, Stanton J. *Darke Hierogliphicks: Alchemy in English Literature from Chaucer to the Restoration.* Lexington: University Press of Kentucky, 1996.

Longsworth, Robert M. "Privileged Knowledge: St. Cecilia and the Alchemist in the *Canterbury Tales.*" *Chaucer Review* 27 (1992): 87–96.

Lowes, John Livingston. "The Loveres Maladye of Hereos." *Modern Philology* 11 (1914): 491–546.

Luengo, Anthony E. "Magic and Illusion in *The Franklin's Tale.*" *JEGP* 77 (1978): 1–16.

Lydgate, John. *The Translation of the Second Epistle that King Alexander sent to his Master Aristotle.* In *Theatrum Chemicum Britannicum. . . .* New York: Johnson Reprint Corporation, 1967.

Lynch, Kathryn. "Despoiling Griselda: Chaucer's Walter and the Problem of Knowledge in *The Clerk's Tale.*" *Studies in the Age of Chaucer* 10 (1988): 41–70.

Mandel, Jerome. "Governance in the *Physician's Tale.*" *Chaucer Review* 10 (1976): 316–25.

McAlindon, T. "Cosmology, Contrariety, and the 'Knight's Tale.'" *Medium Aevum* 55 (1986): 41–57.

McAlpine, Monica. "The Pardoner's Homosexuality and How It Matters." *PMLA* 95 (1980): 8–22.

McCall, John P. "The *Clerk's Tale* and the Theme of Obedience." *Modern Language Quarterly* 27 (1966): 260–69.

McGerr, Rosemarie Potz. "Retraction and Memory: Retrospective Structure in the *Canterbury Tales.*" *Comparative Literature* 37 (1985): 97–113.

McNamara, John. "Chaucer's Use of the Epistle of St. James in the *Clerk's Tale.*" *Chaucer Review* 7 (1972): 184–93.

Memoriale Credencium. Ed. J. H. L. Kengen. 1979.

Miller, Robert P. "The Epicurean Homily on Marriage by Chaucer's Franklin." *Mediaevalia* 6 (1980): 151–86.

———. *Chaucer Sources and Backgrounds.* New York: Oxford University Press, 1977.

Minnis, Alistair. *Chaucer and Pagan Antiquity.* Cambridge: D. S. Brewer, 1982.

———. "Chaucer's Pardoner and the 'Office of Preacher.'" In *Intellectuals and Writers in Fourteenth Century Europe,* ed. Piero Boitani and Anna Torti, 88–119. Cambridge: D. S. Brewer, 1986.

———. "Langland's Ymaginatif and Late-Medieval Theories of Imagination." In *Comparative Criticism: A Yearbook,* ed. E. S. Shaffer, 71–103. Cambridge: Cambridge University Press, 1981.

The Mirror of Alchimy Composed by the Thrice-Famous and Learned Fryer, Roger Bacon. Ed. Stanton J. Linden. New York: Garland, 1992.

Mitchell, Susan. "Deception and Self-Deception in 'The Franklin's Tale.'" In

Proceedings of the Patristic, Medieval, and Renaissance Conference, 67–72. Villanova: Augustinian Historical Institute, 1976.

Molland, A. G. "Roger Bacon as Magician." *Traditio* 30 (1974): 445–60.

Montgomery, Robert L. *The Reader's Eye: Studies in Didactic Literary Theory from Dante to Tasso.* Berkeley and Los Angeles: University of California Press, 1979.

Morse, Charlotte. "Critical Approaches to the Clerk's Tale." In *Chaucer's Religious Tales,* ed. C. David Benson and Elizabeth Robertson, 71–83. Cambridge: D. S. Brewer, 1990.

Muscatine, Charles. "Form, Texture, and Meaning in Chaucer's *Knight's Tale.*" *PMLA* 65 (1950): 911–29.

Myrc, John. *Instructions for Parish Priests.* Ed. Edward Peacock. Early English Text Society, 31. London, 1902.

Neuse, Richard. "The Knight: The First Mover in Chaucer's Human Comedy." *University of Toronto Quarterly* 31 (1962): 299–315.

———. "Marriage and the Question of Allegory in 'The Merchant's Tale.'" *Chaucer Review* 24 (1989): 115–29.

Ogrinc, Will H. L. "Western Society and Alchemy from 1200 to 1500." *Journal of Medieval History* 6 (1980): 103–32.

Olson, Glending. "Chaucer, Dante, and the Structure of Fragment VIII (G) of the *Canterbury Tales.*" *Chaucer Review* 16 (1981): 222–36.

Otten, Charlotte F. "Proserpine: *Liberatrix Suae Gentis.*" *Chaucer Review* 5 (1971): 277–87.

Owst, G. R. *Literature and Pulpit in Medieval England.* Cambridge: Cambridge University Press, 1933.

Patterson, Lee. *Chaucer and the Subject of History.* Madison: University of Wisconsin Press, 1991.

———. "The 'Parson's Tale' and the Quitting of the 'Canterbury Tales'." *Traditio* 34 (1978): 331–80.

———. "Perpetual Motion: Alchemy and the Technology of the Self." *Studies in the Age of Chaucer* 15 (1993): 25–57.

———. "'For the Wyves Love of Bath': Feminine Rhetoric and Poetic Resolution in the *Roman de la Rose* and the *Canterbury Tales.*" *Speculum* 58 (1983): 656–95.

Pearlman, E. "The Psychological Basis of the *Clerk's Tale.*" *Chaucer Review* 11 (1977): 248–57.

Pearsall, Derek. *The Canterbury Tales.* London: Allen and Unwin, 1985.

———. "Chaucer's Pardoner: The Death of a Salesman." *Chaucer Review* 17 (1983): 358–65.

Peck, Russell A. "Chaucer and the Imagination." *Studies in the Age of Chaucer.* Proceedings 2 (1986): 33–48.

———. "Chaucer and the Nominalist Question." *Speculum* 53 (1978): 745–60.

———. "Chaucerian Poetics and the Prologue to the *Legend of Good Women*." In *Chaucer in the Eighties,* ed. Julian N. Wasserman and Robert J. Blanch, 39–55. Syracuse: Syracuse University Press, 1986.

———. "The Ideas of 'Entente' and Translation in Chaucer's *Second Nun's Tale*." *Annuale Mediaevale* 8 (1967): 17–37.

———. "St. Paul and the *Canterbury Tales*." *Mediaevalia* 7 (1981): 91–131.

Pfander, H. G. "Some Medieval Manuals of Religious Instruction." *JEGP* 35 (1936): 243–58.

Phillips, Heather. "John Wyclif and the Optics of the Eucharist." In *From Ockham to Wyclif,* ed. Anne Hudson and Michael Wilks, 245–58. Oxford: Ecclesiastical History Society, 1987.

Rahman, F., ed. *Avicenna's Psychology.* Oxford: Oxford University Press, 1952.

Ramsey, Lee C. "'The Sentence of It Sooth Is': Chaucer's *Physician's Tale*." *Chaucer Review* 6 (1972): 185–97.

Reiss, Edmund. "The Final Irony of the Pardoner's Tale." *College English* 25 (1964): 260–66.

Rhodes, James. "Motivation in Chaucer's *Pardoner's Tale:* Winner Take Nothing." *Chaucer Review* 17 (1982): 40–61.

Riehle, Wolfgang. *The Middle English Mystics.* Trans. Bernard Standring. London: Routledge, 1981.

Riffaterre, Michael. "The Mind's Eye: Memory and Textuality." In *The New Medievalism,* ed. Marina S. Brownlee, Kevin Brownlee, and Stephen G. Nichols, 29–45. Baltimore: Johns Hopkins University Press, 1991.

Robertson, D. W. "The Physician's Comic Tale." *Chaucer Review* 23 (1988): 129–39.

Roney, Lois. *Chaucer's Knight's Tale and Theories of Scholastic Psychology.* Tampa: University of South Florida Press, 1990.

Rosenberg, Bruce A. "The Contrary Tales of the Second Nun and the Canon's Yeoman." *Chaucer Review* 2 (1968): 278–91.

———. "Swindling Alchemist, Antichrist." *Centennial Review* 6 (1962): 566–80.

Rowland, Beryl. "Sermon and Penitential in *The Parson's Tale* and Their Effect on Style." *Florilegium* 9 (1987): 125–45.

Russell-Smith, Joy M. "Walter Hilton and a Tract in Defence of the Veneration of Images." *Dominican Studies* 7 (1954): 180–214.

Ruud, Jay. "Natural Law and Chaucer's *Physician's Tale*." *Journal of the Rocky Mountain Medieval and Renaissance Association* 9 (1988): 29–45.

Salter, Elizabeth. *Chaucer: The Knight's Tale and the Clerk's Tale.* London: Edward Arnold, 1962.

Schroeder, Mary C. "Fantasy in the 'Merchant's Tale.'" *Criticism* 12 (1970): 167–79.

Schweitzer, Edward C. "Fate and Freedom in 'The Knight's Tale.'" *Studies in the Age of Chaucer* 3 (1981): 13–45.

Smith, A. Mark. "Getting the Big Picture in Perspectivist Optics." *Isis* 72 (1981): 568–89.

Speculum Christiani. Ed. Gustaf Holmstedt. Early English Text Society, 182. London, 1933.

Speed, Diane. "Language and Perspective in the *Physician's Tale.*" In *Words and Wordsmiths: A Volume for H. L. Rogers,* ed. Geraldine Barnes et al., 119–36. Sydney: University of Sydney Press, 1989.

Stanbury, Sarah. *Seeing the Gawain Poet: Description and the Act of Perception.* Philadelphia: University of Pennsylvania Press, 1991.

Tachau, Katherine. *Vision and Certitude in the Age of Ockham: Optics, Epistemology and the Foundations of Semantics 1250–1345.* Leiden: E. J. Brill, 1988.

Tatlock, John S. P., and Arthur G. Kennedy, eds. *A Concordance to the Complete Works of Geoffrey Chaucer and to the Romaunt of the Rose.* Washington, DC: Carnegie Institution of Washington, 1927.

Taylor, Paul Beekman. "The Parson's Amyable Tongue." *English Studies* 64 (1983): 401–9.

Theatrum Chemicum Britannicum, Containing Severall Poeticall Pieces of our Famous English Philosophers, who have written the Hermetique Mysteries in their owne Ancient Language Faithfully Collected into one Volume with Annotations thereon by Elias Ashmole, Esq. London, 1652. Reprint, with introduction by Allen G. Debus. Sources of Science Series, 39. New York: Johnson Reprint Corporation, 1967.

Thomas Norton's Ordinal of Alchemy. Ed. John Reidy. Early English Text Society, 272. Oxford: Oxford University Press, 1975.

Thorndike, Lynn. *A History of Magic and Experimental Science.* 8 vols. New York: Macmillan, 1923–58.

Thynne, Francis. *Animadversions Upon Speght's First (1598) Edition of Chaucer's Works.* Ed. G. H. Kingsley. Early English Text Society, 9. London, 1875.

Travis, Peter. "Deconstructing Chaucer's Retraction." *Exemplaria* 3 (1991): 135–58.

Trevisa, John, trans. *On the Properties of Things: John Trevisa's Translation of Bartholomaeus Anglicus De Proprietatibus Rerum.* Ed. M. C. Seymour et al. 3 vols. Oxford: Clarendon Press, 1975.

Tucker, Edward F. J. "'Parfite Blisses Two': January's Dilemma and the Themes of Temptation and Doublemindedness in *The Merchant's Tale.*" *American Benedictine Review* 33 (1982): 172–81.

Vance, Eugene. "Chaucer's Pardoner: Relics, Discourse, and Frames of Propriety." *New Literary History* 20 (1989): 723–45.

Vincent of Beauvais. *Speculum Naturale.* In *Bibliotheca Mundi Vincenti Burgundi.* 4 vols. Douay, 1624. Reprint 1964.

von Nolcken, Christina, ed. *The Middle English Translation of the Rosarium Theologie.* Heidelberg: Carl Winter, 1979.

Wack, Mary Frances. *Lovesickness in the Middle Ages: The* Viaticum *and Its Commentaries.* Philadelphia: University of Pennsylvania Press, 1990.

Wallace, David. *Chaucerian Polity: Absolutist Lineages and Associational Forms in England and Italy.* Stanford: Stanford University Press, 1997.

Wentersdorf, Karl P. "Theme and Structure in *The Merchant's Tale:* The Function of the Pluto Episode." *PMLA* 80 (1965): 522–27.

Wenzel, Siegfried. "Notes on the *Parson's Tale.*" *Chaucer Review* 16 (1981): 237–56.

———. "The Source for the 'Remedia' of the Parson's Tale." *Traditio* 27 (1971): 433–53.

———. "The Source of Chaucer's Seven Deadly Sins." *Traditio* 30 (1974): 351–78.

Westlund, Joseph. "The *Knight's Tale* as an Impetus for Pilgrimage." *Philological Quarterly* 43 (1964): 526–37.

Wetherbee, Winthrop. "The Theme of Imagination in Medieval Poetry and the Allegorical Figure 'Genius.'" *Medievalia et Humanistica,* n.s. 7 (1976): 45–64.

Wolfson, Henry Austryn. "The Internal Senses in Latin, Arabic, and Hebrew Philosophic Texts." *Harvard Theological Review* 28 (1935): 69–133.

Wood, Chauncey. "Chaucer's Most Gowerian Tale." In *Chaucer and Gower: Difference, Mutuality, Exchange,* ed. R. F. Yeager, 75–84. Victoria, B.C.: University of Victoria Press, 1991.

Wurtele, Douglas J. "The Anti-Lollardry of Chaucer's Parson." *Mediaevalia* 11 (1985): 151–68.

Index